Japanese Americans

THE FORMATION AND TRANSFORMATIONS
OF AN ETHNIC GROUP

Twayne's Immigrant Heritage of America Series

Thomas J. Archdeacon, General Editor

Japanese Americans

THE FORMATION AND TRANSFORMATIONS OF AN ETHNIC GROUP

Paul R. Spickard

Brigham Young University—Hawai'i

TWAYNE PUBLISHERS

An Imprint of Simon & Schuster Macmillan

New York

PRENTICE HALL INTERNATIONAL

London • Mexico City • New Delhi • Singapore • Sydney • Toronto

Japanese Americans
Paul R. Spickard

Copyright © 1996 by Paul R. Spickard

Library of Congress Cataloging-in-Publication Data
Spickard, Paul R., 1950–
    Japanese Americans : the formation and transformations of an
ethnic group / by Paul R. Spickard.
        p.   cm. — (Twayne's immigrant heritage of America series)
    Includes bibliographical references and index.
    ISBN 0–8057–7841–1 (cloth). — ISBN 0–8057–9242–2 (paper)
    1. Japanese Americans—History.   2. Immigrants—United States—
History.   I. Title. II. Series.
    E184.J3S7   1996
    973'.04956—dc20   96–15111
                                                                          CIP

10 9 8 7 6 5 4 3 2 1 (hc)
10 9 8 7 6 5 4 3   (pb)

Printed in the United States of America

To Naomi Spickard and Daniel Spickard

Contents

Illustrations

Tables

Figures

Acknowledgments

First thanks must go to the many hundreds of Japanese Americans with whom I grew up and who have shared their lives with me in ways large and small over the years. Jim Morishima was my first mentor and has guided me through many treacherous passages in my intellectual wanderings. He was the first to teach me in a formal way about Japanese Americans. He has been ever a perceptive critic and ever a faithful friend.

I have written several books and many articles, but I have written nothing that does not bear the intellectual imprint of my associations with Jim Morishima, Lawrence Levine, and Winthrop Jordan. Behind them stands a small group of scholars whom I never was privileged to meet but whose methods and ideas framed the intellectual world in which I grew. They are in some respects my intellectual ancestors: E. P. Thompson, Joseph Levenson, Emory Bogardus, Robert E. Park, Franz Boas, E. Franklin Frazier, and W. E. B. Du Bois. Their attention to structure and to culture, to the person and also to the class, to social forces and to individual human choices, and especially to hearing the voices of people many other writers have taken to be voiceless, is the goal after which I strive in my own work.

The footnotes and bibliographical essay suggest the breadth of my intellectual debts in applying my faculties to Japanese American history. Roger Daniels is not only the foremost historian of Japanese America, he has also been a generous and patient guide, on this project and on several related ones, to me as to so many scholars of my generation. Thanks, too, to Roger Dingman, Diane Wong, Albert Craig, and the late Edwin Reischauer, who helped me get started thinking systematically about Japanese American history some decades ago. At a late stage of this project, Laurie Mengel's perceptive reading saved me from several errors, as her friendship sustained me.

In addition, many kind individuals have offered suggestions, perspectives on important issues, copies of documents, and miscellaneous encouragement as I have struggled to understand Japanese American history and to build this narrative. They include Elaine Aoki, Art Hansen, Donald Hata, Lane Hirabayashi, Shirley Hune, Paul Igasaki, Harry Kitano, Ben Kobashigawa, Chalsa Loo, Patrick Miller, Dale Minami, Darrel Montero, Kiyo Morimoto, Don Nakanishi, Lisa Nakata, Franklin Odo, Gary Okihiro, Ken Oye, Gloria Saito, Robyn Sonomura

Chadderton, Eileen Tamura, Diane Taniguchi, Mayumi Tsutakawa, the late
Edison Uno, Alex Yamato, and Alice Yang-Murray.

Librarians and archivists are wizards—guardians of treasures who nonethe-
less can whip them out and share them at the slightest provocation. In pursuing
Japanese American history and producing this book, I have been treated kindly
by the good people at the following libraries and archives: Doe Library and
Bancroft Library, University of California, Berkeley; Hoover Institution Archives,
Stanford; National Archives, Washington, D.C., and Suitland, Maryland;
Hamilton Library, University of Hawai'i; Joseph F. Smith Library, Brigham Young
University-Hawai'i; Macalester College Library; University Research Library and
Special Collections, UCLA; Oral History Program, California State University,
Fullerton; Suzallo Library and University Archives, University of Washington. In
addition, I must thank all those nameless people across the country and the
globe who bring me books through interlibrary loan. Series editor Thomas
Archdeacon and a number of staff editors at Twayne Publishers waited patiently
for the manuscript and labored diligently to produce a good book.

Finally, I am grateful for the love and patience of Naomi Spickard and Daniel
Spickard, once again.

one

Japanese Americans and Ethnicity

The year is 1904. Hiroshi* is picking apricots near Wenatchee, Washington. He is 23 and single. He completed the sixth grade in Japan and farmed there for a while before he decided to go to America to make some money and finish his education. He has been here six years now but has made little progress on his educational agenda. He is making good money, however, and is saving up to go back to Japan, marry, and open a store in his home village. His family writes that they think they can arrange a good match if he comes home soon.

It is 1936. Yuriyo* is about to graduate from Galileo High School in San Francisco. Her father and mother run a residential hotel in Nihonmachi, the Japanese neighborhood just over the hill from downtown. She would like to go to college next year and has been admitted to the University of California, but it is the Depression and there is no scholarship. Besides, she needs to go to work to help support her four younger sisters and brothers. She is looking for a job as a secretary and planning to marry her boyfriend.

In 1976, Bob* is four years out of Stanford Law School. Back home in a southern California suburb, he is working in the legal department of a large corporation. But he is thinking about leaving it to open a small firm of his own with two Chinese friends who are interested in serving the city's growing Asian immigrant community. Bob is active in the Democratic Party and was recently approached about running for the town council. His parents think that is a great idea. But his grandmother is not so sure. Her friends at the Japanese community nursing home remember discrimination and prison camps; they are doubtful that America is ready for Japanese American politicians. Bob, they say, will serve his wife and baby better by sticking with his good job and steering clear of anything that will put him in the public eye.

Mariko's* long hair flies behind her as she dribbles down the court. One of her high school teammates is also from Japan—like her, the daughter of an executive at the Honda plant in Marysville, Ohio. Her father is due to go back to Japan next year, 1991. Mariko likes America. She listens to Milli Vanilli and shops at the Gap. But four years has been a long time away from home. Her mother worries that Mariko may have become too American, and that she may not be admitted to a first-rate Japanese university because of what the mother regards as an inferior American education.

*Asterisks denote pseudonyms.

These four young people are all Japanese Americans. Their lifetimes span the history of their people in the United States. Most Japanese Americans (Mariko is a recent exception) can point to ancestors like Hiroshi who came to America between 1890 and 1910. The Japanese who came then were just one small ripple in a gigantic wave of over 20 million immigrants who entered the United States between the Civil War and World War I. Others—Europeans—settled midwestern farms and provided the muscle for America's industrial revolution. Most Japanese immigrants, like Hiroshi (and like more Europeans than their descendants would like to acknowledge), thought of themselves as sojourners. They came to work, make money, and go back to the old country. Many did go back. But others stayed and raised families of children and grandchildren like Yuriyo and Bob.

This book is their story. It is the story of a people who left their country reeling under the impact of Western imperialism and the first sprouts of industrial capitalism. They came to another industrial, capitalist place, but most entered agriculture in the American West, not industry in the Northeast. They and their children moved quickly out of body labor and into small business, whether urban or agricultural. This they achieved despite energetic efforts on the part of White Americans to keep them in a subservient place. Whites passed laws to hurt Japanese and to drive them out, and at times they took up clubs and guns to punish them for daring to be in America. The ultimate attack came during World War II, when Whites forced nearly the entire Japanese American population into prison camps, merely on account of their race and their ancestral nationality. It took America nearly half a century to apologize and begin to make some small restitution for that extraordinary violation of civil rights.

But this book does not stop there. It also tells the story of Japanese Americans' return to their homes and communities after the war, their struggles to rebuild their lives, and the entry of a large part of the third and fourth generations into the American middle class. It tells of a revival of Japanese American ethnic assertiveness in the 1970s and 1980s, and the arrival of a new generation of immigrants like Mariko and her family. Finally, it considers the fate of Japanese American ethnic identity in an age when countervailing forces both encourage and work to wipe out individual ethnic groups in the United States.

Race and Ethnic Groups: The Traditional Way of Thinking

First, however, a few words are in order about the nature of ethnic groups.[1] Frequently, in talking about ethnic issues, people divide humankind up into large groups that they call "races" and smaller subgroups that they call "ethnic groups." According to that way of thinking, a partial listing of racial and ethnic groups might look like this:

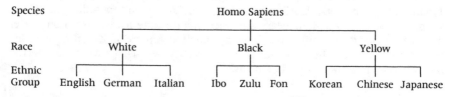

There are at least two problems with this way of thinking about race and ethnicity. In the first place, although it purports to be a biological classification system, "race" as defined here has only a tiny basis in biology. It is, in fact, primarily a social construct, as are the ethnic groups that are subdivisions of the races in this schema. Races do divide people into groups that are, on the average, physically distinct from each other. For example, Black people do, on the average, have darker skin, longer limbs, and wirier hair than do White people, on the average. And Asians do, on the average, have shorter limbs and darker hair than Caucasians, on the average. But those averages disguise a great deal of overlap. Let us take just one marker that is supposed to divide races biologically: skin color. Suppose people could be arranged according to the color of their skin along a continuum:

Darkest   2   3   4   5   6   7   Lightest

The people we call Black would nearly all fall on the darker end of the continuum, while the people we call White would nearly all fall on the lighter end, thus:

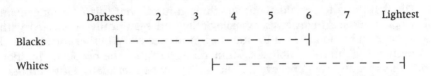

On the *average*, the White and Black populations are distinct from each other in skin color. But a very large number of the individuals classified as White have darker skin color than some people classified as Black, and vice versa. This fact inevitably leads one to the suspicion that so-called races are not biological categories at all, but rather that they are primarily social divisions that rely only partly on physical markers such as skin color to identify group membership.

The second problem with the notion of large "races" subdivided into smaller "ethnic groups" is that races, so defined, do not classify very much that is important. According to this way of thinking, Vietnamese and Koreans are of the same race. If one grants that they may look a bit similar to outsiders (they certainly do not to themselves), in what other ways are they similar? In what other ways is grouping them into one race significant? Do they act alike? Do they worship in the same way? Are their governments or family systems similar? Are they more like each other in action, thought, worship, and political behavior than either is like Swedes or Danes? Insofar as they may in fact be similar, is it because of their biology or because of centuries of contact and sharing of Chinese imperial culture?

All of this is not to argue that race is an unimportant category in human relationships, only that race, like ethnic grouping, is primarily a social and not a biological means of classifying people—indeed, that race is just a particular kind of ethnic group. The mechanisms that divide races from each other are the same mechanisms that divide ethnic groups from each another. The processes that bind a race together are the same processes that bind an ethnic group together. The generic term is "ethnic group," and that is what will be used in this book.

Race as Ethnic Group

Japanese Americans are an ethnic group, as are African Americans, Jewish Americans, and Croatian Americans. Rather than the old-fashioned, inaccurate image of ethnicity discussed thus far, the reader is encouraged to consider American ethnic groups like this:

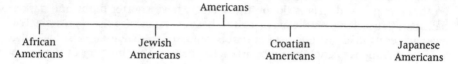

This is the way ethnic groups function in the United States. It will be significant for our study of Japanese Americans to understand what makes ethnic groups work—what holds ethnic groups together and what may cause them to fall apart. In this book, we shall see the Japanese American ethnic group being formed, we shall see it change the bases that hold it together, and we shall see what some would regard as the first stages of its demise.

The first thing to be said about an ethnic group is that it is an arrangement of people who see themselves as biologically and historically connected with each other, and who are seen by others as so connected. Whether the biological connection is accurate or not is less important than that the people in question and others around them believe it to be so. It may be that many East European Jews were not in fact biological descendants of the ancient Israelites but the descendants of Central Asian Khazar tribes who converted to Judaism in the Middle Ages. Nonetheless, they have believed themselves to be descended from the loins of Abraham, Isaac, and Jacob, and non-Jews have believed it, too. That sense of *shared ancestry,* and the thousands of years of shared history that go with it, form the basis of Jewish ethnic identity.

Ethnicity, then, is kinship writ large. But one can also identify three other forces that shape the creation, sustenance, dissolution, and reformation of ethnic groups: shared interests, shared institutions, and shared culture. All three are important. No one force is more fundamental than the others to the nature of an ethnic group. Each has a role to play in shaping group consciousness and action at various times in the history of the ethnic group.[2]

Shared interests, political or economic, are usually the force that pulls an ethnic group together in the first place. That is, if a set of people perceive themselves as sharing a common heritage and also have concrete economic or political reasons for affiliating, they may begin to form an ethnic group.

This type of group formation is occurring, for example, among "Hispanics" in the United States today. Hispanics, of course, are not yet a single group. The three largest groups—Mexicans, Puerto Ricans, and Cubans—have very little in common. Mexican Americans live throughout the country but are concentrated in the Southwest, exhibit an ancestral mixture of Spanish and Indian, are concentrated in the lower and middle classes, and vote heavily for the Democratic Party. Some have been in what is now the United States since before the American Revolution, while others arrived yesterday. Puerto Rican Americans are concentrated in the industrial cities of the Northeast, mix Black ancestry with Spanish and Indian, are heavily working-class, and generally vote

Democratic. Cuban Americans are concentrated in Florida, are visibly lighter-skinned on the average than the other two groups, include many more members of the upper-middle class, and usually vote for the Republican Party. Each of these groups came to the United States at a different time and for very different reasons. Each spoke a different variety of Spanish.

What all three groups have in common is an *interest*. Independently, none of the groups is large enough to attract much attention from government or the public at large outside the locale of its highest concentration. But together they can muster millions of voters. Thus, Mexican, Cuban, and Puerto Rican Americans have a political interest in banding together as "Hispanics." In time we may see Hispanics forming shared institutions and creating shared culture that will sustain their group. Another example of shared interests as the basis of ethnic group formation may have occurred in the decades surrounding 1900, when immigrants from Hiroshima and Wakayama and other Japanese prefectures banded together as Japanese Americans.

While interests may bring a group together initially, they change easily—they are external to the group and can be short-lived. Hispanics are becoming a single ethnic group in America, not because of any substantial natural commonality among them, but because there is a major tangible advantage to be gained by acting as a single group. If an ethnic group endures, it is usually because it forms shared institutions and builds up shared culture.

People within an ethnic group organize themselves to achieve their interests, practice their culture, and maintain their group identity by organizing *shared institutions*. There are any number of examples of ethnic institutions. The United Farm Workers is a Mexican American ethnic institution that expresses and protects the interests of laboring Chicanos. Cumberland Presbyterian Church in San Francisco is an ethnic institution where Chinese Americans come together to worship and socialize. Hadassah is an ethnic institution where Jewish women gather to connect with each other, reinforce their Jewishness, and serve their ethnic community. The National Association for the Advancement of Colored People is an ethnic institution that acts to legislate and defend the rights of African Americans. The family is the most powerful ethnic institution of all: family members come together for many purposes, among them to pass on their ethnic group's understandings of the world from one generation to the next.

Members of an ethnic group come together to pursue group interests within ethnic institutions—the United Negro College Fund is an example, as is the Anti-Defamation League of B'nai B'rith. But ethnic institutions are also places where *shared culture* is created and maintained. It is in Korean churches, Korean families, and Korean neighborhoods that the Korean language—an item of culture—is spoken and the ability to speak it is passed on. The culture is not just what people do in institutions, however. In and of itself, it is an important binding agent that keeps group identity alive. What do an Israeli farmer, a New York journalist, and a London businessman have in common? Nothing at all in terms of interests or institutions. Yet once a year they all say the same words at a Passover seder, and that ritual act—that piece of culture—binds them strongly together. Because they share culture, they all see themselves as Jews and as fundamentally related, indeed, as essential to each other.

Shared culture may be outward and visible to the noninvolved observer. Italian food, the Polish language, and Vietnamese Buddhism are examples. On the other hand, shared culture may be inward and more or less invisible. It can have to do with shared values, orientations, worldviews, attitudes. A trivial example will illustrate. Most Americans flip a switch and say they "turned on the light." But most Chinese Americans, down to the third generation, on performing the same act, say they "opened the light." Most American-born Chinese do not even realize that the expression derives from the Chinese-language term, which connotes opening a gate to allow a current to flow. This is an example of inward shared culture; others include patterns of child-rearing, facial affect, or talking with one's hands.

A New Model of Ethnic Group Formation

Most ethnic groups form initially on the basis of a tangible shared interest, as Hispanics seem to be doing today. They create ethnic institutions by which they organize themselves to pursue their common interests. As people come together in those institutions, they interact and create shared culture—rituals, habitual turns of phrase, behaviors, and understandings that bind them together. Institutions and cultures are much longer-lived than interests. They enable ethnic groups to survive changing circumstances. After an initially shared interest changes or disappears, culture and institutions may even hold the group together long enough for a new set of interests to emerge.

The model of ethnic group formation, persistence, and change offered here is rather different from the models found in many other books.[3] Most writers emphasize either interests, institutions, or culture and regard the other two as secondary or derivative. The contention here is that all three are equally important to the life of an ethnic group, though one or more may be the focus of a group's activities at a particular point in its history.

At any given point in the history of an ethnic group, one ought to be able to locate that group with respect to each factor along a continuum from low to high saliency. One of the underlying tasks of this study shall be to decide, at each point in time, whether shared interests, culture, or institutions formed the primary basis of Japanese American ethnic solidarity. We will attempt to assay the state of Japanese American ethnicity in the frontier phase (before about 1910), the immigrant community phase (from 1910 to about 1935), the early second generation (1930 to 1945), the later second generation (1945 to 1965), and the era of the third and fourth generations (since 1965). At times we may find a high degree of shared interests, at other times mainly shared culture or institutions. When two or more factors are strong, we will see that Japanese American ethnic solidarity is strong. If none of the factors seems very important, then we may conclude that Japanese American ethnic solidarity is weakening, reforming into a new shape, or even disappearing.

But that is getting ahead of the story. And it is important to remember that this is a story. History is neither a simple recital of the play of impersonal social and economic forces—although those are important—nor merely a recounting of the deeds of diplomats and politicians. The history of Japanese Americans is the story of Hiroshi and Yuriyo and Bob and Mariko and thousands of other Japanese Americans over the last century and more. Let the story begin.

two

The Japan They Left

Japan was a closed country for more than two centuries. From 1636 to 1853, the government, controlled by *shoguns,* or military rulers from the Tokugawa family, kept foreigners away from Japanese shores. The only exceptions were a few Chinese and Dutch traders, who were tightly limited in their contacts with Japanese people, plus the odd shipwrecked sailor. Down to 1885, it was illegal for any ordinary Japanese citizen to go abroad.

Japan in those centuries was not so much a modern nation as a collection of feudal baronies, dominated but not run by the powerful shogun in Edo (modern Tokyo). The barons were called *daimyo,* their fiefs were *han,* and their knights were known as *samurai* or *bushi.* Over the Tokugawa period, from 1600 through the 1860s, signs of a national culture and economy gradually emerged. Like Germany and Italy, however, Japan in the early modern era remained a loose collection of localities. For most Japanese, the focus of economics, social life, and identity was local, or at most regional.[1]

Not only was travel abroad forbidden, even travel within Japan was unusual for a Japanese peasant man, and eight out of ten Japanese were peasants. Men typically spent their whole lives within the confines of their village and family and their immediate neighborhood. The family was the unit of society, but the early modern Japanese family was larger and more complex than 20th-century families in Japan or Europe or North America. Three or even four generations in the male line might live under one roof, with collateral kin and servants as well as members of the core family. This *ie,* or extended family household, was dominated by its patriarch. Cultivation rights in farmland and family leadership passed from father to eldest son. Younger sons usually struck out on their own, but if the family were prosperous they could remain on the property and share in the inheritance. A woman would receive nothing, as she was expected to marry into another family. Surrounding this family might be several related *ie,* which together made up a *dozoku,* or clan. A village would ordinarily contain no more than a few *dozoku.* A male Japanese peasant would likely grow to maturity, marry, raise a family, and die all within walking distance of the place he was born. A peasant woman would migrate once, at marriage, from her family's village to that of her husband.

Changes in the Meiji Era

Change came rapidly to rural Japan in the second half of the 19th century. Economic change had been brewing in castle towns for several generations, but many rural areas remained unaffected. In the 1850s and 1860s, the Tokugawa system of economics and politics, which had prevailed for two centuries, collapsed. One contributing factor was the visit of an American fleet commanded by Commodore Matthew Perry. In 1853, and again in 1854, Perry's tall "Black Ships" sailed into Tokyo Bay and demanded that Japan open its doors to trade and contact with the outside world. The Tokugawa government held on for a decade and a half, but finally external and internal pressures brought it down in an 1868 revolution called the Meiji Restoration. Power was seized by bright, young samurai from Satsuma, Tosa, and Choshu, three marginally connected han in southwest Japan. Inside of a generation, they brought about a social revolution. They created new governmental institutions, a new social structure, and a new economy. They even created a new, unified Japanese national identity that extended to include the four main islands of Honshu, Shikoko, Kyushu, and Hokkaido, but not Okinawa, which remained in Japanese minds a separate, colonized entity.

The first task of the reformers was to create national unity where none had existed before. They sought to create in the people's minds a national sense of identity to replace the local and regional loyalties that had circumscribed their lives. To this end, they replaced the feudal han with a new set of prefectures controlled closely by the central government in Tokyo. They revived Shinto, an ancient Japanese religion, and made it into a national cult, with the emperor as its figurehead. He was a political figurehead as well. The Imperial Rescript on Education of 1890 incorporated Shinto and veneration of the emperor into the education of every Japanese schoolchild. "Kimigaiyo," the hauntingly beautiful national anthem, taken from a tenth-century poem, was promulgated as an expression of the Japanese national essence:

> *Thousands of years of happy reign be thine;*
> *Rule on, my lord, till what are pebbles now*
> *By age united to mighty rocks shall grow*
> *Whose venerable sides the moss doth line.*[2]

The makers of Meiji Japan also moved to forestall challenges from other political quarters. They disbanded the han and pensioned off daimyo and samurai. Then they made those formerly distinguished castes over into only slightly privileged commoners who, like other Japanese, had to go to work to earn a living. Equally important was the political task of keeping the foreign barbarians at bay. Japan's leaders were mindful of the nearby example of China. There European imperialists were destroying the country's sovereignty—forcing trade in opium on the Chinese, defeating them in a series of aggressive wars, demanding unequal treaties that limited China's right to govern its own affairs, seizing territory and spheres of influence. The Meiji leaders did not want Japan to fall into the same trap. They had to submit for a time to unequal treaties that surrendered part of their sovereignty, but they hoped to convince the Western powers to rescind the hated documents in a generation or two. They built a strong army and navy to make the Europeans think twice about attacking Japan, and they built modern political institutions they hoped Europeans would respect. They thus avoided the worst aspects of the Chinese fate and laid the foundation for becoming a major world power in the 20th century.

A necessary part of the change was a rapid overhaul of the Japanese economy. In one of the most amazing transformations in world history, mainly agricultural Japan became an industrial powerhouse in the space of two generations. The social costs were enormous, as we shall see. The Meiji government freed peasants to own land and to sell their crops and their labor in a market economy. A strong agricultural sector quickly grew, which the government then taxed brutally to pay for industrializing the country. After building a textile industry, then heavy industries such as steel and shipbuilding on the backs of tens of thousands of workers, the government and private entrepreneurs connected Japan with world markets. By the turn of the century, Japan was the foremost industrial and military power in Asia.

In the midst of this maelstrom of change, the Japanese people made their first sustained contacts with the West. Learning from Europe and the United States was the policy of the Meiji oligarchs, and it began very early. The Tokugawa government and various han had sent abroad about 150 students prior to the Meiji Restoration of 1868—nearly all to Europe. In 1871 several of the new Meiji rulers went abroad themselves at the head of the Iwakura Mission. For two years more than 100 government officials and students— Japan's best and brightest young men—toured the United States, Britain, and the European continent. They examined Western science, technology, government, law, education, and culture, then went home to plan Japan's future. Japanese businesspeople, too, became parties to international interchange. As Japan's economy became enmeshed with the world market, traveling businesspeople brought back knowledge of foreign ways.

Western people and culture also came to Japan. Following the Meiji Restoration, a rage for things Western swept the country. People adopted Western suits and dresses for public occasions. They imitated Western painting, and Japanese woodblock prints could be had for a pittance. Baseball made its Japanese debut in 1872 and had become a standard high school sport a decade later. Some people suggested abandoning the Japanese script for the Roman alphabet. Others wanted to junk the Japanese language altogether and replace it with English. Some leaders suggested a program to encourage intermarriage with Europeans and Americans in order to invigorate the Japanese gene pool. A reaction to all this worship of the West set in during the latter 1880s, when Japanese people gained more self-confidence on the international stage and a nationalist movement took over. But Western culture had made its mark on Japan.

Part of that mark was made by the American Christian missionaries who flocked to the country in the 1870s and 1880s. Although their long-term conversion rate was low, they started schools and had a strong impact on Japanese education. In the first generation, they made a number of key converts among the intellectual class. Some of these Japanese converts sooner or later followed their hearts and emigrated to their mentors' homeland. Others stayed in Japan and helped create Japan's small but active labor and socialist movements around the turn of the century.

Economic Change and Migration

Other Americans who came to Japan were not looking for converts. American labor contractors such as Robert W. Irwin and diplomats such as Eugene Van Reed, working for the owners of Hawaiian sugar plantations, came to Japan starting in 1868 to look for workers. Their first start was a false one. Van Reed illegally recruited 150 Japanese people (all but seven of them young men) off the streets of Yokohama in 1868. He sneaked them out of the country and sent them to work in Hawai'i's plantations. Few were farmers, however, and they did not last long. They were badly treated by their overseers and quickly quit and moved to Honolulu. When the Japanese government learned of the mal-treatment of its citizens, it pressed them to come home; most chose to stay on and thereafter merged into the Hawaiian population.

The Wakamatsu Tea and Silk Colony of 1869 was another failed venture. John Henry Schnell was a German who traded in Japan in the late Tokugawa years. He became friends with some Japanese who found themselves on the los-ing side of the conflict leading up to the Meiji Restoration. At least 22 of them went to California (how is not known) and tried to establish a tea and silk-farm-ing operation on land that Schnell and his brother owned near Gold Hill, north of Sacramento. What happened to the colony is unclear. It did not succeed as a farming venture—the climate is not right for tea or mulberry trees, and neither the Schnells nor their Japanese colleagues seem to have known much about farming. Schnell, his Japanese wife, and their children left the colony, perhaps in 1872. A few members of the colony are remembered by their headstones. One read:

> *In Memory of Okei.*
> *Died in 1871.*
> *Age 19 years.*
> *A Japanese girl.*[3]

Another recalls the life of Sakurai Matsunosuke, who worked nearby as a carpenter for the next three decades. The only Wakamatsu person whose history is known is Masumizu Kuninosuke, who married a Black woman, fathered a family whose descendants live in the Sacramento area today, and lived until 1915.

If these early, furtive expeditions to the United States ended in failure, there was one successful venture: the program inaugurated by the Meiji government in the wake of the Iwakura Mission to send students abroad to school. The idea was to learn as much as possible about Western science, technology, and culture and to return home full of knowledge that would enable Japan to grow strong. The Meiji government sent several hundred students to Britain, France, Germany, and the United States in the 1870s and 1880s. Others went on their own: about 900 studied in the United States between 1868 and 1900. The most famous of the returned students was Niijima Jo. In 1865, Niijima, at age 22, sneaked out of Japan and went to Massachusetts. There he studied at Phillips Academy, Amherst College, and Andover Theological Seminary. On his return to Japan in 1874, he became that country's foremost Christian and one of its most renowned educators. The prime promoter of all this activity was the educator and journalist Fukuzawa Yukichi.[4] Fukuzawa published a newspaper in which he described America to the Japanese and encouraged able young men to go abroad. Quite a number did. Many of the young men sent by the government were sons of former samurai families. On their return, they took up positions in government and business. An increasing number of others in the 1880s and 1890s were ambitious young commoners who scraped together some money and went abroad under their own sponsorship to better themselves.

Large-scale emigration did not begin until the 1880s, after Japan made it legal and social forces compelled certain young people to seek their fortunes abroad. Primary among these forces was economic distress. The early Meiji years were hard economic times for nearly all Japanese. While the economy stagnated, the population was growing rapidly. Samurai lost their lands and titles and had to subsist on fixed government stipends. The inflation of the 1870s eroded those stipends and threw many former samurai into poverty. Farmers suffered from inflation and also from the government's heavy land tax that was used to build Japan's industrial base. The first seven years of the Meiji era saw 190 riots by farmers. As Japan entered the world capitalist market system, that system intruded into the countryside. Farmers' income was further reduced when cheap foreign cotton textiles were imported into Japan, displacing the supplemental income farm families had made by weaving cloth. Violent swings of the economy—inflation in the 1870s was followed by depression in the 1880s—reduced landowners to tenants, and tenants to landless wanderers. In 1884 the Kanagawa farmer-leader Sunaga Renzo submitted the following petition to the government:

> The 200,000 people of this prefecture are unable to repay their debts because of declining prices and the depressed state of the silkworm business and textile industry in general. They are plagued day and night with worries, sorrow, frustration, and hardship. People are being crushed underfoot by the usurers as if they were ants. The demonstration by the members of the Debtors' party in this prefecture in mid-1884 proved to be fruitless; all we got was a lecture from the authorities. No lenience or generosity was forthcoming. . . . Under current conditions [the debtors] can find no way to repay their debts. I beg your excellencies to allow sentiments of morality and benevolence to come forth and, even if the letter of the law has to be distorted a little, to adopt measures that would aid the impoverished people.[5]

Many went to the cities, only to discover that industrial wages were low, the labor movement was being ruthlessly suppressed by the Japanese government, and industry did not have enough job slots to absorb all the landless laborers. Those who found jobs often had to work in wretched conditions:

> From morning, while it was still dark, we worked in the lamplit factory till ten at night. After work, we hardly had the strength to stand on our feet. When we worked late into the night, they occasionally gave us a yam. We then had to do our washing, fix our hair, and so on. By then it would be eleven o'clock. There was no heat even in the winter, and so we had to sleep huddled together. Several of the girls ran

back to Hida. I was told the girls who went to work before my time had a harder time. We were not paid the first year. In the second year I got 35 yen, and the following year, 50 yen. I felt that it was not a place for a weak-willed person like me. If we didn't do the job right we were scolded, and, if we did better than others, the others resented it.[6]

Between 1884 and 1886, one-seventh of Japan's rice land was taken in mortgage foreclosures. In 1885, Japanese working people, faced with economic crisis, began legal emigration on a large scale. The Japanese government gave in to the importunings of the kingdom of Hawai'i and agreed to send the first of tens of thousands of people who would go abroad under labor contracts. That agreement was not a formal repeal of the edict of 1636. There had been some leakage—like Niijima and Fukuzawa—for years. Theirs was simply a pragmatic decision to allow some carefully selected workers to go abroad and thereby lessen economic pressures at home.

Other motives besides economic ones caused people to leave Japan. Some *imin* (emigrants) were political refugees—losing supporters of the Tokugawa (like the Wakamatsu colony people), participants in the popular rights movement of the 1870s, socialists, or labor activists. They went abroad to take refuge from their government. Others, especially during the Sino-Japanese War (1894–95) and the Russo-Japanese War (1904–5), were draft dodgers. In 1873 the Meiji oligarchs established a national conscription law, a necessary step to build a modern army after the abolition of the samurai class. Later amendments gave deferments to students and people living abroad; this was a powerful incentive for young men to go abroad and stay there until age 37, when one became too old for the draft.

The emigrants picked the United States as their destination for three reasons: image, financial advantage, and personal connections. Since the first years of the Meiji era, the United States had enjoyed a very positive image in Japan. That image was enhanced by the writing of people like Fukuzawa Yukichi and Niijima Jo and by the activities of American missionary educators in Japan—all of them apostles of American culture. Perhaps the most compelling reason for choosing the United States as a destination, however, lay in what one could earn there. In 1885 a male farmworker in Japan could expect to make about $1.72 per month. A female laborer could earn 84¢ as a domestic or 95¢ as a farmworker. The first Hawaiian labor contracts, by contrast, promised the male laborer $15 a month and a female $10. Wage differentials varied by time and the degree and type of skill required, but American wages ranged between five and twenty-five times as high as Japanese wages.[7]

A lot of imin went to America because they knew someone who had gone to America earlier and succeeded. Typically, one person from a village would go abroad—to work, to study, or just for adventure. If he returned home rich or wrote back describing the splendors of life in Hawai'i or America, others from the village might follow his path. (This pattern of chain migration was also typical of Irish, Italian, and many other immigrants in the 19th and 20th centuries.) Some prefectures—Hiroshima, Yamaguchi, and Wakayama, for instance—sent thousands of people abroad, while others sent almost none. And people from different parts of Japan tended to follow their neighbors to certain destinations.

For example, many Okinawans went to Hawai'i, but very few went to the American mainland.

Not all the emigrants went abroad. Probably even more were driven by economic or other circumstances to move to other parts of Japan. Since early in the Tokugawa period, some Japanese peasants had been *dekasegi-nin,* people who go out to work. Typically, they were young women or men who left their villages to work in nearby towns when farmwork was slack. They would return to their homes and families when planting or harvesting demanded their labor. The cash they earned and brought or sent back provided a valuable supplement to the family's income. Others were migrant agricultural workers. They would go out to work during the labor-intensive rice-planting season and follow the crops, starting in the mountains and moving to the lowland paddies, where planting is done later. Such movements were restricted during the Tokugawa period. But in Meiji Japan, some farm people began to travel quite long distances, from one end of the archipelago to the other. Loggers and fisherfolk also increasingly moved from place to place as their livelihoods became depleted and they had to seek new places to work. In the late Meiji era, the dekasegi pattern of going out to earn money and return was extended overseas.

Emigrant Characteristics

Which Japanese people went abroad and which stayed home? In the first place, the overwhelming majority of emigrants came from only a handful of prefectures in southwestern Japan: Hiroshima, Wakayama, Kumamoto, Fukuoka, Yamaguchi, Okayama, Nagasaki, Saga, Kagoshima, and, somewhat later, the Japanese dependency of Okinawa. Notably absent were emigrants from the major population centers around Tokyo and Osaka. This regional concentration seems to have been attributable not to any particular hardships suffered in these prefectures during Japan's industrialization, but to the fact that labor recruiters, such as Hawai'i's Robert Irwin, were especially active in those places. Irwin did most of his recruiting in Yamaguchi Prefecture because his Japanese contacts, Inoue Kaoru and Masuda Takashi, were from there. Once labor agents—Japanese or foreign—met success in particular regions, they tended to go back to those places. And once the people of a particular locality had established a pattern of successful emigration and return, their neighbors found it easy to venture forth, even without the facilitating presence of a labor agent. Not only particular Japanese prefectures but certain villages within those prefectures were the fountainheads of emigration. For example, the villages of Jigozen and Kuchida in Hiroshima Prefecture sent large numbers of people abroad, whereas neighboring villages sent far fewer. A 1925 survey of Jigozen found that half the population resided abroad.[8]

The imin ranged up and down the social ladder, from ex-samurai to poor outcasts, and across the occupations, from farmer to fisher to *sake* brewer to Buddhist priest. But patterns are discernible. The three largest groups were farmers, merchants, and students. Depending on the year and place of departure, between 45 and 80 percent of those emigrating had been farmers. That percentage was higher in the early years, among those who signed labor contracts to work in Hawai'i, than in later years, when most people went as free

Figure 2.1   Japanese prefectures that sent the largest number of emigrants to Hawai'i and the United States
SOURCE: Franklin Odo and Kazuko Sinoto, A *Pictorial History of the Japanese in Hawai'i, 1885–1924* (Honolulu: Bishop Museum Press).

14

individuals. Because Hawaiian labor agents wanted to avoid repeating the fiasco of 1868, when big-city street people did not work out on Hawaiian plantations, 90 percent of the workers they recruited in the 1880s were farmers. Over the entire period of emigration, a somewhat smaller percentage of the emigrants were farmers than was true of the whole Japanese population.[9]

Before the 1890s, most of the emigrants came from the lower economic strata of tenant farmers, agricultural laborers, and owners of very small plots of land. As such people succeeded abroad, middling farmers with more substantial stakes in Japan joined the flow of emigration. Partly the shift reflected changing recruitment practices: in the early years, when most of the dekasegi-nin went under contract to Hawai'i, expenses were paid by the employer. By the end of the century, most emigrants were going on their own and had to pay their own expenses.

Merchants, the second group of emigrants, made up between 5 and 20 percent of the outward flow, depending on time and place. Some were connected with major merchant houses and were sent to cultivate new markets abroad. But most were the proprietors of small and often marginal family businesses who went abroad in search of capital to improve their situation at home.

Students also made up between 5 and 20 percent of the emigrants. Many were recent graduates who went to the United States to work, not to study. Others had been working and went abroad to further their education. Students made up the majority of Japanese emigrants to America in the first generation after Meiji, and their absolute numbers increased steadily through the 1920s. But they declined as a *percentage* of the total emigrant population when the number of agricultural laborers going to the U.S. mainland exploded in the 1890s. Between 1868 and 1881, about 45 percent of the more than 300 Japanese students who went abroad did so under government sponsorship. Between 1882 and 1896, the government cut back its funding as the number of students who left independently soared: of the 2,478 students who traveled abroad in that period, only 15 were supported by the government.[10]

As we shall see in chapter 3, Americans viewed the Japanese who came to their country as a crude, ill-educated lot. This perception may have arisen partly from the fact that most Japanese were forced to work in menial jobs in the United States. But native American Whites were also predisposed to make negative and condescending evaluations of immigrant peoples. In fact, Japanese emigrants were quite well educated. Those who left Hyogo Prefecture for Hawai'i were on the low end: 90 percent had only the government-mandated six years of primary education. But those who went to the American mainland were much better educated, on the average, than the general Japanese public and in fact compared well with the turn-of-the-century American population. Sixty percent had at least completed middle school, and 21 percent were high school graduates.[11]

Yasuo Wakatsuki argues plausibly that a large minority of the emigrants were rural elementary schoolteachers. They were bright and ambitious people who took advantage of free tuition to attend normal school but then found their way to higher education and lucrative government and business careers blocked. By going abroad, they hoped to forge ahead with their careers in a society where, unlike Japan, ability counted for more than education.

There were a few people from samurai families among the earliest student emigrants of the 1860s and 1870s, but the mass migration of the 1880s included few ex-samurai. More ex-samurai joined the overseas movement late in the Meiji period, when samurai fortunes declined and more middling people emigrated.

One might suppose that the poorest members of Japanese society—people then called *eta* and now called *burakumin* ("village people") euphemistically— would have strong motivation to leave Japan and try to make lives for themselves unburdened by their status as members of a hereditary outcast class. But such was not the case. There were burakumin in America, and it was widely rumored that they formed the majority in a few Japanese American communities, such as one small town near Sacramento, California.[12] But in fact, burakumin constituted far less than 1 percent of the imin population, significantly less than in Japan as a whole. Many burakumin probably could not afford the fare, and in any case, they were not usually connected to the village and family networks that facilitated the migration of so many others.

Scholars have long assumed that almost all the Japanese migrants were men and that those women who went abroad did so as wives of male migrants. The best recent scholarship, however, suggests that perhaps 20 percent of early immigrants were women and that many if not most of them traveled abroad on their own, independent of male emigrants. Much has been made of the fact that some worked as prostitutes, for Japanese or non-Japanese clients. But it seems that sex work was usually a temporary occupation for women, who later entered occupations with higher social status.[13]

Christians were more likely to emigrate to the United States than Buddhists or Japanese who practiced other religions. Some, like Niijima Jo, went abroad to pursue their Christian commitment. Others went primarily for economic reasons but were encouraged by missionary mentors or the desire to live for a time in what they understood to be a Christian nation. In the modern era, Christians never made up so much as 1 percent of the Japanese population. But by about 1910, there were substantial Christian minorities in Japanese communities in the United States. Many had emigrated as Christians; others were proselytized in the United States. By World War II, 22 percent of first-generation Japanese Americans were Christians.[14]

Given the strict system of primogeniture in Tokugawa and Meiji Japan, one would expect that younger sons, with no prospect of inheriting family property, would have been the ones to go off to seek their fortunes while the family scions stayed home. Certainly many families followed that pattern. But the only studies of family status among Japanese emigrants to America suggest just the opposite: 41 percent of emigrant men whose family status is known were family heads; 28 percent were eldest sons; 31 percent were younger sons. More than two-thirds either controlled or stood next in line for the family property.[15]

As to the emigrants' average age, it was a very young population, as one would expect of any group of emigrants. Many were in their teens, most were in their twenties, and almost none were past 40 when they ventured forth.[16]

What It Took to Migrate

From 1885 and the beginning of formal contract labor in Hawai'i, straight through the 1920s, the Japanese government exercised very stringent controls over the issuing of passports. Details varied over the decades, but a typical set of strictures read like this one for Hawaiian contract laborers:

(1) The emigrant laborer shall meet the following conditions:
(a) The person shall be a bona fide farmer.
(b) The person shall abide by the terms of the agreement on emigrant labor and shall be in a state of health to withstand farm work.
(c) The person shall be between 25 and 30 years of age. However, when a person under 40 years of age qualifies under Article 2, he shall be classified as a substitute and may be accepted by the examiners after due deliberation.
(d) The person(s) shall be a single person or a married couple with no dependents.
(2) A person who falls under any of the under-mentioned categories shall not be eligible for recruitment:
(a) *Shizoku* (person of the *samurai* social class), a merchant, a craftsman, a handyman, or a farmer who at the same time engages in trading, handicrafts, or miscellaneous services.
(b) A person who will reach the age of conscription during the contract period and has military service obligation.
(c) A person who is under 20 or older than 40 years in age.
(d) A female who is more than four months pregnant.
(e) Any suffering from chronic or hereditary diseases.
(f) A person who is without a wife but with an infant.[17]

Many more requests for passports were denied than were granted. The percentage of acceptances ranged from 10 to perhaps 40 or 50 percent. In the first recruitment drive in Yamaguchi, several thousand people applied for 600 places. The final emigrants were chosen by lot from among the qualified applicants. In 1888, in the village of Kuga in Yamaguchi, 99 people applied and 39 were accepted. In the village of Okukuga in Kumamoto, 34 applied and 3 were accepted. Nearby in the village of Ujiguchi, 75 applied and 12 were accepted.

The national and prefectural governments demanded that emigrants find two or three propertied citizens who would stand guarantee. One letter of guarantee from 1906 read:

To the Governor of Fukushima Prefecture
Name and Address of Applicant:
In connection with the travel to the United States of the above-mentioned person to undergo commercial training, funds necessary for the above person to attain his objective should, without fail, be borne by his parental family, but in case of unforeseen disaster, sickness, etc., we the undersigned shall, as a matter of course, be jointly responsible for all liabilities and shall guarantee against any eventuality that might invite national disgrace.
Month _____ Day _____
Guarantors:
Address:_____ Name:_____
Address:_____ Name:_____
Address:_____ Name:_____ [18]

All this reflected the Japanese government's concern over avoiding international embarrassments that would dampen its hopes of convincing Western nations to rescind the unequal treaties. The apparatus of control meant that when, shortly after 1900, American Whites began to complain about the immigration of Japanese laborers, the Japanese government had the means to curtail the flow quickly.

Once an emigrant's documents were in order, he or she had to get to America. If he was going to Hawai'i under contract, the agent handled the transportation and took the cost (plus interest) out of the worker's wages later on. If the emigrant was on his own, he had to pay his expenses to the port of embarkation and then the fare across the Pacific. In 1897 the trans-Pacific fare was $32.50 to Hawai'i and $44.50 to the American West Coast, third-class. If the emigrant went to the mainland, he had to demonstrate to U.S. immigration officials that he would not become a public charge. This usually meant that he had to show that he had $30 to $50 in cash. The total amount that an independent emigrant needed for the trip around 1900, with nothing left over upon landing, would be on the order of $100.

To gather such a huge sum was beyond the means of a Japanese peasant. Some sold land or businesses. Families went into debt, at 30 to 40 percent annual interest, in order to send one member abroad. In Wakayama Prefecture, aspiring emigrants formed mutual credit associations. Eight or ten would pool their money to send one person to the United States. That person, able to earn more money in the New World, would make remittances, along with the contributions of the remaining members, until a second person could go. Then both would send money and cut the time before a third person could join them. With any luck, in a matter of ten years or so, all members of the credit association might be at work in America.

In the 1880s most emigrants had only a very imperfect idea of what they were getting into. But by around 1900, enough people had returned and told their stories that quite a bit of information was available. Colonization societies were formed to encourage emigration and share information about travel, documents, jobs, housing, and social relations in the United States. Guide books were printed that included such information, as well as detailed descriptions of various locations and of the U.S. banking, currency, postal, and education systems. By the height of Japanese emigration to the United States in the years 1900–1910, an emigrant could board ship with a fairly good idea of what lay in store.

What did the Japanese who stayed home think about those who went abroad? On the whole, their evaluations tended to be negative. To be sure, villages appreciated the money sent back by those who had gone out to work. And those villages that sent many sons and daughters to America must have had a positive attitude toward emigration. But for centuries Japanese people had done very little moving around, except for the dekasegi minority, and certainly none had gone halfway around the globe for decades at a time. Most viewed the imin as trash, as cowards, as people who had failed to make it in Japan and so were forced to go abroad. It was by no means an accurate assessment, but it colored the attitude of many stay-at-home Japanese. One such, named Chikuzan, visited America briefly around 1911 and came back to write the following:

The Japanese emigrants on the American West Coast are not representative of the real Japanese people. . . . I do not say that there are not some among them who are worthy of respect, but they are only a handful. The reputation of the vast majority is that there is not a good one among the lot. . . .

These people escape from the scrutiny of the Japanese people and live a life that is, in effect, a long journey abroad. Because they believe only in earning the maximum amount of money with the least amount of work, their behavior can be easily imagined. These are the people who boast that they are citizens of a first-class nation, so even the American cannot help but be exasperated. . . .

There may be some who will resent my words as being too insulting toward the Japanese. But I believe even now that the unpleasant impressions I gained on the trip across the ocean and immediately after landing on the West Coast were such that even these words are inadequate. The fact that the Japanese consul in America has termed the Japanese emigrants as a national disgrace is by no means unjustified.[19]

Such a negative Japanese attitude toward the emigrants as failures and disreputable people persisted well into the second half of the 20th century. Yet as we shall see in the next chapter, the imin were, on the whole, talented, brave, and energetic people who struggled and succeeded in wresting a living from a hostile nation.

three

Emigrants and Frontiersmen

Few came as immigrants at first. Most came to make some money and then go home. Bunji Suemori of Hiroshima recalled years afterward: "I went to Hawai'i in 1904 when I was 16. I was an adopted son, and my father-in-law told me, 'Come back in three years.' I intended to return after saving $500 in that period."[1] This motive was not unusual; it was shared by most turn-of-the-century immigrants to the United States from Italy, Greece, and the Balkan states as well. Most of the Japanese who came to America saw themselves initially as involved in *dekasegi* (going out to work), not *teiju* (emigrating permanently). Nearly all of them were young men, restless to get ahead, moving from job to job.

The Japanese who came to America were only one tiny ripple on a vast wave of immigrants who surged out of the Old World and into the United States around the turn of this century. Japanese immigrants began to come in earnest in the 1890s, somewhat later than the southern and eastern Europeans who made up what historians call the New Immigration, and much later than the majority of the northern and western Europeans who had taken part in the Old Immigration. At the crest in the first decade of this century, about 13,000 Japanese came to America each year, compared with 34,000 Germans, 205,000 Italians, 215,000 from the Austro-Hungarian Empire, 25,000 Norwegians, 17,000 Greeks, and 16,000 Turks annually during the same decade. Between 1881 and 1930, more than 27 million immigrants came to these shores. Of that number, 275,308—barely 1 percent—were Japanese.[2] Yet the Japanese were a special target for abuse from other Americans and assumed political importance far beyond their numbers.

Hawai'i

The Japanese American story begins in Hawai'i, for it was in Hawaiian cane-fields that large numbers of Japanese immigrants first worked. In the early years, Hawai'i had a larger Japanese population than the U.S. mainland, and even today, nearly one-third of all Japanese Americans live in the 50th state. Japanese Hawaiian history is largely a separate story from Japanese American history on the mainland, the primary focus of this book. It is useful to look at developments in Hawai'i, however, because they helped form the experiences

Table 3.1   *Japanese and Total Immigration to the United States, by Decades*

Decade	Total Immigration	Japanese Immigration	Japanese as Percent of Total
1861–70	2,314,824	186	0.01%
1871–80	2,812,191	149	0.01
1881–90	5,246,613	2,270	0.04
1891–1900	3,687,564	25,942	0.70
1901–10	8,795,386	129,797	1.48
1911–20	5,735,811	83,837	1.46
1921–30	4,107,209	33,462	0.81
1931–40	528,431	1,948	0.37
1941–50	1,035,039	1,555	0.15
1951–60	2,515,479	46,250	1.84
1961–70	3,321,677	39,988	1.20
1971–80	4,493,314	49,775	1.11
1981–89	5,801,579	40,654	0.70
1861–1980	50,390,117	455,813	0.90

SOURCE: Leonard Dinnerstein and David M. Reimers, *Ethnic Americans,* 3d ed. (New York: Harper & Row, 1988), 206–12; U.S. Department of Justice, *1989 Statistical Yearbook of The Immigration and Naturalization Service* (Washington, D.C.: Dept. of Justice, 1990), 4.

of mainland Japanese Americans. Many Japanese experiences in Hawai'i are parallel to their mainland experiences; others stand in sharp contrast. The main features that set the Hawaiian Japanese experience off from that on the mainland were the islands' plantation economy, the limited geographical movement available to Hawaiian Japanese, the contract labor system, the islands' colonial status after the American takeover, a complex racial hierarchy, and the presence of a larger percentage of women in the Japanese population in the islands (between 20 and 40 percent in the 19th century; see Mengel reference in note 13 to ch. 2).

The migration to Hawai'i began before the flow to the mainland United States. More than 12,000 Japanese lived in the Hawaiian kingdom in 1890. A decade later, after the U.S. annexation in 1898, more than 60,000 lived in the new territory of Hawai'i. These numbers continued to rise by approximately 30 percent per decade through the 1930s. By contrast, the main migration of Japanese to the U.S. mainland came during the 1900s and 1910s, and the numbers leveled off thereafter (see appendix, table 2).

Those who went to Hawai'i entered the world of the plantation. They were recruited by agents who worked for about 50 different emigration companies in Japan. The companies signed contracts to provide workers for Hawaiian sugar plantations. Their agents then traveled the back roads of rural Japan, recruiting laborers. The companies helped the would-be emigrants arrange passports and paperwork and booked their passage to Hawai'i, in return for a portion of their earnings for the life of their contracts. Between 1891 and 1908, these companies sent over 124,000 Japanese farm laborers to Hawai'i.[3]

3.1   Women cane workers in Hawai'i, 1890s. *Courtesy of Bishop Museum.*

The labor contracts amounted to indentured servitude, usually for a period of three years. During that time, the worker was a virtual slave of the plantation owner. Hours were long, labor was bone-crushing, discipline was harsh, and a worker's time was not his or her own. One field worker lamented, "In Japan we could say, 'It's okay to take the day off today,' since it was our own work. We were free to do what we wanted. We didn't have that freedom on the plantation. We had to work ten hours every day"—planting, hoeing, stripping leaves, cutting cane, and processing the harvest.[4] Women as well as men worked the fields and felt the lash of the *luna*, or overseer.

The plantations were multiracial places, but not melting pots. From 1892 to 1915, between one-half and three-quarters of the plantation workforce was Japanese.[5] But there were also large numbers of Filipinos and Chinese, as well as Hawaiians, Haoles (Whites), Koreans, and Portuguese. An ethnic hierarchy prevailed: owners were Haoles, Portuguese filled the luna spot, and the darker races did the manual work. Owners divided the field laborers into separate ethnic gangs, each typically with its own living quarters and each paid a different wage. The separate quarters gave people a place to speak their native languages, cook their native foods, and keep company with people from their homelands. They also helped the planters rule, by dividing the working class. Some mixing did occur in the workplace, however. One fruit of that mixing was *pidgin*, a polyglot language built on Hawaiian grammar using words from all the languages of the plantation, a Creole derivative of which is still spoken in Hawai'i.[6]

After Hawai'i became a U.S. territory, the Organic Act of 1900 incorporated U.S. law into Hawai'i. This effectively outlawed the contract system, because it created unfree labor that reminded Americans of slavery. Nonetheless, exploitation continued. The planters dominated Hawaiian territorial politics, as they had during the late years of the monarchy. They maintained their hold on their workers by cooperating with each other to fix wages and prices and by calling on the territorial government when needed to retain their grip.

Workers resisted this oppression in a number of ways, from malingering to retreat into drugs and alcohol to staging strikes. Most, however, served out their contracts and then left the plantation. As one Japanese work song put it,

> *I hate "hole hole" work [stripping cane stalks]*
> *Let's finish cutting cane*
> *And go to Honolulu.*[7]

Thousands left the plantations and sought work in Honolulu.[8] Probably as many went back to Japan. More moved on to the American West Coast, until that avenue of migration was cut off in 1907.

The Mainland Diaspora

On the mainland, migrants from Hawai'i were joined by thousands more coming directly from Japan. In the period 1891–1900, 27,440 laborers went straight from Japan to the American West Coast. In the period 1901–7, that number jumped to 42,457, with over 38,000 more coming via Hawai'i.[9] Chojiro Kubo described the journey:

[I]n August of 1897 I went to the U.S. by the cargo boat, "Yamaguchi Maru" (3,000 tons) from Kobe. I was then 16. The third class accommodations were crowded with more than 160 passengers and there wasn't any bunk in which to rest. I slept spreading my own mat and blanket on the wooden floor in the front hatch where there were no windows and no lights. Overhead a piece of net was hung, and when the boat rolled we clung to the net to keep from being thrown around. Day after day the weather was bad and the sea stormy. The hatch was tightly closed and there was no circulation of air, so we were all tortured by the bad odor. As the boat was small, whenever a high wave hit us the top deck was submerged and the sound of the screw grinding in empty space chilled us. The food was second class Nankin rice and salted kelp, with dirty clams preserved by boiling in soy sauce. It was impossible fare which now I wouldn't dare to eat. I shivered, thinking that I would probably go back to Japan some years later in just such a boat. Everyone was groggy with seasickness. On the 27th day we arrived in Port Angeles [Washington], opposite Victoria [British Columbia]. We were given a severe health examination and our baggage and possessions were all collected and put into one room where they were fumigated with sulphur combined with other disinfectants. Consequently my shoes shrunk and my coat was so wrinkled that I couldn't use it any more. We sailed from Victoria and arrived at our destination, Seattle, on the 5th of October, docking at Pier 5.[10]

Seattle was the main port of entry for all Japanese coming to the U.S. main-land. The key people there were labor contractors. Men like Kumamoto Hifumi and Takahashi Tetsuo opened offices on Puget Sound and negotiated contracts to provide section hands for the Great Northern and Northern Pacific Railroads, which were just then building rail networks across the northwest quarter of the United States. Recruited in Japan and in Hawai'i, young men were sent out in teams from Japanese-owned boardinghouses in Seattle and San Francisco to work in gangs laying track. Soon the contractors were also finding jobs for workers in Alaskan fish canneries, Wyoming coal mines, and the lumber mills of the Northwest.

The contractors made a lot of money. They typically took 10¢ out of each rail-road worker's $1.10 daily wage, and a similar percentage out of the much higher wages of miners and lumber workers. They also charged workers fees for provi-sions, minimal health care, letter-writing services, and sending remittances home. Some employers paid finder's fees to the contractors as well. Workers put up with the exploitation because they were at the contractors' mercy: few work-ers spoke much English yet or knew their way around the American geographi-cal and economic landscape. But turnover was rapid as Japanese workers got their bearings and struck out on their own.

The Japanese American population of this period was more spread out than at any later time until after World War II. The 1900 census missed a lot of the ever-moving men. Most of the 5,617 in Washington the census did find lived in rural areas; the same was true for the 10,151 in California. The census also found 2,441 Japanese in Montana, 2,501 in Oregon, and 2,291 in Idaho (see appendix, table 2). The experience of Inota Tawa was typical of workers in this frontier period:

It was 1893 when I entered Idaho as a member of Tadashichi Tanaka's group of workers. . . . We dressed like American railroad workers in shirts and dungarees and American shoes. . . . We worked ten hours a day and made $1.15, out of which 10 cents was withheld as employ-ment commission. White workers got $1.45 per day. Two or three months every winter we were out of a job. . . . One or two hundred workers waited in the Nampa camp until the snow melted in spring. Room and board there cost approximately $7 or $8 per month, and the system was that we would pay it back when we started working again in spring. . . .

The section life at that time was very crude. Between six and ten people were living together per section. The foremen were all whites, and they lived by twos in separate buildings. They were high-salaried men making $60 to $70 per month. Since it was a camp in the moun-tains, there was no recreation available. . . . The only pleasure was pay day once a month. Receiving our checks, we went off into town, bought bourbon at $1 or $2 a bottle, canned salmon and—secretly— rice. We cooked the rice, put vinegar over the salmon and piled that on top of the rice. We called it "sushi" and enjoyed it gleefully. Getting drunk on the cheap whiskey, we sang the songs of our homeland and talked about the memories of home. . . .

For three years and a half I worked this way and sent the money—nearly three thousand yen—to my father in Okayama. He bought about a five-acre field [a large farm by Japanese standards] and suddenly became a rich man in the village. As I had realized the first goal of coming to the States, I decided to work for myself after that, and went down south to San Francisco.[11]

In this unsettled frontier period, young male Japanese workers quickly learned survival English, moved out from under the thumb of the labor contractors, and found jobs on their own. Although large numbers continued to work in railroad construction, lumbering, mining, and cannery work, in the first decade of this century the majority of Japanese Americans gradually moved into agriculture. They were still a mobile lot, young men living in migrant labor camps and following the crops from vegetable fields near the Mexican border up through California, Oregon, and Washington into British Columbia's orchard country. By 1910 Japanese were the largest single population group among agricultural laborers in California, as in Hawai'i.[12] It was only later, after about 1910, that this frontier phase gradually came to an end and Japanese men settled down as owners and managers of farms and businesses.

The social life of this young, male, transient population revolved around gambling, drink, and hired sex. An Alaska worker described the scene there:

Liquor was limited to one cup of low class stuff a day, there was a regulation against making or keeping liquor secretly, and there were no women in the camp. Nevertheless, some smart boys extended a hand to native women. . . . Japanese called them "saibashi." Some of them were mixed White Russians, and from time to time I saw astonishingly glamorous or coquettish girls. Their husbands were all absent from home, doing fishing, and so some of the Japanese, making any kind of excuse, approached these mixed-blood girls. . . . However, the number of Alaskan girls was limited, and since that was the case, it was not

Table 3.2   Japanese American Occupations, 1909

Farming and allied agricultural work	39,525
Domestics, including "schoolboys" and hotel and restaurant establishments	12,000
Small business establishments	10,000
Railroads	10,000
Salmon canneries	3,300
Lumber mills	2,200
Mining and smelting	2,000
Total	39,025

SOURCE: U.S. immigration reports, cited in Bill Hosokawa, *Nisei: The Quiet Americans* (New York: Morrow, 1969), 60.

3.2   Some worked in the Northwest lumber industry. *Courtesy of Japanese American National Museum.*

surprising that some Alaska boys put all their energy into gambling, naturally. Day after day they played endless poker, with no money limit. Even if one made $150 a month—the highest income among Japanese at that time—if he played poker, the money soon disappeared. I myself had a bitter experience when I lost all my money.[13]

When they passed through wide-open cities like Seattle and San Francisco, men had the luxury of choosing Japanese prostitutes from the bawdy houses run by Japanese businessmen, as well as a choice between many gambling and drinking establishments.[14]

Very few Japanese women ventured to the U.S. mainland in the frontier period, and we know little about them. Scholars have tended to assume that many were witting or unwitting prostitutes, who came to serve the expatriate males. Their pimps—men who had bought them from indigent families or tricked them with promises of marriage, jobs, or the high life abroad—often had connections with Japanese labor contractors or hotel owners who helped them market the women's services. Some Japanese prostitutes served only Japanese clients, some served only Whites, and some had a mixed clientele.[15]

The story of Yamada Waka is not untypical, save for its redemptive ending. She was born Asaba Waka in 1879, in a village in Kanagawa Prefecture, not far from Tokyo, to a family whose fortunes were in decline. After four years of primary education—half the legal requirement—she worked in sugar cane fields until age 16, when her family married her off to a rich but miserly man much her senior. Soon thereafter, she fled the marriage and took ship for America, where a woman she met said Waka could earn money to send back to her family. On arriving in America, Waka was seized by the woman's accomplices and made to work in brothels in San Francisco and Seattle. Several years later, she made a break for freedom with the aid of San Francisco settlement-house workers and a student and teacher named Yamada Kakichi. She married Yamada in 1904 or 1905. A few years later, the couple returned to Japan, where they were central figures in intellectual circles of the 1920s. Yamada Waka eventually became one of the most forceful writers and speakers in Japan's early feminist movement.[16]

Titillating as the prostitute theme is—and surely it contains elements of truth—it denies the agency of Japanese women and assumes they were passive objects summoned by males. The best recent research on Japanese immigrant women in Hawai'i suggests that many came as independent migrants and that, though some engaged in sex work at least briefly, their lives were much more complex than this stereotype.

Early Opposition to Japanese Immigrants

The Japanese were just one small group among the hundreds of thousands of other people—many of them immigrants—working in the fields and forests, the mines and mills, of the American West at the turn of the century. There were Punjabis and Armenians in the fields of California, Swedes in the north woods, Italians in the San Francisco fishing fleet. Yet the Japanese were singled out by other Americans for particular abuse, beginning in the early 1890s. They were victims of the anti-Chinese feeling that had boiled over periodically for the previous four decades. Starting in the 1850s, Chinese immigrants had been the objects of verbal diatribes and physical attacks by White Americans, not just on the West Coast but throughout the country. The Chinese were legislated against in California, driven from the mines in Wyoming, expelled from the cities of Washington state, assaulted when they came to work in the factories of Massachusetts. In 1882 Congress passed a law barring further immigration by Chinese laborers.

Mindful of this abuse, the Japanese government had carefully tried to control who went abroad and to monitor their behavior and reception in the United States. The Japanese government cared no more for the welfare of working people than did the American government. But Japan was trying to avoid China's quasi-colonial fate and guarding its own international image as it sought to enter the growing world market economy: the Japanese government did not want overseas Japanese to be perceived as a problem in their host countries. So it was with shock and dismay that Japanese foreign service officials witnessed the growth of the first anti-Japanese movement in America.

The post-1900 drive to renew the Chinese exclusion act spilled over into more generalized protests against, and calls for the expulsion of, all Asian immigrants. Since Chinese numbers were dwindling—aging immigrants were dying or going home—much of the animus fell on the Japanese. Labor organizations took the lead in whipping up a frenzy of anti-Japanese sentiment. White working people did not want competition from any Asian workers they could find a way to exclude. Forming the Asiatic Exclusion League in San Francisco in 1905, they lumped Japanese and Chinese together as a threat to the welfare of American workers:

> The conditions of life are, in the last analysis, determined by the conditions of labor. . . . The Caucasian and Asiatic races are unassimilable. Contact between these races must result, under the conditions of industrial life obtaining in North America, in injury to the former, proportioned to the extent to which such contact prevails. The preservation of the Caucasian race upon American soil, and particularly upon the West shore thereof, necessitates the adoption of all possible measures to prevent or minimize the immigration of Asiatics to America.[17]

The workers' organizations were joined quickly by newspapers, most notably the influential *San Francisco Chronicle.* Chester H. Rowell, a Fresno editor and later a prominent Progressive, gave voice to a subtler source of opposition—fear of able and aggressive Japanese:

> We find the Chinese fitting much better than the Japanese into the status which the white American prefers them both to occupy—that of biped domestic animals in the white man's service. The Chinese coolie is the ideal industrial machine, the perfect human ox. He will transform less food into more work, with less administrative friction, than any other creature. . . . They are patient, docile, industrious. . . .
>
> The Japanese are a very different people. As laborers they are less patient but quicker and brighter than the Chinese. . . . But the Japanese do not confine themselves to "Japtown," nor permit the white man to determine the limits of their residence. . . . The Japanese problem is only beginning, and the end is not wholly within our control. . . .
>
> The Pacific Coast is the frontier of the white man's world, the culmination of the westward migration which is the white man's whole history. It will remain the frontier so long as we guard it as such; . . . The multitudes of Asia are already awake. . . . [A]gainst Asian immigration we could not survive.[18]

Behind the media's fears lay the startling realization that Japan had just pummeled Russia, a European power, in the Russo-Japanese War of 1904–5. Fear of aggressive Japanese who did not know their proper place spurred on the racist agitators. The *Chronicle* whipped up its readers with lurid headlines:

> "Japanese a Menace to American Women"
> "The Yellow Peril—How Japanese Crowd out the White Race"
> "Brown Men an Evil in the Public Schools"
> "Brown Artisans Steal Brains of Whites"
> "Crime and Poverty Go Hand in Hand with Asiatic Labor"[19]

There followed a campaign of harassment, picketing, and beatings administered by members of the Asiatic Exclusion League and like-minded thugs. In

June 1906, a group of Japanese seismologists who were inspecting the damage caused by San Francisco's famous earthquake were harassed and pelted with rocks by young toughs. In October, the league organized a boycott of Japanese restaurants in which more than picketing took place: windows were broken and owners were beaten. M. Sugawa described his experience:

> As I was passing on Sutter Street, near Scott, three boys, 21 or 22 years of age, attacked my person. I nearly fainted. Upon rising to my feet they again assaulted me. This time they smashed my nose. I grabbed the coat of one of the trio, and after having my nose dressed at one of the nearby hospitals, I went home. The next day a policeman came, requesting me to give up the coat. I at first refused, but finally, upon his assuring me that it would be deposited at the police station, I gave it up. I reported the matter to the police. When the case came up for trial the youngster was dismissed on the plea of insufficiency of evidence.[20]

That dismissal was typical of the courts' responses to White assaults on Japanese in this period.

Meanwhile, the Asiatic Exclusion League recruited California members of Congress to introduce legislation that would extend the ban on Chinese laborers to include Japanese and other Asians. Then a small administrative decision blew up into an international incident. The anti-Japanese forces, in San Francisco and elsewhere, were especially bothered by the presence of Japanese people in schools. There was an undercurrent of sexual fear at work here. Some Japanese immigrants—boys and men—were trying to learn English. Since there were few adult classes in those years, teenagers and adults were placed in primary school classrooms with American-born students whose English skills were similar to their own. The Progressive politician Grover Johnson complained: "I am responsible to the mothers and fathers of Sacramento County who have their little daughters sitting side by side in the school rooms with matured Japs, with their base minds, their lascivious thoughts, multiplied by their race and strengthened by their mode of life. . . . I have seen Japanese twenty-five years old sitting in the seats next to the pure maids of California. . . . I shudder to think of such a condition."[21] But the sexual theme did not predominate. Members of the Asiatic Exclusion League and their fellow travelers simply looked for any way they could find to take a slap at Japanese Americans.

Under mounting public pressure, the San Francisco school board acted, on 11 October 1906, to segregate Japanese (and Korean) children by requiring them to go to the city's school for Chinese children. The excuse was that the April 1906 earthquake and fire had damaged a number of school buildings and students therefore had to be transferred. The racial intent, however, was obvious to all and satisfying to the anti-Japanese lobby.

Japanese immigrants were not happy. Some sent reports to Tokyo newspapers. The Japanese government lodged a furious protest with President Theodore Roosevelt. Roosevelt shared the exclusionists' belief in Anglo-Saxon racial superiority, but as one who spoke loudly and carried a very small stick, he was loathe to offend the leaders of Asia's new military powerhouse. He had no constitutional authority to intervene in the San Francisco schools crisis, so he resorted to persuasion. He sent a cabinet member to San Francisco to investigate. In his annual message to Congress in December, he said nice things about Japan and castigated the White people of San Francisco for their anti-Japanese actions. By 13 March 1907, the president and his helpers had managed to persuade the San Francisco school board to reverse their segregation order.

In return, Roosevelt persuaded the Japanese government to sign the Gentlemen's Agreement, as it was called, in which Japan promised to tighten up its already restrictive emigration policy:

> This understanding contemplates that the Japanese government shall issue passports to continental United States only to such of its subjects as are non-laborers or are laborers who, in coming to the continent, seek to resume a formerly acquired domicile, to join a parent, wife, or children residing there, or to assume active control of an already possessed interest in a farming enterprise in this country, so that the three classes of laborers entitled to receive passports have come to be designated "former residents," "parents, wives, or children of residents," and "settled agriculturists."[22]

In fact, the Japanese government had been tightly monitoring emigration for several years already. The Gentlemen's Agreement went on to stipulate that the Japanese government would apply similar restraint in authorizing passports to Hawai'i. Meanwhile, Congress authorized, and Roosevelt ordered, that all movement of Japanese workers from Hawai'i, Canada, and Mexico to the U.S mainland be stopped, effective in the summer of 1908.

The anti-Japanese race-baiters were mollified, at least for the moment. Little did they suspect that the flow of Japanese immigrants would continue, made up not of men but of the wives and children of men already in the U.S. Some Japanese immigrants breathed a sigh of relief, in anticipation that the harassment would stop. But others, discouraged by all the harassment, headed for home. In the three years after the Gentlemen's Agreement took effect in 1908, 9,312 Japanese citizens were admitted to the United States, but 15,897 chose to depart (see appendix, table 3).

Thus ended the frontier phase of Japanese American history. Those Japanese who stayed on after the Gentlemen's Agreement looked toward settling down, toward making a transition from *dekasegi-nin* to *Issei*—from sojourners to first-generation Japanese Americans.

Japanese American Ethnicity in the Frontier Phase

It is now possible to estimate the state of Japanese American ethnicity during the frontier period in Japanese American history.[23] In the period before about

Table 3.3   *Japanese American Ethnicity in the Frontier Phase, 1881–1910*

Interests	low	**medium**	high
Culture	low	medium	**high**
Institutions	**low**	medium	high

1910, Japanese American group ethnicity was not strong. Japanese immigrants as a group were high on shared Japanese culture, medium on shared interests, and low on shared institutions, which were not yet clearly formed. Nearly all the early immigrants were young men, unmarried or at least with no family responsibilities in the United States. They came to America intending to work for a time and then return in a few years to Japan to establish middle-class family lives. Except for concentrations on Hawaiian plantations, they scattered across the western landscape. They mined in Colorado, built railroads in Washington, lumbered in Oregon, engaged in fishing and cannery work in Alaska, and worked the farms of California. They pursued not just one line of work but moved from one place and occupation to another without pause. They connected through informal networks of kin and acquaintance and through the labor contractors but formed few lasting ties to place and no permanent institutions.

The culture they shared was Japanese—not a new Japanese American culture—and it was a limited bonding agent. In fact, their identity as Japanese nationals was as yet only imperfectly formed. Japan, like Germany and Italy, was a nation in the making, recently formed out of quasi-feudal domains. The immigrants came to the United States as Hiroshima-*jin* or Wakayama-*jin* or people from other prefectures, and most of their economic and social relations were within prefectural boundaries. As Yasuo Wakatsuki writes of the early imin, "It is doubtful whether the emigrants had any consciousness of being Japanese nationals."[24] Nonetheless, they did speak mutually intelligible dialects of Japanese, most were Buddhist coreligionists, and they shared many of the common aspects of the national culture that was developing in Meiji Japan.

four

Immigrants and Family Folk

T he lives of Japanese Americans changed dramatically in the years after the Gentlemen's Agreement. Prior to that time, the immigrants were made up almost exclusively of transient young people, most of them men. Afterwards, immigrants increasingly became a settled group of people, with wives and children, stable jobs and addresses, and a rising number of small businesses. The emigrants from Japan of the frontier period became the Japanese immigrants to America. They called themselves *Issei*—the first generation—and some began to consider America their home. White Americans, however, still did not see the Issei as entitled to full partnership in the American experiment and tried to drive them out.

Starting Families

The change from male to family society is reflected in the demography of Japanese immigration. In the frontier phase, men typically came to America and women stayed in Japan. Eighty-four percent of the Japanese who arrived in America in 1898 were men; in 1900 the figure was 91 percent. In 1907, the year the Gentlemen's Agreement was negotiated, 78 percent of Japanese immigrants were male. Then, in the period of settling and family building, women began to come. By 1911 nearly half the immigrants were women streaming in to rejoin their husbands or to meet them for the first time (see appendix, table 4).[1] Married women formed a steadily growing part of the Japanese American population until the late 1920s, by which time all new immigration from Japan had been banned and the second generation had begun to grow.

The change to a family society is also reflected in the rapid rise in the number of children born to Issei couples in the years after the Gentlemen's Agreement. The number of *Nisei*—second-generation Japanese Americans—born in California each year leaped more than 20-fold between 1907 and 1920:

Much has been written about "picture brides" (*shashin kekkon*). Here is a typical situation. An Issei man who has been working for some years in the United States finds himself approaching middle age. Although his original intention was to go back to Japan and marry, he has not yet made as much money as he had intended to, or perhaps he is beginning to think of the United States as his

Table 4.1 Issei Population, 1900–1930

Year	Japanese Population	Married Women	Married Women as Percent of Total
1900	24,326	410	1.7%
1910	72,157	5,581	7.7
1920	111,010	22,193	20.0
1930	138,834	23,930	17.2

SOURCE: Yuji Ichioka, "Amerika Nadeshiko: Japanese Immigrant Women in the United States, 1900–1924," Pacific Historical Review, 49 (1980), 341.

Table 4.2 Japanese American Births, California, 1906–1930

1906	134	1919	4,458
1907	221	1920	4,971
1908	455	1921	5,275
1909	682	1922	5,066
1910	719	1923	5,010
1911	995	1924	4,481
1912	1,467	1925	4,016
1913	2,215	1926	3,597
1914	2,874	1927	3,241
1915	3,342	1928	2,833
1916	3,721	1929	2,353
1917	4,108	1930	2,220
1918	4,218		

SOURCE: Edward K. Strong, *Japanese in California* (Stanford, Calif.: Stanford University Press, 1933), 62.

home. He decides to stay in America for a while longer, but he is lonely or desires an heir. He is forbidden by a 1905 California law to marry a White woman, and in any case, Japanese social pressure precludes marrying anyone who is not Japanese.

The thing to do was to return to Japan and find a wife, then bring her back to join him in his work in America. Probably most Issei marriages happened that way. The man might write ahead to relatives, who would hire a *baishakunin*, or marriage arranger, to search out a likely candidate. The Issei man would go home for a brief visit—a couple of weeks to a few months—meet and marry his bride, and bring her back to the United States.

For their part, migration to America was attractive to some Japanese women, even if they had to marry to make the trip. It was an adventure. Living standards were higher in North America. Sex roles were less hierarchical. Responsibilities to extended kin were less onerous. In the more fluid social situation of a migrant community, a woman had a greater chance than in Japan of carving out a degree of autonomy for herself.

Other men married before they went abroad and left their wives at home. Typically, such an emigrant returned three or four times over a dozen years. Each time he would visit for a few weeks or months, perhaps sire a child, then leave the family in Japan and go back to work in America. Only later, when it looked uncertain when or if he would ever be able to go home, did he send for his family to join him. So it was not just brides but also children who went abroad to make up the newly settled family society in Japanese America after 1908.

Many Issei referred to themselves as *yobiyose*—"summoned" immigrants. They were children of pioneer fathers who were left with their mothers in Japan and then called to come over in the 1910s.[2] Before the Gentlemen's Agreement, only 5 percent of Japanese immigrants had parents who already lived in the United States at the time they arrived; after the agreement, 58 percent came to join a parent or parents already in America (see appendix, table 5). Taken together, wives and yobiyose children made up almost all of the Japanese American immigration after 1908.

By comparison with the relatively mundane, if difficult, business of building a family on both sides of the Pacific, the picture bride phenomenon was simple and filled with human drama. To save money or avoid exposing himself to the Japanese military draft by going home, an Issei man working in America would write home and have relatives arrange a bride. He would send money and presents for her and her family, along with a picture of himself that showed him at his best—sometimes even better than his best. He would send her courtship letters describing the success he was having and the wonderful life they would lead together in America. She would send letters and pictures, too, and he would send a ticket. There might or might not be a proxy wedding in Japan before the bride boarded the ship. On disembarking in Seattle or San Francisco, she met the man she had agreed to marry. Yoshiko Ueda described the picture bride scene:

> When I was aboard the "Kashima Maru" bound for Seattle in 1918, I met many picture brides. Having plenty of free time, we talked about our personal affairs, and they spoke about their husbands whom they had never seen. Some of them proudly said such things as: "My husband is the president of a company." Or, "Mine is the manager of a large store."
>
> But when the boat finally landed, the "president" and the "manager" turned out to be unbearably disgusting, about 40 or 50 years old, and their humble job was working on the railroads. The brides were between 18 and 23. Some of them upon meeting their disappointing "president" and "manager" promptly said "No!" and pled to return on the same boat. Such refusals invariably put their husbands at a complete loss.
>
> This sort of case most frequently occurred when the man had sent a picture of himself which was taken when he was young. Some brides therefore, seeing their husbands darkened with sunburn, and with gnarled hands, found the images in their minds so different that they claimed to the immigration officials, "This one is not my husband,"—which got the husbands into trouble with the law. But even under such discouraging circumstances some of them gave up and went on

into the marriage. There were others, however, who insisted "No, no!" and stayed in Seattle hotels for over a month, crying and begging to go back to Japan. Still others in the interim of waiting for the next boat, got pregnant and then gave up. And of course there were some who, while refusing their husbands, found a better man and changed over to him.[3]

Although proxy weddings had been legally recognized in prior years, through most of this period American state governments no longer recognized proxy wedding ceremonies. As a result, some husbands married their wives at dockside, or in religious or civil ceremonies a few days later. Some wives, feeling defrauded, insisted on returning home. Some swapped husbands on the dock; others were swapped by the men who had paid their passage. But most women and men honored the commitment they had made and quietly settled down to their new lives. It is worth noting that, first, except for the distance traveled, the picture bride arrangement was not all that different from the way people had been getting married in Japan for some generations: the choice was made by one's family and one lived with that choice and did not disgrace the family name by running away. Second, Japanese Americans were not the only ones in America marrying in such a way: there were also Chinese picture brides and Italian picture brides. In fact, an early group of White Seattle women—the Mercer girls—came from Massachusetts expressly to marry men whom they had never met.[4] Finally, although the picture bride story is memorable, it was not true of all Issei women. Interviews with Issei in recent decades have turned up many who say they knew one or two picture brides when they were young and heard of others. But very few women interviewed will admit to having been picture brides themselves, and very few men say they were picture grooms—in fact, there seem to be very few people who knew more than one or two picture brides.[5] It seems likely that the more common practice was for Issei men to return and bring wives over than simply to send for them sight unseen. In addition, an unknown number of women appear to have the family unification process allowed by the Gentlemen's Agreement as a cover for migrating on their own.

However couples got together in America, theirs were marriages that had already endured a difficult beginning. Some couples were strangers. Others had suffered years of separation. Wives had to get to know their husbands, children had to learn to live with their fathers. The age difference between husband and wife—nearly ten years, on the average—was not unusual for the Japanese but added to the distance between Issei wives and husbands (see appendix, table 6).

The couples had to establish a common bond of duty, love, or resignation very quickly, for pressures were intense and resources were few. In America, as in Japan, the Issei had to work very hard to make even a meager living. Women found themselves working for wages outside the home or working alongside their husbands on farms or in businesses.

Having no extended family—no older generation and few collateral kin—in America liberated the Issei woman from the legendary tyranny of the Japanese mother-in-law. But being alone also tended to isolate her. Lacking extended family, she was left in the company of her husband and his male friends. By 1930, 85 percent of the Issei men had found wives, but in the 1910s the number

4.1   An Issei couple in Western dress. *Courtesy of Japanese American National Museum.*

was only a fraction of that.[6] There were lots of loose, lonely males around to be fended off. Most Issei women who immigrated in those years could tell stories like the one told by Michiko Tanaka to her daughter Akemi: "Everywhere we worked there were few married couples and the rest were single men. Those who had wives bragged. Consequently, the women without children had many men pursuing them. A woman could take advantage of the situation and make good money. Yanagi-san did. She took up with other men because of financial problems. . . . Many times men approached me and said, 'Let me do it with you and I'll give you money,' but I was hard—I never gave in. What an insult! I wasn't a whore."[7]

Still, Tanaka was stuck in a loveless marriage to a man who, hard though he worked, drank and gambled away the money they earned. Some Issei women in similar straits left their husbands. But nearly all, like Michiko Tanaka, stayed—if not out of personal devotion, then out of a sense of duty to the wifely role, as they understood it. She told of her Buddhist schooling in Japan: "They also taught us womanly things. Women do not stand above men and flaunt their authority; in the house the man is the most important person; a woman must raise her husband up in front of others."[8] As the Japanese population settled down, and as Japanese communities grew in the 1910s and 1920s, a gossip system bloomed that effectively tied women dutifully to their husbands. If men took up with other people's spouses, drank, gambled, or frequented prostitutes, that was understandable. If women did similar things, their sins were likely to make the pages of the local Japanese newspaper and result in ostracism.

In this difficult situation, husband and wife endured—and many couples thrived—by living out values they had brought with them from Japan. Chief among these was *gaman*, which can be translated roughly as perseverance. G. Sato, a Nisei, told of his parents' attitude: "*Gaman?* Oh yes, we had that very much so. Well, just like when we had that fire, burned down my dad's boarding house and all we had. You know, my folks didn't say much except *shikataganai* [it can't be helped] . . . and *gaman* . . . you have to be patient 'cuz you know what happened has happened. Nothing you can do to remedy it. You just have to go on."[9]

Making a Living

And on they did go, working hard to build lives in America. The 1910s and 1920s saw a startling change, not only in gender demographics but also in the pattern of Issei employment. The major change was from wage work to small-scale, private entrepreneurship. A 1915 study estimated that 82 percent of California Issei farmers were farmhands, and only 18 percent were owners or managers. Nine years later, another survey found the farmhand percentage had declined to 61 percent, with 39 percent of Japanese agricultural workers having become owners or managers. In a 1930 survey, 41 percent were farmworkers and 59 percent were owners or managers.[10] A survey of older Issei taken in the 1960s described a steady march during the 1920s out of the ranks of wage labor and into ownership of farms and small businesses (even though, because of discriminatory land laws, property had to be placed formally in the hands of American-born children). By the time Japanese Americans reached their occupational peak before World War II, more than 40 percent, and perhaps as many as half the Issei, operated their own businesses or farms (see appendix, table 8).[11] That is an amazing economic achievement, one matched by the first generation of no other American immigrant group of their era except Jews.

"Schoolboys"

Some Issei began their time in America as students. Perhaps one-quarter had been students immediately before leaving Japan, and many—women as well as men—cited a desire to continue their studies when they applied for visas. Stating this intention was possible in part because, after the Gentlemen's Agreement, the Japanese government was less reluctant to send students abroad than it was people who said they were going out to work. Soon, however, the difficulty of both studying and supporting themselves caught up with most of the so-called schoolboys. While the average Issei man had eight years of education in Japan, he succeeded in adding less than a single year of schooling in the United States—usually English classes in night school.[12] The story of Shige Kushida is fairly typical. She came to the United States to study, with the promise of a scholarship from the Women's Christian Temperance Union. The scholarship never materialized, and she took work as a domestic. Kushida eventually married and raised a well-educated set of children but never completed her own academic ambitions.[13]

Of course, there were exceptions. Sen Katayama, founder of the social work profession in Japan and also of the Japanese Communist Party, managed to attend Grinnell College, Andover Seminary, and Yale before returning to Japan.[14] James M. Unosawa worked for a coal mine, an iron mill, an orange ranch, and a railroad to earn money to support himself through high school, college, and medical school. A small cadre of doctors like Unosawa, as well as dentists, lawyers, and other professionals, served Japanese American communities after acquiring their education by their bootstraps.[15] But such people were exceptions.

Farmers

Very quickly, even those who started out as students made their way into the working world. The greatest number found work in agriculture: they made up 54 percent of the Japanese in California in 1930.[16] Even people from town and city backgrounds in Japan found themselves farming in America about one-third of the time. As it had been for European immigrants, one of the allures of America for the Issei was the possibility of owning and farming their own land.[17]

Already by 1910, Japanese men had become the largest single group of laborers in the California fields. In the following decade, they became the owners (or at least the operators) of a significant number of farms as well. Between 1910 and 1920, the number of Japanese-run farms in Los Angeles County tripled; their acreage multiplied by a factor of seven; and their holdings grew to 5 percent of the county's total farmland.[18] So Issei were both bosses and workers in the West Coast's factories in the fields. One 1929 survey counted more than 64,000 Japanese Americans working in California agriculture: 13,000 field hands and 51,000 independent farmers exercising various degrees of ownership.[19]

4.2   Women and children also worked in the fields. *Courtesy of Japanese American National Museum.*

The average farm run by a non-Japanese Californian was 200 acres or more in the 1910s; the average Issei farm was less than 20 acres. Yet Issei farmers managed to turn small, steady profits by working extremely hard. Short on capital and mindful of their unpopularity in American society, many Issei had to rent or buy marginal lands on which they struggled to make a living. They used irrigation to make the desert bloom in the Imperial and San Joaquin Valleys. George Shima, the "Potato King," made a fortune reclaiming marshland in the Sacramento River delta. There were few technological advances in all this—just energy, flexibility, group solidarity, imagination, and willingness to work hard.

There was some carryover from Japanese farming techniques that prepared the Issei for what they faced in America. Rice farming in Japan was labor-intensive and performed without machinery or draft animals. Lacking capital, Japanese farmers in America looked for crops, such as berries, that could be grown with the same intensity. Yet the crops, the soil, the climate, the market— all were very different from Japan. Some Whites attributed the success of the Japanese at farming to the fact that many of them were built close to the ground (a racist characterization that was later used to justify exploitation of Mexican American farm laborers). Jack Takayama, a farmer from the Yakima Valley, recalled: "Every Japanese worked about four times as hard as any white man, from early in the morning till late at night." A neighbor, Sakitaro Takei, described the work in more detail:

I went to Wapato. At that time the Yakima Valley was nothing but sagebrush as far as I looked. Empty-handed we began clearing the land, having borrowed for everything. Brokers advanced the money against the coming harvest—a kind of contract farming—$20 for one acre of cantaloupes, or $200 for ten acres, for example. As for food, the stores issued a $50 coupon book. Therefore without having a cent of capital, a person could struggle with the sagebrush desert. Fortunately, probably because they were also suppressed by the whites as colored people, the Indians were very friendly toward Japanese and glad to lease their land. First we knocked down the clumps of sagebrush with a mattock and, piling them up, we set fire to them. As it was troublesome to dig them out one by one, I shaved them down with a long iron rail pulled by eight horses. This horse-drawn rail mowed them down very easily, just like shaving your beard with a razor. Sage, which has shallow roots, was easy to wipe out. We burned it all. In this way I cleared five acres and grew cantaloupe, tomatoes and onions. . . . The house was a tent-house with apple-boxes for tables and chairs. I took a bath with water heated in a tub. As for green vegetables, I picked wild grass called "Jimmy Hill mustard"—named after the president of the railroad. It grew alongside the tracks and out of it I made hot salad, boiled greens and pickles. I worked like a horse or a cow; I went to the field before dawn and came back when it got too dark to see. The truth is I worked about eighteen hours a day with no recreation—nothing—simply work.[20]

Soon there were enclaves of Japanese American farmers all over the West—from the Texas rice lands to the strawberry fields near Watsonville, California, north through the hop fields in Oregon's Willamette Valley, all the way to the fruit orchards of the Okanogan country of British Columbia. In each area, Japanese American farmers tended to specialize in certain crops, which they often came to dominate: truck farming in southern California, onions and celery in northern California, and berries all up and down the West Coast. There were Japanese farm colonies in remote areas, such as Kern County, California, where the Issei worked alongside immigrants from the Punjab, and the area around Phoenix, where they mixed with Chicanos. But the largest rural concentrations were near big cities, where crops could easily be taken to market by wagon, truck, or even commuter train. Thus, Gardena and Moneta near Los Angeles, Gresham near Portland, and Bainbridge Island near Seattle all became home to significant numbers of Japanese American farmers. Frank Tomori remembered coming to such a colony:

I took a train at Portland and after four or five hours I arrived at Hood River station. There, in the car belonging to Mankichi Inukai who came to meet me, I went to the Inukai brothers' farm in Dee. This was a farm that Mankichi and his younger brother Kazuo were managing.

It happened to be July 4, American Independence Day, and many Japanese neighbors got together at the farm and welcomed me with a feast for which they had killed some chickens. We also had watermelon and *makizushi* (vinegared rice rolled in seaweed). I felt as if I had come to a rural area in Japan. . . .

The village of Dee was on a high plateau like the summit of mountains, and some hundreds of feet below on the east ran the Middle Fork and on the west, the West Fork. The plateau was really a strange place where, if you dug down fifteen feet, you hit a bubbling spring full of crystal water. Seventy percent of this plateau was owned by less than twenty Japanese families, and when I went there they were still clearing the land. Cutting down the big trees, they put powder at the roots of the stumps and exploded them. Then they dug around the roots, braced kindling wood against the stumpwood, and burned the stumps for two or three days. The Douglas firs were so big it took three people to span them. For this kind of huge stump they set thirty or thirty-five charges, and they counted the reports on their fingers. Only after all the charges had exploded could they approach the spot again. It wasn't rare that people, without knowing that some charges were unexploded, came close too soon and were killed. After burning the roots they filled in and levelled the land and planted young apple or pear trees. Between the rows they grew strawberries and, living on the income from these for eight or ten years, they waited till the trees produced.[21]

Outside such isolated oases of Japanese company, the Issei were surrounded by seas of White faces with whose owners they did not connect. Cho Nishikata remembered:

We worked for ten or eleven hours a day, and when the day's work was over we bathed in the river or poured heated water into the washtub and took a tub bath. I was so tired that when I woke up in the morning I didn't even feel like shaving. Our only pleasure in this life was the County Fair which was held twice a year. It was a kind of village festival, and, wearing ten-gallon hats and dungarees which cost less than a dollar a pair, we went to watch the events. Young and vigorous fellows took part in rodeos, riding bareback and hitting the horse's rump with their hat. We Japanese just vacantly stared at them, leaning against a fence. In the fair grounds they exhibited piles of all kinds of prize vegetables. Besides the exhibits, they sold sandwiches, hotdogs, ice cream, peanuts, popcorn and so on, and the white village girls were all dressed in their best outfits, so it was an impromptu fashion-show. Japanese-Americans after the war would be able to take part in such an atmosphere, eating and drinking easily together with the whites, but we who were obviously poorly dressed and didn't know English were on the outside looking in, and stuck together in twos and threes, watching this foreign festival wordlessly.[22]

The years between the Gentlemen's Agreement and 1920 saw a steady growth of Issei ownership and operation of farms. There were five stages in this process.[23] Upon first coming to America, an Issei worked as a field laborer. Many stopped at that point or were prevented from going further by the endless round of toil. But if an ambitious immigrant wanted to go into business for himself, the next step was to become a contract farmer, working someone else's land for a set wage. He might also act as a labor contractor, hiring some of his erstwhile workmates to help him farm the land. Contract farming offered a way up from simple manual labor in the fields, and it required no capital of one's own.

The third step was share tenancy: the tenant worked a piece of someone else's land and paid the landowner a share—usually half—of the crop. This sharecropping system, also common in the South, afforded greater risks but also greater profits than contract farming for a set wage.

Next came cash leasing. A tenant leased a farm for a set rent and number of years, perhaps three to five. By leasing land for cash, Issei became independent farmers, assuming all risks and reaping all profits. The final stage was outright ownership. Only a small number of Issei achieved this stage, and non-Japanese Americans tried hard to keep any Japanese from succeeding.

Each year up to 1920, the amount of land under Issei cultivation increased, and nearly every year a larger number of Japanese Americans made the transition from laborer to contract farmer, from contract farmer to share tenant, from share tenant to cash lessee, and from lessee to owner (see appendix, table 9).

This gradual move from laborer to owner or operator took Japanese American farmers over to the other side in agricultural labor disputes. The Issei field labor force was never highly organized, but there were unions and strikes, such as the Hawaiian strikes of 1909 and 1920. By the 1930s in California, however, Japanese American farmworkers stood more on the side of management than of labor. Although some Issei and Nisei workers still labored in the fields, when the Mexican and Japanese berry pickers of El Monte went out on strike in 1933, it was Japanese growers who broke the strike.[24]

Many Japanese Americans continued in agriculture. But with the coming of wives and families, with the consolidation of the Japanese American population into settled communities by the 1920s, ever more Issei turned to city trades. The progression from farm to city was made over and over in countless individual lives, and at different rates in different parts of the country. As late as 1930, 54 percent of Japanese Californians worked in agriculture. But only 40 percent of those who had been in the United States 20 years or more were still farming. As one Issei put it: "I saw little future in farm work. . . . [F]or the first five years I had to work in the farms, picking fruit, vegetables, and I saved some money. Then I came to live in the city permanently."[25]

Small Business Owners

Just as rural Issei moved from being farm laborers to farm owners and operators in the 1910s and 1920s, city Japanese Americans over the same period made the transition from hired workers to small-scale entrepreneurs. In 1909, according to a study by the U.S. Immigration Commission, 15 percent of Japanese Americans worked in small businesses, either as owners or as workers. Twenty years later, in Seattle, the figure was 76 percent.[26]

Los Angeles and Seattle were the urban centers with the largest concentrations, but most towns and cities along the West Coast had growing Japanese American populations (see appendix, table 10). In each city, one could find a *Nihonmachi,* or Japan Town, as well as growing networks of Japanese American

4.3   T. Takayoshi hustled to make a living running a small store/laundry/photography studio in Port Blakely, Washington. *Courtesy of Japanese American National Museum.*

businesses. There were Japanese-run hotels and boardinghouses, grocery stores, fruit and vegetable stands, restaurants, and nurseries in abundance. Japanese Americans also ran a fair number of pool halls, tailor shops, barbershops, and other service establishments. Some of the service businesses catered mainly to Japanese American customers, but most of the Issei businesses served an interracial clientele toward the lower end of the economic scale.

How did city Japanese Americans come to concentrate so heavily in small business? Discrimination is part of the answer: they could find wage work as domestic servants but could not break into the higher-paying industrial labor force because they were kept out by both employers and unions. The angle of their entry into the West Coast economy also tended to favor small business, as one Issei interviewed in the 1930s explained:

> These Japanese came here with nothing but a blanket on their back— they had no money, they didn't know any English, they didn't know how to do any of the things that the Americans know, nor how the Americans made their living—so they had to start from the bottom. But, of course, the restaurant cooking of that day was relatively simple; all one had to know was how to fry an egg, toast bread, and fry a steak. It was known as "fry cook." Mr. T. was the first to get started in that line of business. And then other Japanese worked in his place, learned the trade, and started businesses of their own. They catered to the many laborers who lived down near the lower end of the city at the time, and they did very well, for the white men found these lunch-counter services cheap and convenient.[27]

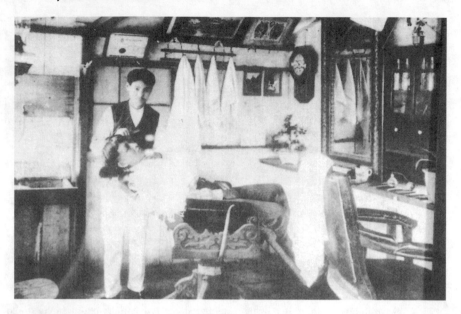

4.4   Some Issei worked in personal service to one another, as in this barbershop. *Courtesy of Bishop Museum.*

Suggested here is a certain openness in the expanding western economy to people who carved out small niches for themselves.

Groups of Japanese Americans worked together to get each other launched in business. Families and the *kenjinkai* (people from the same *ken*, or prefecture, in Japan) helped each other along. Another Issei interviewed in the late 1930s said:

> There was a tendency towards the concentration of people from the same prefectures in Japan at the same places, and in the same lines of work. For example, the barbers in Seattle, at least in the old days, all tended to be people from the Yamaguchi-*ken*, for Mr. I. came first and established himself in that line, and then helped his friends from Japan to get started. Then again, in the restaurant business, the majority of them are Ehime-*ken*, for men like Mr. K. first got into this, and then aided his *ken* friends to follow in the same field. Homes like those of Mr. I. were places of congregation for the young men who were eager to learn things and to discuss them, and in the course of their association learned such trades as their friends knew.[28]

The critical need for capital to get started was handled by creating *tanomoshi*, or rotating credit associations. Frank Miyamoto described how they worked:

> If some individual, who we shall call A, needs monetary aid, he calls upon one of his close friends, B, to start a *tanomoshi*. B then goes around to several of their common friends and induces a group of fifteen or twenty who are interested in such a *tanomoshi* to gather at a dinner on

an appointed date. Each contributes an agreed sum, such as $25 or $50, and the pool is rented to A *gratis* since the object of it is primarily to help him. A ordinarily reciprocates by paying the cost of the dinner, and he later pays off his obligations with a small monetary gift to each of the members. His debt is paid back in monthly installments. Thereafter, monthly meetings are called in which new pools are set up, and the remaining members bid for its use, the bid representing the interest upon the principal which the individuals agree to pay. With the passing of each monthly meeting, the circle of bidders is gradually narrowed down. The *tanomoshi* closes when each member has paid his debt.[29]

Once up and running, Japanese small businesses provided steady work—for long hours at low wages—for family members and kenjin and helped glue Japanese communities together. It was not just that Japanese Americans worked hard. It was that they worked together. They went beyond the sharing of capital exemplified by the tanomoshi and coordinated their work in related industries. Japanese American farmers from the Kent-Auburn Valley sold their produce to Japanese American grocery stores and vegetable stands in Seattle and formed business organizations to foster their common interests. Similar vertical and horizontal integration operated in the flower and nursery industry of southern California and, to a lesser extent, in fishing and other areas of commerce.[30]

As on the farm, so in the city—the work was hard. Henry T. Kubota recalled:

It was 1930 when I began a hotel business. The first place I had was the New Home Hotel on Charles Street at the south end of Dearborn. It was a two-story wooden building and the guests were white workers. Soon after, I also began to manage Crown Hotel two blocks away. It had forty-nine rooms. Asking an old man to be a watchman, I worked by myself at both hotels alternately. I did everything from making beds to cleaning toilets. From nine in the morning till eleven at night I was continually on the run except at mealtimes. One room rented for about $7 a month, and those were Depression days, so all the rooms were not filled. Consequently I couldn't afford to hire anyone to help and pay them wages. Since I was managing two hotels alone, no matter how hard I worked, one of them was always left short of care. In such cases I asked some old men living in one hotel on welfare to become watchmen and paid them 25 cents a day. I didn't even have holidays, let alone vacations. My only recreation was at most one evening a week when I went to Atlas Theater to see a movie or fall asleep in the seat.[31]

Domestics

No work was harder than that done by Issei who worked as domestic servants. The majority were young men who lived in and cooked, cleaned, kept house, and tended gardens for well-to-do families. Many Issei men who took such jobs did so shortly after their arrival in the United States as a way of learning English through daily contact with non-Japanese. Most had aspirations to use their English skills to go on to school. In fact, the term "schoolboy" sometimes was taken to mean the same thing as "servant," as in this recollection by Shizuma Takeshita: "I went to work as a schoolboy and received a dollar twenty-five per week with meals and lodging."[32] Such jobs were obtained through informal networks—someone at church or the pool hall moving on to a new job would pass his servant's position on to a friend.

Personal service was a low-status occupation in Japan, however, and most Issei men were eager to move on once they had acquired a little cash and some English. The number of Japanese American domestics—mostly live-ins—reached a high of 12,000–15,000, according to a 1909 report. After about 1915, the number dropped rapidly as many Japanese men shifted from wage labor to small-time entrepreneurship. But the White western middle class was growing in those years, and with it a demand for servants. What the White middle class wanted in this new era, however, were not live-in servants such as only the rich could afford. They wanted day workers who would come in and cook and clean and tend the garden, and then go home. This demand gave rise to two parallel developments. In the late 1910s and 1920s, quite a few Japanese American men went into route gardening. A smaller but significant number of Issei women cooked and cleaned on a part-time basis, often for several households in rotation. The number of Issei women domestic workers was always tiny—almost all Issei women worked very hard, but they did so in family enterprises and not for pay. For the few Issei women who took the step into wage work, it represented independence, even as it also ushered them into a low-paying, dead-end occupational ghetto (see appendix, table 11).[33]

What did all this mean about the economic fortunes of Japanese Americans? A high percentage were entrepreneurs—higher than for any other ethnic minority in the West, or for most immigrant groups in other parts of the country. They had made a significant step away from manual labor for wages. But they were not rich people. The average size of an Issei farm—20 acres—was one-tenth the size of the average non-Japanese-owned farm in the 1910s. The hotels the Issei ran were not the Hilton or the Ritz; they were flophouses in run-down neighborhoods that served a poor, transient, and sometimes criminal clientele. Very few Japanese businesses employed more than one or two people who were not related to the owner or manager. The best current analogues to Issei businesspeople early in the century are Korean and Asian Indian entrepreneurs. In cities like Los Angeles and New York, Korean families have scraped together money to buy small groceries that serve poor neighborhoods. In various out-of-the-way locations across the country, Asian Indian families have bought broken-down mom-and-pop motels and restored and run them. By dint of extended family cooperation and hard work, Koreans and Asian Indians use such establishments to make a living that puts them in the ranks of the lower-middle class. In similar fashion, the Issei entrepreneurs of the 1910s and 1920s were the petitest of the petite bourgeoisie.

Geographical Differences

The life experiences of Japanese American immigrants differed substantially from one area to another. One very big difference was between the U.S. mainland and Hawai'i. In the frontier period, Japanese Hawaiians and mainland

Japanese Americans were part of the same migration process. Many early Issei first came to Hawai'i and then made their way to the West Coast. A web of labor recruiters connected the two places, and the mountain West as well. But in 1907, as part of the Gentlemen's Agreement, President Theodore Roosevelt stopped allowing Japanese citizens to move from Hawai'i to the mainland states. By the 1920s the Japanese American population on the West Coast was large enough and well enough established that mainland Japanese American history had begun to diverge substantially from the island experience. As early as 1910, the West Coast Issei constituted 38 percent of the total Japanese American population, and the Hawaiian Japanese constituted 53 percent. Except for the years surrounding the Depression and World War II, the West Coast Japanese Americans maintained roughly that percentage of the population, while the Japanese Hawaiian people declined slightly as a proportion of the total Japanese American population.

In the Hawaiian Islands, Japanese Americans had become the largest ethnic group, making up more than one-third of the territory's population on the eve of World War II. Many remained in plantation towns, such as Kona on the island of Hawai'i, where the population was almost all Japanese. Others lived in Honolulu in situations more like those of Issei and Nisei in West Coast cities yet with lots more Japanese around them. Not only did many Japanese Hawaiians live in environments dominated ethnically by their countrypeople, but they constituted a settled agricultural working class, unlike the small entrepreneurs on the West Coast. Very few Hawaiian Japanese farmers owned or leased land or ran their own farms. Hawaiian agricultural land was almost all in the hands of a few very large landowners who ran their estates as quasi-feudal fiefs. Japanese Hawaiians as a group were manual laborers longer than their West Coast cousins. Add to these structural differences an acculturational difference: Japanese Hawaiians had been in U.S. territory about a half-generation longer than West Coast Japanese. The Hawaiian Nisei generation was large and maturing by the late 1920s; at that time, the Nisei on the mainland were children.

There were also significant differences on the West Coast between city Japanese and those on the farm, many of which were mentioned earlier. One trend that deserves to be highlighted here is the movement from countryside to city after the close of the frontier period. Over the period 1910–30, most rural California counties registered either a slow rise or an actual decline in their

Table 4.3 Regional Japanese American Population, 1890–1990 *(percentages)*

Region	1890	1900	1910	1920	1930	1940	1950	1960	1970	1980	1990
West Coast	10	21	38	42	43	39	30	39	41	43	43
Hawaii	86	72	53	50	50	55	57	44	37	33	29
Mountain West	*	6	7	5	4	3	4	4	3	4	4
North Central	1	*	1	1	1	1	6	6	7	6	7
South	1	*	*	*	*	*	1	4	5	7	8
Northeast	2	1	1	2	1	1	2	4	6	7	9

*less than 0.5%.
SOURCE: See appendix, table 2.

Table 4.4   Japanese American Population in Rural and
Urban California Counties, 1900–1930

	1900	1910	1920	1930
Rural Counties[a]				
Butte	365	295	423	307
Colusa	53	140	275	211
Contra Costa	276	1,009	846	796
Imperial	0	217	1,986	2,241
Kern	48	273	338	712
Marin	52	199	140	158
Merced	43	98	420	768
Monterey	710	1,121	1,614	2,271
Orange	3	641	1,491	1,613
Placer	133	862	1,474	1,874
Riverside	97	765	626	589
San Benito	15	286	427	559
San Bernardino	148	946	533	578
San Luis Obispo	16	434	501	868
San Mateo	46	358	663	1,169
Santa Barbara	114	863	930	1,889
Santa Cruz	235	689	1,019	1,407
Urban Counties[b]				
Alameda (Berkeley, Oakland)	1,149	3,266	5,221	5,715
Fresno (Fresno)	598	2,233	5,732	5,280
Los Angeles (Los Angeles, Long Beach)	204	8,461	19,911	35,390
Sacramento (Sacramento)	1,209	3,874	5,800	8,114
San Diego (San Diego)	25	520	1,431	1,722
San Francisco (San Francisco)	1,781	4,518	5,358	6,250
San Joaquin (Stockton)	313	1,804	4,354	4,339
Santa Clara (San Jose)	284	2,299	2,981	4,320

[a] Counties with very small Japanese American populations have been omitted.
[b] Some of the urban counties (e.g., Fresno) had substantial rural areas.
SOURCE: Strong, *Japanese in America*, 37.

Japanese American population, while all the urban counties showed sharp increases. The farm areas also witnessed increased concentrations of Japanese Americans, as that population came to be located mainly in a few rural counties, such as Imperial, Monterey, Placer, and Santa Barbara.

Even more significant in percentage terms was the movement from the backcountry in states such as Idaho and Montana and into the cities of the West Coast (see appendix, table 2).

The Pacific Northwest Japanese were distinct in some ways. Their numbers were never so large as those of the Japanese in California or Hawai'i. There were no completely Japanese Northwest communities or neighborhoods. As a result, the average Japanese Washingtonian or Oregonian, whether discriminated against or not, had a bit more experience dealing with Whites and other non-Japanese than did the Issei of California and Hawai'i.

Japanese Americans in the mountain West, the Southwest, and Alaska remained in the frontier phase long after West Coast Issei had settled down to start businesses and raise families. More than 10,000 Japanese Americans lived in the mountain West in 1920, most of them men who still worked in the mines and railroads or planted and harvested other people's fields. Hundreds more worked in the canneries, forests, and fishing towns of Alaska. It was only in the 1930s that many of them began to work farms of their own or start small businesses, as had their countrymen on the West Coast a decade or two earlier. Many inland Issei married Japanese women somewhere along the line, but many never got the chance. The United States outlawed further Japanese immigration before those men settled down. Faced with the prospect of a lonely old age and surrounded by non-Japanese Americans, Issei men in Texas and Arizona frequently married Mexican women, and some Alaska Issei married Indians. Japanese Americans in such remote outplaces tended to lose contact with their countrypeople on the West Coast, in Hawai'i, and in Japan. Only in the larger Japanese population centers in the mountain states, such as Denver and Salt Lake City, did the connection to the broader Japanese American population persist.

There were always a certain number of Issei on the East Coast. Many were young men who had gone east in search of better educational opportunities and relief from the anti-Japanese agitation on the West Coast. The eastern Issei population, however, was scattered and never very large. There was a consulate in New York, where a certain number of businessmen engaged in international trade. But as Eleanor Gluck reported, "the Japanese in this city do not know each other." Outside New York, the Issei were isolated. When Michiji Ishikawa went looking for them in the early 1930s, he found no more than several hundred Issei, mostly erstwhile schoolboys whose dreams of education had faded and who were working as servants or factory workers. About one-third had married non-Japanese women.[34]

Japanese American Communities

If New York Issei did not connect with each other, that emphatically was not true for Japanese Americans on the West Coast. Perhaps the most distinctive characteristic of the Issei generation was an intense level of community organization. The first agents who facilitated community organization were the contract labor bosses of the frontier period; they drew together teams of Issei workers, housed them in hotels and bunkhouses, secured transportation and jobs, and frequently provided medical and mail services. Most early immigrants had their initial entry into American society managed by a labor boss. But with the shift to a more settled Japanese American society of families, farms, and businesses, the boss's role declined.

The part played by the kenjinkai did not decrease. Frank Miyamoto described the importance of the ken in the 1930s:

In Japan, the *ken* as a social organization has relatively little importance, except as an administrative unit of the nation. It is only when the Japanese leave their native land and congregate in large numbers in alien places that the differences of *ken* become noticeable and make for a degree of intimacy among those of the same *ken* that has a certain clannishness about it. The chief reason for this felt difference is, of course, the fact that over long centuries of relatively immobile social organization, the people living in different areas developed different traits of culture which differ so greatly from one another that even from the standpoint of language alone there are occasions of great difficulty in understanding.

People from different ken were reputed to have different character qualities. According to Miyamoto, "Common belief is that the Hiroshima people are sharp business men, the Gumma people are quiet, and so on."[35]

Many labor bosses recruited mainly people from their home ken. Hotel owners tended to rent to kenjin. Nearly all Issei men married women from their own ken, even when they met them in America. People from the same ken tended to live near each other and follow the same occupations. People from Okinawa made up a large portion of the Hawaiian Japanese population, but almost no Okinawans lived on the mainland. The largest sending ken, Hiroshima, had sons and daughters in every Japanese community. But within southern California, most of the Hiroshima-jin lived in Gardena (Moneta), Little Tokyo near downtown Los Angeles, and Hawthorne, and many were vegetable farmers. By contrast, Wakayama-jin were concentrated in San Pedro near Los Angeles Harbor and entered fishing and related trades. Fresno was mainly a Hiroshima town. Walnut Grove was heavily populated by people from both Kumamoto and Hiroshima. And the Tenth Street neighborhood of Los Angeles was full of former residents of Tottori Prefecture.[36]

Ken affiliation shaped business opportunities, as described by a Seattle Japanese American:

> Unless the agent happens to belong to the right *ken* group, it is very difficult for him to sell insurance. For example, I happen to belong to the Kanagawa *ken* which has only a small representation here in Seattle. If I go to the people of the Hiroshima *ken,* or the Okayama *ken,* or any others of such large *ken* group, and if there happens to be an agent from their own group, they will buy from him in preference to me. There is not any personal antagonism against me, but it is simply an expression of their desire to help a member of their *ken* first. I might present any number of arguments showing why they should buy from me, yet they would very likely say vaguely that they will consider it and give me an answer later, and let it go at that. Inevitably, they will buy from a member of their own or related ken. Because of these difficulties, and the trouble of attempting to overcome the handicap of my belonging to a minor ken group here, I have given up the effort to sell life insurance although I still have a license for selling it.[37]

With the exception of religious institutions (for some Issei), the kenjinkai organized more of a person's social life than any institution except family. It was, in essence, the family writ large. The kenjinkai fulfilled at a higher level many of the welfare functions performed by the extended family in Japan. Ivan Light, a student of Japanese American business, described this function: "As a relief organization, the prefectural club stood at the apex of a pyramid of community agencies expected to aid needy Japanese. . . . The close family was conventionally expected to constitute the lowest level relief agency. Appeals for aid beyond this circle were then to be directed to extended relatives, friends and so forth up the ladder of informal agencies, until finally the needy person lacking other resources might petition his prefectural club."[38]

The kenjinkai helped people land jobs and tided them over in hard times. Mainly because of them, together with a cultural imperative to avoid disgracing the family name, Japanese Americans did not appear on the rolls of public welfare agencies. They also organized recreational activities and gave people a place to belong. In the words of a Los Angeles storekeeper: "You know, we have a store which is run by my family. We are poor, busy, and have many children. We cannot go out like other families. But we have never missed a *Kenjinkai* picnic; it is the only occasion when we can meet many friends and hear about them. Children always make good friends at the picnic. We eat, drink, and chat in our native dialect."[39]

We have already described the tanomoshi, or rotating credit clubs, that groups of Issei (often kenjin) formed to meet their needs for start-up capital. Once in business, farmers and entrepreneurs quickly formed associations with other Japanese Americans in their industry. Thus, each rural district had at least one Japanese American farmers' association, often subdivided by crop: there were 31 farmers' groups in Los Angeles and Orange Counties in 1937, all brought together under the Japanese Southern California Farm Federation. Masakazu Iwata, the authority on Japanese American agriculture, described the functions of farmers' organizations: "The early Japanese farm organizations, local in character, aided their members in finding ranches, served to limit the competition for land by fixing maximum rental that a Japanese should pay, assisted in marketing the crops and obtaining supplies, interested themselves where disputes arose between a landlord and tenant, and disseminated scientific knowledge of agriculture and horticulture through publications of their own. Many of these local associations served as mutual benefit societies as well."[40]

Japanese city merchants grouped themselves no less intentionally than the farmers. There were formal and informal organizations of Issei businesspeople—for instance, hotel owners, barbers, and restaurateurs. And Japanese American businesspeople of all stripes came together to defend themselves against anti-Japanese actions by Whites. S. Frank Miyamoto described the actions of Seattle businesspeople: "[A]ttempts to drive out the Japanese were never successful, for the Japanese themselves formed associations and returned the fight by threats of boycott against those who refused to sell to their people. These threats were made effective by promising certain wholesale houses having large Japanese trade the concentration of all Japanese business with them if they would continue their sale of goods."[41] By the 1930s, Seattle had 22 Japanese trade associations and an overarching Japanese Chamber of Commerce. Some organizations transcended the boundary between farm and city. One such was the Southern California Flower Market Association, which integrated growers, shippers, and sellers into one large, cooperating group.

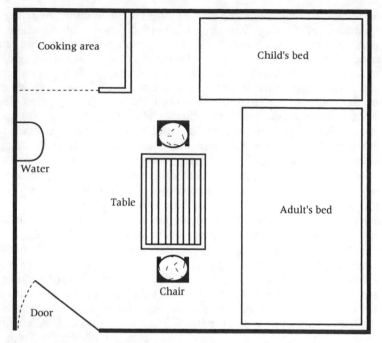

Figure 4.1   A one-room apartment for a Japanese American family.
SOURCE: Kazuo Ito, *Issei* (Seattle: Japanese Community Service, 1973).

By contrast to this high degree of business organization, Japanese American working people never achieved a strong, enduring union presence. There were exceptions, of course. Issei and Nisei farmworkers took part in union movements and some large strikes in Hawai'i and California. And there were outstanding individual labor organizers, such as the legendary Karl Yoneda.[42] But most Issei workers relied more on kin and ken connections than on class consciousness to meet their needs for mutual support.

Every Japanese community had at least one Japanese-language newspaper, which brought news of the world and especially of Japan, along with schedules of community events, gossip about other Japanese Americans, and news from Japanese communities up and down the coast. These newspapers, along with many short-lived special interest magazines, engaged in hearty debate with one another over community issues and international relations between Japan and the United States. At the height of their activity in the 1920s, the three largest of Seattle's five Japanese newspapers—the *Hokubei Jiji, Asahi Shimbun,* and *Taijoku Nippo*—had a combined circulation larger than the Japanese population of the entire state of Washington.[43] Such newspapers provided not just information and a public forum but a good bit of the glue that held Japanese American communities together.

Outsiders knew little or nothing about the organizational life of Japanese American communities. A mayor or White newspaper reporter who wanted to know about Japanese Americans went, not to the kenjinkai or growers' association, but to the Japanese consul or the Japanese association. The major West

Coast cities—Seattle, Portland, San Francisco, and Los Angeles—had consular offices. Officials there took it as their duty to look out for Japanese immigrants who got in trouble and to protest if discrimination occurred. The consuls were respected by Japanese Americans. For instance, they were invited to community festivals and placed in positions of honor. But they had almost nothing to do with the daily lives of ordinary Issei. They were Japanese abroad, not Japanese Americans.

Over the first third of this century, consular functions increasingly were delegated to *Nihonjinkai*, or Japanese associations, located in major Japanese American population centers. The first was formed in San Francisco in 1900, not to coordinate intracommunity functions but to defend Japanese Americans against the anti-Japanese movement of that year. Especially after the Gentlemen's Agreement of 1907–8, the Japanese associations acted as overseas arms of the Japanese government. They processed papers for immigrants, arranged the bureaucratic aspects of bringing wives and children over, and registered marriages, births, and deaths. They attempted to scrutinize and control the overseas Japanese, for example by conducting campaigns to stamp out prostitution, gambling, and other behavior the government thought would give a bad name to Japanese people in America. They maintained contacts with the leaders of Japanese American economic and social organizations, especially with the leaders of the larger businesses. When anti-Japanese agitation occurred, they tried to organize a defense. This was the primary role of the Japanese associations and consulates: to face outward from Japanese American communities toward the broader public.[44]

There are some parallels between the organizational structures of Japanese American communities and those of other immigrant groups of the same period. The Italian *padrone*, for instance, performed many of the same functions as the Issei labor boss. Mexican and Chinese immigrants were similarly organized by labor contractors. Few other immigrant nationalities built institutions like the kenjinkai, but East European Jewish communities, particularly in New York City, had *landsmanshaftn*—benevolent societies based on Old World district of origin—which were similar in design and function. Most other immigrants had newspapers and labor unions; among East European Jews, both labor and the press were much more active than among Japanese Americans. Few immigrant peoples created anything like the tanomoshi credit organizations. It is perhaps not accidental, therefore, that no other group entered small entrepreneurship so thoroughly in the first generation. Finally, no other immigrant group received quite so much attention from the government back home. That difference is mainly due to the weakness or inattention of the governments of other sending countries: Italy and China, for example, were not strong enough to do much for their overseas citizens, and Russia was pleased to be rid of its Jewish population. By contrast, Japan was a rising power on the international scene, both able and eager to speak up for (and also control) its citizens abroad. Though neither the consulates nor the Japanese associations organized much of the life inside Japanese American communities, they did provide a constant bureaucratic link between every Japanese American and the Japanese government. They sought to ensure that no Japanese American embarrassed Japan, and that Americans did not abuse the Issei.

Religion

Religion in the formal sense of regular participation in worship rituals and commitment to theological principles has not been a prominent characteristic of Japanese life in modern times. Most Japanese in the Meiji era were Buddhists of a sort, with elements of Confucianism, Taoism, and Shinto mixed in to suit the individual and the occasion. This does not mean that individual Japanese did not experience religion intensely—some did—only that, as a group, flexibility rather than dogmatism was the watchword.

Similarly, most Japanese immigrants brought to the United States a religious sensibility grounded in Buddhism and little experience of regular religious observance beyond the burning of incense in the *butsudan*, an alcove in the home set aside for religious contemplation. Buddhism for most Issei meant the ceremonies conducted at births, weddings, and funerals. It also meant important ethical ideas taught in families about how properly to treat one's kin and neighbors. Religion was not a regular activity in the schedule of most people, but it was an important part of one's identity, linking one to a web of relationships in one's family and community.

During the early years of immigration, there were no Buddhist priests or temples in America, no one to perform the occasional ceremonies and remind the immigrants of their ethical responsibilities. That left pioneer Issei as spiritually disconnected as they were socially disconnected, drifting from place to place in the American West. So it was a relief to many Issei when Buddhist temples began to sprout in Hawai'i in the 1890s. The first mainland temple was built in San Francisco in 1898. A series of temple openings followed (about one a year) in places like Sacramento (1899), Fresno (1901), Seattle (1901), Portland (1903), and other towns, right on through the 1930s.

The early temples were small affairs set up by missionaries sent from Japan to tend the wayward Issei. They were also harbingers of the more settled Japanese American society to come. During the frontier period, Issei men did not have much to do with these infant institutions. Later, as the men brought over their wives, settled down near other Japanese Americans, and formed communities, the Buddhist temples became centers of communal activity. They alone brought together Issei from different ken and different trades. They sponsored *obon* dance festivals and *hanamatsuri*, the flower festival marking the birth of the Buddha. They gave cohesion to Japanese American community life, and few people had more prestige among Japanese Americans than the Buddhist priests.[45]

On the other hand, America was a largely Christian country, and that could not but affect the Issei. The Catholic Church had other fish to fry—it paid more attention to Chinese and Mexican immigrants than to Japanese. But nearly every major Protestant denomination made the Issei a missionary target in the 1900s and 1910s. Baptists, Episcopalians, Presbyterians, Congregationalists, Methodists, the YMCA, the Salvation Army—all set up special teams of White men and women to minister to Japanese immigrants. They offered salvation and Sunday School from the start, but they also provided a host of social welfare activities that won the hearts of many practical Issei: English language classes, help finding jobs as domestic servants, and, in the 1920s, child care for parents who worked. Before long, mission stations became ethnic churches,

4.5 Shinto was a part of the religious life of most Japanese immigrants, but was elaborated into formal institutions only in Hawai'i. *Courtesy of Bishop Museum.*

such as Makiki Christian in Honolulu, or Japanese Baptist in Seattle. Until the 1930s and even beyond, the ministers were often White, but all of the parishioners and most lay leaders were Japanese. A few outstanding individuals, like the Reverend Takie Okumura of Honolulu and Major Masasuke Kobayashi of the California Salvation Army, were Issei pastors who also became community leaders.

The contrast between the welfare concern of the Protestant churches and the socially less active posture of the Buddhist clergy attracted some Issei to Christianity, but that was not the only magnet. Christian churches provided a range of activities that offered Issei women a life outside the home. So many women streamed into the churches that many Protestant Japanese congregations were predominantly female. Then, too, many Issei wanted to learn about America, and White Christian missionaries could teach them better than could Japanese Buddhist priests. There was also something attractive about the Christian emphasis on the individual for some Issei, who, after all, had themselves struck out across the globe alone. One described it this way:

> In Japan I was a Buddhist of deep faith. . . . After coming to America, however, I changed to Christianity because I felt that there was something in it which Buddhism did not have. In Buddhism they talk a great deal about cause and effect, and about destiny, but they have nothing in it which says anything about what one can do himself to change himself or his world. In Christianity, however, we learn that it is possible to alter the way of life and one's destiny by one's own acts. This is the thing which I have come to feel is important, and that is the reason I have given up my Buddhism and taken up Christianity.[46]

Finally, there was the personal appeal of the interested Protestants. Some Issei had come to America in part because of their experiences with Christian missionaries in Japan. One woman described her feeling about her White Christian mentors: "It is very natural for me to have a very friendly attitude toward the American people, because my contacts with them were limited to the missionary teachers in Japan. These missionary teachers were to us students as the living Christ. They were more than teachers; they were our best friends."[47] There were proportionately many times more Christians among the Issei than among the Japanese who stayed in Japan. Christians never reached 1 percent of the population in Japan, but they accounted for 15–20 percent of the Issei (and more of their children) by the 1930s. The majority of Christian Issei— perhaps 90 percent—seem to have become Christians after coming to the United States. But a significant minority converted in Japan and came here partly in pursuit of the imperatives of their faith (see appendix, table 12).[48]

The two religions, Buddhism and Christianity, were not spread evenly across the population. At all times, a majority of the Issei were Buddhists, but a slim majority of city Issei were Christians. Christians tended to be a little younger and to have three or four more years of education than Buddhists. In the country, farmworkers were almost all Buddhists, while about one-third of farm owners were Christians. Issei from the Pacific Northwest were more likely to be Christians; those from California and Hawai'i were more often Buddhists. Women were more likely than men to be Christians, but women were also more likely than men to be Buddhists; Issei women were just more religious than Issei men. Finally, because Christianity demanded the commitment of a personal conversion and churches offered many more activities than temples, Issei who were Christians were likely to be more involved in religious activities on a regular basis than were Buddhists (see appendix, table 12).[49]

Crime and Deviance

Whether Buddhist, Christian, or nonbeliever, the Issei almost never caused trouble for the civil authorities. The arrest rates for Japanese Americans from 1902 (the year of the first survey) down to the 1960s were lower than for any other major West Coast ethnic group, in spite of the fact that, during the frontier period, the Issei constituted the kind of young, male, transient population that might be expected to have a very high crime rate (see appendix, table 13). Such crimes as the Issei did commit stemmed from the different cultural mores of Japan and America with regard to drink, gambling, and prostitution.

Several explanations for the low Japanese immigrant crime rate offer themselves. One is cultural: Buddhist social ethics were so firmly ingrained that Japanese overseas obeyed their inner voices and refrained from antisocial behavior. Whatever the merits of this argument for a Japanese cultural orientation toward self-discipline, there quickly emerged structural factors that added to the effective control of antisocial impulses. One was the intense concern of the Japanese government that the national image not be sullied by misbehavior abroad. This concern led the government very early to select only model citizens to go overseas. It also led the Japanese consuls and Japanese associations to keep tabs on the Issei and to engage in campaigns against gambling and prostitution when it became apparent that Japanese mores in these areas offended

Table 4.5   *Crimes by Japanese Americans in California,* 1900–1927

Type of Crime	Number	Percentage
Offenses against persons	393	2.3
Offenses against property	632	3.7
Offenses against public policy and morals	7,275	42.5
Offenses against public health and safety	8,803	51.5
Total	17,103	100.0

SOURCE: Walter G. Beach, *Oriental Crime in California* (Stanford, Calif.: Stanford University Press, 1932), Table 44.

some Americans. Once Japanese American communities formed, newspapers published gossip about people who misbehaved, and informal networks passed around similar information. All these served to keep Issei upstanding and law-abiding.[50]

The Japanese Must Go!

That was not enough for White Americans. The Issei were models of middle-class American ideals—hardworking, law-abiding, devoted to family and community, exemplars of small-scale, free-market capitalism. Yet other Americans refused to believe these were Issei virtues. Instead, they created for themselves a fictional view of Japanese Americans as by their very nature obnoxious to American values. White Americans engaged in repeated, and finally successful, campaigns to thrust them out. In the words of the historian Robert Higgs, "Seldom have so few innocuous people inspired so much irrational hatred."[51]

The complaint against the Issei was fourfold. One charge was that the Japanese were very un-American and "unassimilable"—incapable of becoming good Americans. At the height of the 1900 anti-Asian activity, San Francisco Mayor James D. Phelan said: "The Chinese and Japanese are not bona fide citizens. They are not the stuff of which American citizens can be made. . . . Personally we have nothing against Japanese, but as they will not assimilate with us and their social life is so different from ours, let them keep at a respectful distance."[52] Phelan and others made much of the fact that Japanese immigrants had not taken out citizenship papers—ignoring the fact that Japanese people were forbidden by law to become U.S. citizens. The first American immigration law, in 1790, provided that any "free white person" could be naturalized. In 1870, after the demise of slavery, people of African descent were added to the naturalization clause. But Asians remained "aliens ineligible to citizenship." It is not clear how many Issei would have sought to become American citizens, given the opportunity, but it is clear that they were not afforded the opportunity. Thus, the anti-Japanese argument that the Issei had perversely chosen not to become U.S. citizens and were therefore "unassimilable" was specious, even hypocritical.

In 1924, V. S. McClatchy, a Sacramento newspaper editor and a leader of the political movement to halt Japanese immigration, expanded the image: "The Japanese are unassimilable and more dangerous as residents in this country

4.6   The Hollywood Protective Association tried to keep Japanese Americans out. *Courtesy of William Morrow and Company.*

than any other of the people ineligible under our laws. . . . With great pride of race, they have no idea of assimilating in the sense of amalgamation [i.e., inter-marriage and disappearance as a biologically distinct group]. They do not come here with any desire or any intent to lose their racial or national identity. They come here specifically and professedly for the purpose of colonizing and estab-lishing here permanently the proud Yamato race. They never cease being Japanese."[53] In fairness to the critics, since most Issei came to America as sojourners, not as settlers, it is true that they did not intend to assimilate into the American mainstream. Yet that was equally true of many immigrants from southern and eastern Europe, who occasioned less venemous opposition. In any case, this is a very different issue from the argument of Phelan and McClatchy, that Japanese immigrants were *incapable* of assimilating. George P. Clements of the Los Angeles Chamber of Commerce was more candid than most when he told a congressional committee in 1921: "It is not a question of whether the Jap is assimilable or not, we do not want to assimilate him."[54]

The second complaint about the Japanese was that they were filthy and degraded people who by their very presence (and their willingness to work at difficult jobs for lower wages than Whites) tended to degrade the Whites around them. The *American Defender* wrote: "Whenever the Japanese have set-tled, their nests pollute the communities like the running sores of leprosy. They exist like the yellowed, smoldering discarded butts in an over-full ash tray vilify-ing the air with their loathsome smells, filling all who have misfortune to look upon them with a wholesome disgust and a desire to wash."[55] Congressman E. A. Haynes said: "As is well known, no white man can compete with the Japanese laborers. They are satisfied to be housed in such cramped and squalid quarters as few white men . . . could live in, and the food that keeps them in condition would be too cheap and poor to satisfy the most common labor in this country."[56] Thus, the willingness of many Japanese Americans to work hard and endure hardship was turned rhetorically into a character flaw by those who opposed them.

A third theme in the anti-Japanese barrage was fear of sexual aggressiveness by Issei men. According to this fiction, Japanese men ached with lust for White women. The *Los Angeles Times* wrote in 1920: "The Japanese boys are taught by their elders to look upon . . . American girls with a view to future sex relations. . . . What answer will the fathers and mothers of America make? . . . The proposed assimilation of the two races is unthinkable. It is morally indefensible and biologically impossible. American womanhood is by far too sacred to be subjected to such degeneracy. An American who would not die fighting rather than yield to that infamy does not deserve the name."[57] Such statements usually came coupled with exaggerated statistics on Japanese American fecundity and sounded the theme of White America being overwhelmed by aggressive Asian hordes. White people like the *L.A. Times* editors might have been shocked to learn that most Japanese men had no interest in White women. Joe Tominaga, a schoolboy, bluntly refused the offers of his White classmates to get him a date: "Why should American girls think Jap boys want to marry them? I came here to study, not to marry. . . . We do not want American wives anyway— they are . . . always talking about self. We do not think them so pretty, either, as they think themselves."[58]

The fourth complaint was that the Issei were the advance wave of a new Japan, rebelling against justly deserved quasi-colonial domination and grabbing a place on the world stage, often by devious means. Newspapers—chief among them the Hearst chain—trumpeted stories of sneaky Japanese infiltrating the Western Hemisphere and plotting to steal from the United States what the United States had once stolen from other nations: California and Hawai'i. The *Los Angeles Examiner* in 1916 printed a "Hymn of Hate," which read in part:

> *They've battle ships, they say,*
> *On Magdalena Bay! [a harbor in Baja California where the*
> *Japanese navy was supposedly building a base]*
> *Uncle Sam, won't you listen when we warn you?*
> *They meet us with a smile,*
> *But they're working all the while,*
> *And they're waiting just to steal our California!*
> *So just keep your eyes on Togo,*
> *With his pockets full of maps,*
> *For we've found out we can't trust the Japs!*[59]

From *Patria* (1916) to *Shadows of the West* (1920) and *Seeds of the Sun* (1920), movies depicted Japanese spies scheming to take over American territory, Japanese troops invading California, and Japanese men attacking White women. In 1909, Homer Lea published the best-selling book *The Valor of Ignorance*, about a future war between Japan and the United States in which Japanese invaders overwhelm American forces in the Philippines and on the West Coast. All this concern about an expansionist military power in Japan was not wholly misplaced—witness the events of the 1930s and 1940s. But its emphasis on the sinister role of Japanese Americans was fantasy.

To members of the anti-Japanese lobby, which opposed and harassed Japanese Americans at every turn in the 1910s and 1920s, the Gentlemen's Agreement was no solution; it was a betrayal. They had called for Japanese exclusion to match the earlier exclusion of the Chinese, and they thought they had achieved it. Yet Japanese wives and children kept coming. Crying foul, they agitated for other restrictions.

They met their first success in 1913, when the California Assembly passed the Alien Land Law. The law, quickly copied in Washington and several other states, did not mention Japanese Americans specifically. Instead, it forbade "aliens ineligible to citizenship"—Asians—to buy land or lease it for more than three years. Those who already owned land could keep it, but they could not bequeath it to other noncitizens. U. S. Webb, California's attorney general and a coauthor of the law, made clear its intent: "to limit their [Japanese immigrants'] presence by curtailing their privileges which they may enjoy here; for they will not come in large numbers and long abide with us, if they may not acquire land."[60]

Many Issei became discouraged by all this abuse and started planning their return to Japan. Others, however, saw the holes in the law and set about circumventing it. The Issei were ineligible for citizenship, but their children, the Nisei, were American citizens by birth. It was an easy matter to buy land in the name of minor children and appoint oneself as trustee. That is how Jukichi Harada bought a house for his family in Riverside, California, in 1915. The anti-Japanese lobbyists again protested, but the courts backed Harada.[61] Other would-be landowners or renters arranged to borrow or rent the name of an American citizen, either a Nisei or a sympathetic non-Japanese. Some set up dummy corporations: Nisei were the paper leaders but Issei really called the shots. The White population tried to tighten the land law via a 1920 initiative, but the strengthened provisions proved equally unenforceable. The Issei responded to all these legal stratagems with energy and creativity. They hired lawyers and contested discriminatory laws through several levels of appeal, found legal ways to circumvent the laws' intent, and defended themselves to the public in books and magazines.

The net effect of the Alien Land Laws was not to drive the Japanese Americans out of West Coast agriculture. Although some people quit farming and went to the cities or back to Japan, the actual number of acres of Japanese American farmland increased through the 1920s. A decrease after 1920 may be attributed partly to the stricter second Alien Land Law, but it was probably equally a product of the general agricultural depression that began in 1921 and ran throughout the decade (see appendix, table 9).

White Americans took several other steps to encourage Japanese Americans to leave. They agitated against the picture bride system until in 1919 the national Japanese Association took a public position opposing the practice. There followed a storm of protest in Japanese American communities, but neither the Japanese Association nor the Japanese government paid any attention. In 1920 the Japanese foreign ministry stopped issuing passports to picture brides. In 1922 the U.S. Supreme Court denied the petition of Tadeo Ozawa for the right to become a U.S. citizen. He had lived almost all his life in Hawai'i or

California, spoke native English, had graduated from Berkeley High School and attended the University of California, was a Christian, and, in the opinion of the court, was "well qualified by character and education for citizenship," but he had been born in Japan and so was "ineligible to citizenship."[62]

In 1921 labor organizers and businesspeople in Turlock, California, decided to throw out the Issei who worked in the fields around their town. First, they circulated a petition that read in part: "We, the undersigned merchants and business men of Turlock, protest against the annual influx of Japanese into this community and, believing that it is the birthright of American citizens to fill all available jobs, we call upon the growers and farmers of this district to employ white labor exclusively. We call upon the packers and distributors to handle only such fruits and produce as has been produced by American labor exclusively. As evidence of our good faith, we pledge our hearty and unqualified support to the accomplishment of this purpose."[63] Then an armed mob of 50 to 60 White men rousted 18 sleeping Issei cantaloupe pickers, put them in trucks, and had them driven to Stockton and the railroad line with instructions not to return unless they wanted to be lynched. No one was convicted of the crime.

Finally, the anti-Japanese lobby got up enough political momentum to push for outright exclusion. They were not alone in this drive. A national movement had been growing since the middle of World War I, first to try to "Americanize" immigrant peoples, and then to sharply limit or exclude them. The treatment of the Japanese was related to that experienced by immigrants from southern and eastern Europe, but it was harsher. After no small amount of political wrangling, in 1924 Congress passed an immigration law that sharply cut back on the number of people who could come to the United States. It set quotas for most foreign nationalities: commodious ones that never were filled for the countries of northern and western Europe, and very small ones for the nations of southern and eastern Europe. There was no quota at all for Japan, or any other nation whose people were "ineligible to citizenship." The idea behind the law was that America was an Anglo-Saxon nation. People from Scandinavia, Germany, and the British Isles had been coming to the United States since the beginning and were regarded by the framers of this legislation as the main stock of the American people. More recent immigrants from places like Greece, Italy, and Poland were unlike Anglo-Saxons and therefore could be tolerated only in small numbers, and only if they shed their foreign ways. Asians—and Japanese Americans were the lightning rod here—were deemed unassimilable, unfit for U.S. citizenship, and therefore were to be excluded entirely.

The new law did not keep Issei men who had already established residency in the United States from coming and going, but it did stop abruptly any further attempts to bring over wives and children. There was a scramble to reunite families in the 36 days between the date President Calvin Coolidge signed the immigration act and the date it took effect, 1 July 1924. Many families remained irrevocably split.

The Japanese government protested, and people in Japan held nationalistic mass rallies. They proclaimed 1 July "National Humiliation Day," and there was talk of a boycott. The Japanese government was frustrated by the evident failure of their decades-long attempt to command treatment by the United States on a par with that accorded the European nations. Adopting the racist values of the colonial powers, Japanese leaders wanted to be treated like Europeans, not like

4.7   Some Issei men went back and forth to Japan right up to the eve of exclusion. These men landed at Angel Island Quarantine Station in San Francisco Bay in about 1923. *Courtesy of National Archives.*

Asians. Five prominent Japanese leaders wrote the Japanese ambassador in Washington: "Among the countries of the Orient, there are those which still cannot claim to rank among the advanced, civilized world powers. That these lesser nations will be treated differentially by American immigration laws is understandable. But since Japan already ranks among the advanced, civilized nations, it is unfair for her to be treated as an inferior country."[64] Clearly, Americans did not share Japan's estimation of its own level of attainment, and that rankled.

Protest though they might, there was nothing the Japanese government or public could do to change the minds of U.S. lawmakers. The Japanese living in America took a more cautious approach, hunkering down and going on about their business without public protest. In the months and years that followed the exclusion law, many Issei began to reevaluate their commitment to living in America. Some had acquired jobs, homes, businesses, and children and had begun to think of themselves as permanent residents. Tatsumi Taketa described the progression of feelings: "When I had come to the States, I had intended to go back to Japan after saving a certain amount of money, but once I began life in the States, things didn't work out that way. Whenever I had a little bit of savings and was making a profit, I had to use it to buy for this next season. Meanwhile the children grew up and their education became costly. Thinking all the time that I would go back to Japan 'sometime,' I put down roots in America."[65]

For many, however, the accumulated aggravation of all the rejections by other Americans—harassment on the street, bombardment in the press, the Alien Land Laws, denial of citizenship, and finally exclusion—caused them to pull away from America. In 1925 the net figures for Japanese aliens admitted to and departing from the United States plunged into negative numbers, and they stayed there until after World War II. Little by little over the next decade and a half, about one-third of the immigrant generation gave up on America and went back to Japan (see appendix, table 3).[66] During this period, as the Los Angeles newspaper *Rafu Shimpo* noted, "[t]he extreme dejected spirits of the Japanese . . . cannot be concealed. Some people are thinking of returning to Japan. Some are seeking safe havens outside the state or country."[67] The most disappointed Issei went back to Japan. Those who remained began to pin their hopes on a better life for their Nisei children.

Japanese American Ethnicity in the Immigrant Community Phase

Over the first third of this century, as dekasegi-nin became Japanese Americans, as the Issei formed families and communities, the bases and strength of Japanese American ethnicity changed. Early in the century, immigrants from Hiroshima and Wakayama and other prefectures began to band together as Japanese Americans on the basis of a common interest. Their coming together partly reflected the strong national identity that was being built by the Japanese government in the late Meiji years, but it was also a response to attacks by White Americans. Those attacks were not visited only on isolated individuals or groups. They were not aimed at people from particular prefectures. White Americans attacked *Japanese*—for example, in the 1906 San Francisco schools crisis and related physical attacks. The imin, for their part, responded as Japanese nationals. They turned to their national consul for help, they began to form national Japanese associations, and they began to build a pan-Japanese American identity. These activities marked the beginning of the transition to the immigrant community phase, which dated from 1910 to about 1935.

In this period, all three indices of ethnic group cohesion were high. First there was the common, pan-Japanese American *interest* in resisting, or at least surviving, discrimination at the hands of other Americans. This was also the period when Japanese on the West Coast built the ethnic *institutions* that formed their communities. Primary among these perhaps was the family. They also built economic institutions, such as farmers' cooperatives and businessmen's associations. Together with consular officials, the Issei organized the Japanese Association of America, as well as local Japanese associations in various cities. As communities and families grew, they founded Buddhist and Christian churches, language schools, and other ethnic institutions. Some of these organi-

Table 4.6   *Japanese American Ethnicity in the Immigrant Community Phase,*
1910–1935

Interests	low	medium	**high**
Culture	low	medium	**high**
Institutions	low	medium	**high**

zations—in particular, the Japanese associations—constituted channels through which Japanese Americans acted together to oppose discrimination and exclusion.

At the same time, in ways scholars have not yet measured, the Issei were creating a shared Japanese American *culture*. American words and constructions crept into the Japanese language spoken in the United States. Built on Meiji-spoken Japanese, it began to diverge from the language spoken in fast-changing Japan. It is likely that Japanese Buddhism in America also took on forms and vocabulary that varied from Japanese Buddhism. It is certain that Japanese American Christianity was not exactly the same as the Christianity practiced by other sorts of Americans, despite the earnest attempts of Caucasian missionaries to make it so.[68]

Thus, in the decades of Issei maturity and settled living, Japanese American ethnicity was strong—perhaps stronger than at any other time in history.

five

Born in America

Take a walk through central Seattle on a sunny spring afternoon in the late 1930s.[1] Start just south of downtown, in front of Union Station at the corner of Fifth Avenue and Jackson Street. Walk north on Fifth, into the heart of the Japanese business district. On the right, pass the Amor Geo Pool Room, where a pair of unemployed Nisei men are shooting pool with some young Filipinos. Wave to Mrs. Sugitachi in her barbershop, and nod at the middle-aged Issei men coming out of the Osaka Hotel.

As you cross Main Street, look downhill to your left. Three blocks away, you can see the offices of Pacific Commercial Bank and, next door, M. Furuya, the labor agent. Nearer at hand, the staff of the *Great Northern Daily News* is turning out the newspaper. Continuing up Fifth, you pass the Japanese American Tourist Bureau on the right and the bustling office of the *Japanese American Courier.* Inside, Jimmie Sakamoto, the *Courier*'s editor, is yelling at staffers. Pause in front of the Great Northern Hotel. Across the street is the other newspaper, the *North American Times* (*Hokubei Jiji*). The same building houses the New Troy Hotel. The hotel's manager, Izo Kojima, is sweeping the sidewalk. As you continue on to the corner, notice Takahashi and Company Importers, Frank Okada's insurance office, Yorita Printing, and the office of the Cannery Workers and Farm Laborers Union.

Just past the Golden Pheasant Noodle Factory—which makes noodles and cookies for both Japanese and Chinese homes and restaurants—turn right at the vacant lot and head east on Washington Street. All about you here are Japanese American adults, going about their workaday affairs. At the corner of Sixth Avenue, you can stop at the Maneki Cafe for a bowl of noodles and a chat with Tokuzi Sato. Further down Sixth are a string of Japanese-owned businesses, from Ishida's barbershop and Togo Cleaners to Mrs. Shinoda's restaurant and the office where Dr. Fukuda pulls teeth. At the corner of Maynard Avenue, one block past Sixth, stands the Astor Hotel. On the second floor is the Nippon Kan Theater, where plays, concerts, and community meetings are held almost every night.

Turn away from the Nippon Kan and walk down Maynard to Jackson again. This area is completely Japanese—Mrs. Fusayo Tama's Oregon Dye Works, the Togo Hotel, the Northwest American-Japanese Association. Many Japanese people and businesses can still be found south of Jackson, but they begin to mix in

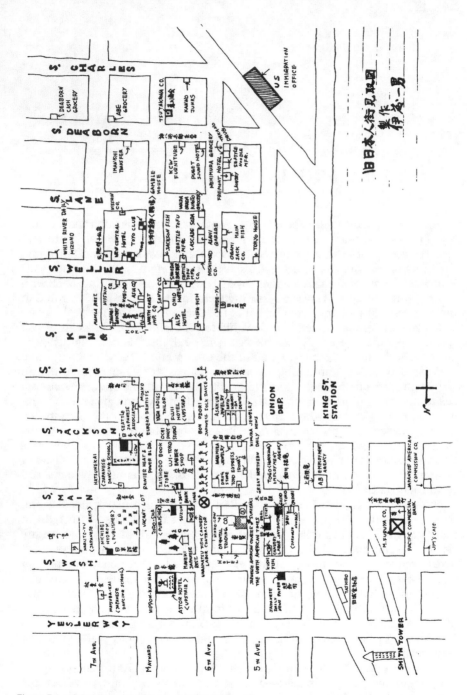

Figure 5.1   A Japanese neighborhood in Seattle
SOURCE: Kazuo Ito, *Issei: A History of Japanese Immigrants in North America*, trans. Shinichiro Nakamura and Jean S. Gerard (Seattle: Japanese Community Service, 1973), frontispiece.

with Chinese establishments, such as Lee Quong Cigar Manufacturers and the Mar Hotel, as well as with vacant lots and rundown houses.

Turn left and head east, uphill, on Jackson Street, the main Japanese thoroughfare. Pass Shizuhara Aoki's shoe store, the Ariizumi Drug Company, Shima's Dry Goods, and the Tokyo Cafe. Walk past Asakura's jewelry store and Hajime Mitsumori's dental office, past Nakahara Massage and Kathleen Mukai's beauty shop. Pause at the corner of Ninth Avenue and look off to your right. Midway down the block is the Japanese Presbyterian Church. Next door is the Oriental Evangelical Night School, where Issei as well as Chinese immigrants will be going tonight to learn English, and coming out with knowledge of Jesus, too.

At John Fujimura's gas station at the corner of Tenth Avenue, stop and look left, to the ornate buildings of the Seattle Buddhist Church, a block north. The Reverend Tatsuya Ichikawa and his flock keep the church in tiptop shape, and something is always going on there. Continue up the hill to the top, at 12th Avenue. Turn right there. Jackson's business district is beginning to fade into apartments and small private homes. The side streets are nearly all residential by this point. Two blocks' walk south on 12th takes you to Weller Street and Bailey Gatzert Elementary School. It is now three o'clock, and students are just getting out of school. About half the students are Chinese. They head back downhill to Chong Wah, the Chinese Benevolent Association building at Seventh and Weller. There they will spend the rest of the afternoon studying Cantonese.

Do not follow them. Instead, turn in the opposite direction (east) and follow the ragtag stream of Japanese kids across 12th, past the Nichiren Buddhist Church, and down Weller Street into Rainier Valley. Two long blocks take you past the Japanese Methodist Episcopal Church to Rainier Avenue. There the Nisei children stop saying "swell" and "gotcha" and begin to talk Japanese. Suddenly quiet, they file into Seattle Gakuen, the Japanese language school, where they will spend the rest of the afternoon rehearsing their parents' tongue.

Leave them to their lessons, turn left just past the school, and head north on 16th Avenue, along the side of the hill. In four blocks, you reach Collins Playfield. The tiny fieldhouse has two baskets and gleaming hardwood floors. It is full of high-school-age Nisei playing basketball—two teams passing crisply and playing earnest defense, while a dozen boys wait their turn to play.

Jog east one more block to 17th and cross Yesler Way—after Jackson Street, the other main drag in this part of town. Japanese people are now becoming more sparse. All around are little, wooden, single-family homes and small apartment houses. About one-third of the people on any of these streets are Japanese. The others fill the ethnic spectrum. Stop a moment and marvel at the bustling energy with which the Reverend Eiji Sushiro and his parishioners prepare for Wednesday night prayer meeting at the Japanese Holiness Mission, in a big frame house between Fir and Spruce. A group of these Christians live on 17th Avenue—in the next block—at the Amelia Apartments; all 14 families are Japanese. But their neighbors include Antonio Ferrara, James Murphy, Rufus Houston, and Moses Genauer. Three blocks farther east, there are no Japanese at all; past 20th is a mostly Jewish neighborhood.

Head back downhill (west) on Alder Street, parallel to Jackson and Yesler. Six blocks of long strides bring you to the Tenrikyo Church of the Reverend

Mitsudo Funo. The block opposite the church is all Japanese, although there are plenty of non-Japanese on the other blocks round about. Two blocks away, on 11th between Yesler and Spruce, stand two apartment houses. There are 32 units in the Abbotsford Apartments, with one Chinese family, one Filipino, and one Japanese. The rest are White and Black. Across the street, 19 of the 26 units in the Star Apartments are filled with Japanese. Roy Okamoto's corner grocery serves both clienteles.

As daylight fades, walk quickly west on Spruce to Broadway. The people at Japanese Baptist Church have just scooted the kids off the basketball floor and brought in folding chairs and a portable pulpit. You made it in time. The people are singing, and the Reverend Shozo Hashimoto is about to start Bible study.

You have made a circuit just inside the perimeter of the Seattle Nisei's world. Their parents and elder siblings worked mainly in Japanese-owned businesses in the district around Jackson and Maynard. That was where Japanese American community life centered, in an almost purely Japanese environment. But most Japanese American families did not reside there. By the 1930s they had moved east, out of the urban district near the harbor and train station, past Rainier Valley and up the hill, into an ethnically mixed neighborhood of small houses and trees. Japanese-run stores and churches had begun to follow them up the hill. Only about one-fifth of the Nisei, in Seattle and across the country, lived in Japanese-dominated neighborhoods. Two-fifths lived in mixed neighborhoods like the one around Collins Playfield and the Japanese Holiness Mission. The other two-fifths lived scattered across non-Japanese parts of town (see appendix, table 14).[2] Yet even though they lived mixed in geographically with lots of non-Japanese, most Nisei inhabited a separate social world, effectively segregated from any intimate contact with the non-Japanese people around them.

The Nisei Generation

The Japanese American population has exhibited a structure of discrete generations unique among American ethnic groups. Immigration began in earnest only in the 1890s, was limited effectively to the wives and children of immigrants by the 1910s, and was cut off completely in 1924. The result was that almost all the Issei were born before 1900, while almost all the Nisei were born between 1915 and 1940. Thus, the experiences of the two groups differed sharply. As the Nisei were growing up in the 1920s and 1930s, there were almost no young Issei their own age, and the Nisei came to see the immigrants as people distinctly different from themselves. So, too, there were almost no Nisei in the parental generation in those years to help interpret the youngsters to the Issei. Thus, the differences of experience between immigrant and native-born were compounded by the generation gap. In the pressured situation of the 1930s and 1940s, this made for a lot of tension and misunderstanding between Issei and Nisei.

Family

The Issei did everything they could to raise their children as good Japanese. Japanese American families replicated Japanese families of the Meiji

Table 5.1   West Coast*ᵃ* *Japanese American Population by*
Age, Sex, and Nativity/Generation, 1940

Age	Issei Men	Women	Nisei Men	Women
0–4	30	25	3,727	3,407
5–9	37	39	4,149	4,231
10–14	64	54	6,473	6,270
15–19	140	105	9,295	8,598
20–24	227	216	7,653	6,540
25–29	341	251	3,964	3,111
30–34	959	812	1,561	1,138
35–39	2,588	2,673	749	371
40–44	2,892	3,782	262	132
45–49	2,169	3,490	132	63
50–54	5,157	2,172	58	25
55–59	4,720	1,160	32	5
60–64	3,662	770	15	3
65–69	1,500	292	6	1
70–74	476	80	9	1
75+	152	54	9	5
Total	25,114	15,975	38,094	33,802

ᵃ "West Coast" here includes California, Washington, Oregon, and Arizona.
    SOURCE: Dorothy S. Thomas, Charles Kikuchi, and James Sakoda, *The Salvage* (Berkeley: University of California Press, 1952), 578.

(1868–1912) and Taisho (1912–1926) eras in most respects.[3] The Japanese family of these eras—in towns as well as on the farm—was based on the *ie*, or household. It included all the people who lived under one roof—frequently three generations, plus collateral kin, even servants. There were connections outside the household to a larger kin network, but the *ie* was the basic unit of society. The *ie* was an economic entity. Land or business was owned in common, and profits were shared. So was work: all members of the *ie* contributed unpaid labor and received sustenance from the household. The *ie* also was the unit of political and religious organization—the entire household was responsible for the misbehavior of any individual, and religious affairs were conducted by the household head on behalf of the entire *ie*.

The Japanese household embodied a three-part hierarchy based on gender, age, and birth in the household. Men took first place over women, the old over the young, people born within the *ie* over those born outside. At the top of all three hierarchies was the eldest male, the household head. Outside, he represented the household not only on religious occasions but in all legal and political, and most social, matters. Inside, at least in theory, his word was law. All authority—and all responsibility—were his. He ran the household economic enterprise, and others were expected to do as he instructed. At his death, his authority and responsibilities passed to his eldest son. The other sons were arranged below the eldest in age rank. Then came the household's women, again ranked by age.

Women had no public position, and no official authority within the household. But a degree of informal power might come to a woman who had a strong will, worked hard, contributed to family prosperity, or became skillful at manipulating others. Since women as well as men were age-graded, and since the relationship between mother and son was the closest bond in the Japanese family, a woman who had reached the station of matriarch often wielded conspicuous (if unofficial) power by virtue of her age and her emotional control over the eldest son. She worked her power most noticeably to the disadvantage of the lowest-status woman in the household, her daughter-in-law. That woman stood beneath even the daughters of the house in rank. All women in a typical Japanese family worked even harder than the men, for they were frequently expected to make economic contributions as well as handle all the child care and household chores—all the while maintaining a pose of cheerful submission.

The Japanese American families of the 1910s, 1920s, and 1930s approximated this Japanese model fairly closely, with one important exception. The families were hierarchical and male-dominated. Deference was always due one's elders. Economic arrangements were communal rather than individual. There was no division between work life and family life. If anything, Japanese women in America were even more overworked than women in Japan. But very few Japanese American families included grandparents or other extended kin. Many Issei couples more or less adopted single men into their households on occasion, to build a kind of artificial kin network, but for the Nisei it was not the same as having grandparents, aunts, and uncles around. As a result, Issei men assumed ultimate familial authority at a much younger age than they might have in Japan. From the point of view of Nisei children, the two-generation Japanese American household lacked a certain flexibility that young Nisei might have been able to exploit had they lived in Japan. If one has two older generations, even in a hierarchical family, there is always the possibility of subtly playing one generation off against the other. If children live only with their parents, their room to maneuver is more restricted. Akemi Kikumura met her Japanese relatives only after she had reached adulthood. On that occasion, she said, "I cried for self-pity—pity that we were deprived all our lives of the warmth and protection of a grandfather and grandmother, of uncles and aunts."[4]

The child-rearing practices of Issei parents reinforced family solidarity. Children were prized, but they were expected to be assets to their families. A small child was the object of joy, pride, and what to another American might seem shameless pampering. Then, beginning at around age four or five, the child was made to feel the weight of duty. Formerly lavish affection was withdrawn, and responsibilities took its place. The child must now behave well, because her behavior reflected on the entire family. One Nisei reported: "Both father and mother impress upon us that they love us so much that they want us to be good and to grow up to be honorable people. Father is very exacting. When he says do something, he wants it done that very minute. If you say, 'I'll do it in a minute,' he says, 'You are not to talk back to me. Do it right now.'"[5]

The emphasis was on shame and dependency, on obligation and responsibility. Most especially, the youngster could never do anything to sully the family name, cause the neighbors to gossip, or bring Japanese people under criticism from non-Japanese Americans. As Harry Kitano, a Nisei sociologist, noted, "A good performance by a child reflects on the goodness of his family, but a bad performance shames the family and produces feelings of guilt in the member who has invited the disgrace."[6] Praise was seldom part of the parenting package past a child's early years; gentle ridicule and reminders of the shame one was about to bring upon the family were much more common.

If these admonitions were not enough to bring the Nisei to heel, the other members of the Japanese American community stood ready to help out. Every town and rural district had a well-oiled Japanese American gossip machine, ready to pounce on tidbits and put them to use encouraging conformity. Toshio Mori set the scene in a story called "Between You and Me": "Inside of a week we knew there were words between Father Horita and Eiichi and the son had left late one night without further trace. Although the Horitas did not know we knew, practically everyone in the community was familiar with the Horita affair. Over and over the folks talked about Eiichi and Father Horita and Mother Horita."[7] Sometimes members of the older generation used gossip to instruct the young people:

> My parents talk about sex only when there is an appropriate example. For instance, when an unmarried girl in the community becomes pregnant there is always a lot of gossip. Mother discusses it when the children are around and says what a terrible disgrace and shame it is to have such ugly things said about one. She goes on to say how disappointed this girl's father and mother must be. Her brothers and sisters, father and mother will never be able to go to Japan again. And worse still, if a parent or some other member of the girl's family has recently died, this person, I am told, must weep beside some kind of stream in heaven or behind some bushes. Then mother ends in a grand finale by saying she would rather go to "Hades" than see her daughter in such a disgraceful state.[8]

Interconnecting gossip networks linked all the West Coast Japanese American communities, so the Nisei could never be free from scrutiny. Rose Hayashi*—a very unusual Nisei—ran away from her Los Angeles home in 1939 at age 16. For the next three years, she drifted up and down the West Coast, from San Diego to Seattle and back again. She worked in a succession of beer parlors, pool halls, and nightclubs and dated dozens of men of various ethnic backgrounds. It is arresting to note that the Japanese American gossip network kept track of Hayashi through all her wanderings, made regular reports to her parents, and put some pressure on her to mend her ways.[9]

Most Nisei understood all this to be just the way things were. But many also experienced it as tyranny. One Nisei woman complained:

> Once at a party, I felt someone pinching me. It was my mother, and I knew immediately that I wasn't doing the right thing. Sometimes it is because I am using my left hand, other times because my ungainly legs are not folded properly. When distance is involved, glaring eyes from mother means "stop laughing so heartily," and glaring eyes plus a sort of point means "use your right hand." A slight shaking of the

head slowly and inconspicuously from left to right means usually, "I want to see you when we reach home." A verbal gesture is also used that is a fast whisper as, "do keep quiet," "be gentle," "take care of the baby," "go call your father," "remember to thank the lady for the nice present," and "take some."[10]

Values

Issei parents used all these techniques to pass on to their children a recognizable set of Japanese values.[11] The first of these, *on*, was an attitude of obligation and respect. One acquired *on* toward one's parents, one's teachers, one's school, one's country. It was an obligation that required loyalty, obedience, and reverence. *On* was for a lifetime; it was not a debt that could be repaid, it was a permanent relationship of obligation.

A second value the Nisei learned was *gaman*, perseverance. No matter how great the obstacles, one must stick to one's task. No matter how obnoxious the taunts of enemies, one must face one's responsibilities with stoic lack of affect. One should not show anger, fear, or other emotions. One should simply stick it out to achieve one's goal.

Mitigating the iron quality of gaman, but not reducing its effectiveness, was the value of *ninjo*. Nisei translate this as "humane sensibility" or "the milk of human kindness." Those who have ninjo are empathetic and understanding of others and extend themselves to help others. One feature of a person with ninjo is the ability to sense when another person might become embarrassed and to adroitly keep that person from losing face.

The fourth value was *enryo*, or modesty on a level that seems extreme to many non-Japanese. Originally, enryo was something a social inferior practiced toward superiors. But in 20th-century practice among Japanese Americans, enryo was practiced by everyone toward everyone else. As part of what Harry Kitano called the *"enryo* syndrome," every Nisei child heard *hazukashi*—"people will laugh at you"—and found it a powerful incentive to be more modest. The effect of enryo was that one rhetorically minimized one's positive attributes and accomplishments, and those of one's family, even if one was in fact competing hard to get ahead. Many a Nisei child heard his father remark, "Oh, this is just my dumb son," when he knew his father was driving him to excel and expected great things of him. Noreen Sakai* described enryo:

> There's this holding back. You even have to be dishonest with yourself in order to not offend. It's self-feeding guilt. Everyone's going out of his way all the time to put himself below others. Being Japanese is going to your neighbor with this thirty-dollar melon that you bought out of season and saying, "Please accept this humble gift from my ugly wife and my stupid children." It's mind-boggling self-deprecation. You keep apologizing even if it's not your fault, even if there's nothing to apologize about.[12]

No Japanese American was fooled by anyone else's modesty, but enryo did ease the tension in competitive situations. Many non-Japanese Americans mistook the meaning of enryo. As Kitano said, "It has helped the Japanese 'look good' in Caucasian eyes because of its lack of aggression and high conformity, but for the Japanese American the cost of the goodness may have been very high. A full development of an individual's potentialities would surely be hindered by such a norm."[13]

Finally, the Issei prized indirection and avoidance of direct conflict. This was not an explicit value, with its own Japanese label, just the outworking of the other values. Seldom would an Issei parent directly command a child. Even less often—almost never—would a child talk back. A gentle suggestion, indirectly delivered, was usually enough to get the job done. A father might say, "Mama, see how Emi-chan studies!" referring to their daughter, but within earshot of their son. The son would likely take the hint and hit the books himself, perhaps noting the self-satisfied smirk on Emi's face as he did so.

Japanese Language Schools

Issei parents sought outside reinforcement as they taught Japanese values to their children. They relied on help from the gossip system and from churches. Most strikingly, they also relied on Japanese language schools (*nihon gakko*). Every Japanese American community had such a school by the mid-1920s, and some had several. Honolulu Japanese Americans built their community's first in 1896, Seattle did the same in 1902, and Los Angeles in 1911. Even tiny Eatonville and Toppenish, Washington, had Japanese language schools.

The schools taught reading, writing, grammar, and pronunciation, as well as Japanese history and geography. Between home and nihon gakko, some Nisei became bilingual; others developed far less skill. But the Issei had deeper, more emotional purposes in founding these schools and making their children attend. Miyoko Tsujikawa of Auburn, Washington, said, "I want them to study Japanese language and understand Japanese culture and history, then transmit to other Americans the good points of Japan. I also want them to respect their parents and their seniors. Further, I want them always to feel pride in being Japanese-Americans, who have inherited blood inferior to none." Seattle's Yoshisada Kawai added, "Although people may say that Issei are out-of-date, I want the children not to forget sincerity, diligence, *giri-ninjo* (the moral code of the days of our youth)." Jitsuo Otoshi, also of Seattle, said, "My hope is that they will inherit as a tradition the indomitable spirit which is considered to be characteristic of Japanese."[14]

A good bit of these schools' curriculum came from Japan. A prominent document for ceremonial occasions was the highly nationalistic Imperial Rescript on Education. But in the 1910s and after, sensitive to pressure from the anti-Japanese movement, the language schools began to speak backhandedly of their task including Americanization along with imparting Japanese culture. A mid-1920s statement by the president of the Southern California Japanese Language School Association reflects this public presentation of the language schools' mission: "Although the moral training of the children can be greatly accomplished by the presentation of good Japanese racial traits, we must not forget that we are educating American citizens. We must study more diligently in order to select character traits which will be suitable to the American nationality."[15]

The Nisei received this Japanese education not exactly as their parents had intended. To be sure, some would echo Mrs. D. Murashima, a Nisei from Del

5.1   A Japanese-language school class. *Courtesy of Japanese American National Museum.*

Rey, California: "We were taught that we owe our respect, our *on* to our teachers, parents and country. We learned this at Japanese school. The teacher always said that. Teacher impressed that on us. It stayed with us for the rest of our lives."[16] Plenty of Japanese values were in fact passed on, but some were barely appreciated. Monica Sone and her friends were bored and unimpressed by the seriousness with which their Issei teachers and parents approached such events as the celebration of the emperor's birthday. She was more concerned with how to maintain two separate personalities—one for what she regarded as her real life, one for Japanese school:

> Nihon Gakko was so different from grammar school I found myself switching my personality back and forth daily like a chameleon. At Bailey Gatzert School I was a jumping, screaming, roustabout Yankee, but at the stroke of three when the school bell rang and doors burst open everywhere, spewing out pupils like jelly beans from a broken bag, I suddenly became a modest, faltering, earnest little Japanese girl with a small, timid voice. I trudged down a steep hill and climbed up another steep hill to Nihon Gakko with other black-haired boys and girls. On the playground, we behaved cautiously. Whenever we spied a teacher within bowing distance, we hissed at each other to stop the game, put our feet neatly together, slid our hands down to our knees and bowed slowly and sanctimoniously. In just the proper, moderate tone, putting in every ounce of respect, we chanted, "*Konichi-wa, sensei.* Good day."

Sone was both confused by and resentful of the teachers' attempts to make her American body behave like a Japanese:

Suddenly Yasuda-sensei stopped me.

"Kazuko-san!"

I looked up at her confused, wondering what mistakes I had made.

"You are holding your book in one hand," she accused me. Indeed, I was. I did not see the need of using two hands to support a thin book which I could balance with two fingers.

"Use both hands!" she commanded me.

Then she peered at me. "And are you leaning against your desk?" Yes, I was, slightly. "Stand up straight!"

"*Hai!* Yes, ma'am!"

I learned that I could stumble all around in my lessons without ruffling sensei's nerves, but it was a personal insult to her if I displayed sloppy posture. I must stand up like a soldier, hold the book high in the air with both hands, and keep my feet still.[17]

Such were the lessons many Nisei children learned in language school.

Nisei Personality: Functioning in Two Worlds

Still, the Nisei as a group did imbibe enough Meiji-era Japanese values and stylistics from their parents, coupled with American imperatives from their surroundings, to develop what many observers insisted was a distinctive Nisei personality type. Frank Miyamoto summarized the evaluations of several prominent social scientists regarding what he called

> special [Nisei] problems of interpersonal style . . . industry, respect for authority, and cleanliness . . . acute sensitivity to the attitudes of others and a consequent restraint of his behavior in the effort to avoid disapproval . . . rigidity, a tendency to react inflexibly to new situations . . . controlling emotions and emotional involvements . . . tendency to employ euphemisms and round-about expressions to avoid emotionally provocative assertions; to dissimulate—that is, to dissemble and make pretenses that things were not as they appeared—in situations where the truth might prove too self-revealing; and to strive for self-composure and "cool" in the face of situations which might prove disruptive or embarrassing . . . a high degree of sensitivity to the attitudes of others toward him, and a tendency to constrain his behavior in order to minimize the risk of criticism.

Miyamoto rightly rejected the notion that these tendencies constituted a Nisei character flaw. Instead, he located the problem "within the interactive process rather than within the personality. . . . That is, the problem is not inherent within the Nisei personality but is a function of the need to interact within American society."[18]

R. A. Sasaki gives us a glimpse, in the story "The Loom," of how many of these personality issues developed in the interactions of one Nisei with the American and Japanese American worlds around her:

5.2   Most Nisei, like this young boy at Raphael Weill Elementary School in San Francisco, grew up among Whites and other ethnic groups, as well as Japanese Americans. *Courtesy of Bancroft Library.*

She had grown up in San Francisco, wearing the two faces of a second-generation child born of immigrant parents. The two faces never met; there was no common thread running through both worlds. The duality was unplanned, untaught. Perhaps it had begun the first day of school when she couldn't understand the teacher and Eleanor Leland had called her a "Jap" and she cried. Before then there had never been a need to sort out her identity. . . .

And from the first instant Eleanor Leland pulled up the corners of her eyes at her, sneering "Jap!", a kind of radar system went to work in her. Afterward she always acted with caution in new surroundings, blending in like a chameleon for survival. There were two things she would never do again: one was to forget the girl's name who called her a Jap, and the other was to cry.

She did her best to blend in. Though separated from the others by her features and her native tongue, she tried to be as inconspicuous as possible. If she didn't understand what the teacher said, she watched the other children and copied them. She listened carefully to the teacher and didn't do anything that might provoke criticism. If she couldn't be outstanding she at least wanted to be invisible.

She succeeded. She muted her colors and blended in. She was a quiet student and the other children got used to her; some were even nice to her. But she was still not really a part of their world because she was not really herself.

At the end of each school day she went home to the dark, narrow corridors of the old Victorian and the soothing, unconscious jumble of two tongues that was the two generations' compromise for the sake of communication. Theirs was a comfortable language, like a comfortable old sweater that had been well washed and rendered shapeless by wear. She would never wear it outside the house. It was a personal thing, like a hole in one's sock, which was perfectly all right at home but would be a horrible embarrassment if seen by *yoso no hito* [those people outside].

In the outside world—the *hakujin* [White] world—there was a watchdog at work who rigorously edited out Japanese words and mannerisms when she spoke. Her words became formal, carefully chosen and somewhat artificial. She never thought they conveyed what she really felt, what she really was, because what she really was was unacceptable. . . . The Japanese who passed through her house could drink, gamble, and philander, but she would never acknowledge it. She would admit no weakness, no peculiarity. She would be irreproachable. She would be American.[19]

That was the problem for the prewar Nisei—to be sufficiently Japanese at home, yet sufficiently American in the outside world.

The Cultural Generation Gap

The differences between Issei and Nesei amounted to a cultural generation gap, compounded not only of the usual differences of experience and outlook between youth and middle age but also of the even larger differences between immigrant and native-born, and of the conflict of loyalties that resulted from these differences. Yoshiko Uchida described the duality that the Nisei felt:

A lot more of me was Japanese than I realized, whether I liked it or not. I was born in California, recited the Pledge of Allegiance to the flag each morning at school, and loved my country as much as any other American—maybe even more. Still, there was a large part of me that was Japanese simply because Mama and Papa had passed on to me so much of their own Japanese spirit and soul. Their own values of loyalty, honor, self-discipline, love, and respect for one's parents, teachers, and superiors were all very much a part of me.[20]

Yet many Nisei chafed against being defined by their parents' Japanese-ness—in their own eyes, in their parents', and most of all in the eyes of White Americans. Like many second-generation members of immigrant groups, the Nisei had a hard time understanding the magnitude of their parents' achievements. The Issei had left home and family to come thousands of miles and wrest a living from a hostile land. They had been attacked verbally, physically, and legally. They had hired some of the best lawyers in the West and fought back, and sometimes they had won. They had worked intelligently and hard and had managed to build homes and secure lives for their children. But most Issei did not speak English very fluently. They did not have their children's easy familiarity with American slang and dance music. They could not help the Nisei with their homework or college applications, for they had not been through American schools.

All this led many Nisei not only to discount their parents' achievements but to disbelieve their competence. According to Yoshito Fujii: "The Nisei, who observed their fathers as youngsters, still don't realize how hard their fathers struggled. They are too subjective to realize what the Issei actually have done."[21] Some Nisei went to great lengths in their rejection of the Issei—and in turn, of the Japanese part of themselves. Daisuke Kitagawa, a Japanese Christian minister who worked with Nisei teenagers, stated the case in extreme, but not incorrect, terms:

> The Nisei in his adolescence. . . . [i]n fact and in practice . . . was in every way a member of the Japanese community, except that his language was English. This irked him not a little; and to counteract it, he turned to an extreme form of Americanism, rejecting everything, with the possible exception of food, which in any way identified him as a Japanese. . . .
>
> A Nisei, in order to be a respectable member of the Nisei community, had to be rebellious against his parents and the Issei in general. . . . The adolescent Nisei revolted against his parents, not only because they belonged to a bygone generation, but also, and more primarily, because they were Issei, an alien group. Here the rebellion took on a complexion of self-hate. In his parents the Nisei found that element in himself which made it difficult for him to be accepted by American society. Consequently, regardless of what kind of persons his parents were, one could not be a Nisei unless he had something approaching a grudge against them.[22]

There were, of course, not only emotional clashes and differences of perspective but also objective cultural differences between the generations. Young Nisei men did not drink or gamble as much, on the average, as did Issei men—in fact, the Nisei were often quite bothered by what they regarded as uncouth Issei habits in these areas. There was also a distinct religious difference between the generations: only about one Issei in five was a Christian, while between one-third and one-half of the Nisei were Christians (see appendix, table 12). The anthropologist Christie Kiefer points to four main areas of cultural difference between Issei and Nisei in the years just before World War II:

1. Nisei were far more interested than their parents in adopting a White, middle-class American lifestyle. For the Issei, it was enough to get along in America. The Nisei wanted to do well and to be accepted as people who belonged in America.

2. Nisei had far greater American cultural skills than the Issei. They spoke better English and knew how to dance. They caught more of the subtle cues of interpersonal behavior when they interacted with non-Japanese Americans.

3. The Nisei lacked their parents' depth of understanding of Japanese culture. They spoke some Japanese and were pretty well behaved, but very few among them would ever be mistaken for Japanese if they went to Japan. From a Japanese perspective, they reeked of America.

4. Not only did the Nisei speak better English than the Issei, they also had a broader intellectual perspective, based on more education and greater interaction with a wider range of people.[23]

For their part, many Issei were not too happy with what they saw developing among the Nisei. In the 1930s, they complained that the Nisei were "ambition-less . . . lazy . . . indolent . . . taking things too easy . . . too Americanized . . . not serious-minded . . . unpatriotic to Japan . . . unappreciative."[24]

Intergenerational conflict came to a head in 1937 at the outbreak of the Sino-Japanese War. Here was a test, in Issei minds at least, of how Japanese the Nisei were. They flunked. The Japanese government news agency, *Domei*, fed what can only be called propaganda to Japanese community newspapers up and down the West Coast. Japanese consular officials visited Japanese American communities and delivered lectures, in English, on the urgency of patriotic support of the motherland. Issei organizations and individuals sent a lot of money to support the war effort in China. Nisei may have contributed as individuals, but the amounts were small and the numbers were few; no Nisei organization publicly endorsed the Japanese attack on China. This response was partly due to where the Nisei got their international news: not from the *Rafu Shimpo* and the *Hokubei Jiji* but from the *Los Angeles Times* and the *Seattle Post-Intelligencer.* They read the Japanese community newspapers, to be sure—but for news of Nisei social events, not information about the world. Issei leaders and the Japanese government viewed the increasingly cosmopolitan Nisei with alarm.

In White America

The conflict of the generations was partly brought on by the experiences Nisei had with White Americans. Japanese Americans lived not far from the small African American neighborhoods in cities like Los Angeles, San Francisco, and Seattle. The Nisei attended school with some Black children, with Chicanos in most California towns, and with Chinese Americans. Yet, of the other peoples of color, it was only the Chinese with whom Nisei had much interaction. In Seattle, Portland, and Los Angeles, the Chinese neighborhoods were closest to the Japanese, and Chinese and Japanese children shared classrooms—in Seattle, from the kindergarten at Bailey Gatzert to the 12th grade at Garfield High School. But there was no small animosity between the Issei and the older generation of Chinese Americans, not only because of the Sino-Japanese

War but because of a long history of insults and attacks going back centuries in Asia. That kept young Chinese and Japanese American people from making common cause, though they knew one another, had similar parental problems, and were often treated as one group by White Americans.[25]

It was primarily the Whites toward whom Nisei directed their attention when they looked outside their own ethnic community. Some even wished, almost, to be White. Yoshiko Uchida recalled her feelings, growing up in Berkeley in the 1920s: "How wonderful it would be, I used to think, if I had blond hair and blue eyes like Marian and Solveig [her Scandinavian neighbors]. Or a name like Mary Anne Brown or Betty Johnson. If only I didn't have to ask such questions as, 'Can we come swim in your pool? We're Japanese.' Or when we were looking for a house, 'Will the neighbors object if we move in next door?'" Daisuke Kitagawa noted that "Japan and Japanese culture, anything that identified him as Japanese, became taboo to the Nisei, simply because it was detrimental to his trying to establish himself as an American." Some Nisei admitted being embarrassed to speak Japanese outside their homes, for fear it would bring censure and lack of acceptance from non-Japanese Americans. Ichiro Yamada, the hero of John Okada's novel *No-No Boy* (1957), expressed this yearning for acceptance by White America. As a child in the bosom of his family, he felt only his Japanese identity. But as he grew up, "[t]here came a time when I was only half Japanese because one is not born in America and raised in America and one does not speak and swear and drink and smoke and play and fight and see and hear in America among Americans in American streets and houses without becoming American and loving it. But I did not love it enough, for . . . I was . . . still half Japanese. . . . I wish with all my heart . . . that I were American." It was not so much that Nisei wanted to be White. There may have been some such people, but most, like Yamada and Uchida, just wanted to be accepted by Whites as Americans.[26]

In some settings, and up to a certain age, Nisei did find a place in White America. This was especially true in school. The Nisei record in West Coast public schools was quite remarkable. Despite the discrimination against Japanese Americans and their relative poverty, by 1940, 58 percent of Nisei men over age 25 had acquired a high school education, and 19 percent had some college. That compared to 46 percent and 19 percent for White men (see appendix, table 15). And they scored higher marks: a 1927–28 survey of Japanese American junior and senior high school students found that Japanese Americans had significantly more As and Bs, and fewer Ds and Fs, than other students.[27]

Schools were a place where many Nisei could interact freely with non-Japanese Americans. Jim Yoshida played fullback for Seattle's Broadway High School in the 1930s alongside White, Black, and Chinese teammates. A Nisei young man recalled, "I always mingled freely with American children while I was in school and never encountered any difficulties. Some of my best friends were American." Another said, "During my early high school years . . . I . . . never thought of myself as Japanese, but always as American; I knew absolutely nothing about it. I knew more of Europe and America than of Japan."[28]

Many Issei parents encouraged their children to throw themselves into school and, some thought, into becoming as American as they could. A Nisei woman told Mei Nakano: "It's a wonder we weren't all schizos. Our parents were always telling us to be 'good Japanese.' Then they'd turn right around and tell us to be 'good Americans.'" Ruth Sasaki described a Nisei girl's pursuit of an American education:

> [Her parents] felt the key was an American education, a college educa-
> tion. Immigrant sons and immigrant daughters would fulfill their
> dream.
>   She and her peers acquiesced in this dream. After all, wasn't it the
> same as their own? To succeed, to be irreproachable, to be
> American? . . .
>   They did everything right. They lived at home to save expenses.
> Each morning they woke up at dawn to catch the bus to the ferry
> building. They studied on the ferry as it made the bay crossing, and
> studied on the train from the Berkeley marina to Shattuck Avenue, a
> few blocks from the majestic buildings of the University of California.
> They studied for hours in the isolation of the library on campus. They
> brought bag lunches from the dark kitchens of old Japantown flats
> and ate on the manicured grass or at the Japanese Students' Club off
> campus. They went to football games and rooted for the home team.
> They wore bobby socks and Cal sweaters. The women had pompadours
> and the men parted their hair in the middle. They did everything cor-
> rectly. But there was one thing they did not do: they did not break out
> of the solace of their own society to establish contact with the outside
> world.[29]

Nisei Society

However well the Nisei did in school, there came a time for almost all of them when further progress among Whites was impossible, unwanted, or both. Discrimination frequently had something to do with it. A Nisei recalled the treatment he received at the YMCA:

> At one time I was playing basket-ball on a Sunday School team of an
> American church and we played at the YMCA. I could tell that I was
> not wanted there but because I played on that team they did not deny
> me any of the privileges. At that time some of the boys proposed my
> name for membership in the YMCA, and for a time it seemed that I
> would be admitted because my last name could pass for European, but
> when they came to my first name they knew that I was Japanese and
> then did not admit me.[30]

For most Nisei, the turning point came in the high school years. They had been looking outward to White America for models and for friends. But as non-Japanese youngsters paired up for dates, Nisei frequently found themselves left out. As they made plans for jobs and colleges, Nisei discovered their prospects were much more limited than those of their White classmates. Kazuo Kawai did not feel the racial line being drawn against him until he entered a Los Angeles high school. But then his former White friends began to turn away and ignore him, as if he did not exist.

I turned for the first time to Japanese friends. . . . By common isolation, we became close friends. . . . In language, in thought, in ideals, in
customs, in everything I was American. But America wouldn't have
me. She wouldn't recognize me in high school, she put the pictures of
those of my race at the tail end of the year book. . . . She won't give me
service when I go to a barber shop. . . . She won't give me a job, unless
it be a menial one that no American wants. I thought I was American,
but America wouldn't have me. Once I was American, but America
made a foreigner of me—not a Japanese, but a foreigner.[31]

Thus, rejected by the American society to which they had thought they
belonged, the Nisei turned inward and created among themselves a separate
social world, an all-Nisei imitation of the White teenage society that had refused
them. Mei Nakano remembered:

In high school, where social interaction and school politics gained
importance, racial division increased in proportion. Nisei made non-
Japanese friends but danced amongst themselves at the high school
hops, went to football games together and dated other Nisei. Social
segregation outside of school remained in force for even the most popular and active girls. Although the recollections of Nisei women are
often couched in terms like "I didn't feel comfortable (dancing with,
dating . . ., etc.) them," putting the onus on themselves, they were
quite conscious that an invisible line barred them from interacting
with white students in those social matters. Thus, if there were a
dozen or more Nisei students attending a high school, they often
formed a Japanese Club, not for political purposes, but mainly to carry
out a social agenda.[32]

The creation of this Nisei society was not merely reactive. Many Nisei took
pride, if not in being Japanese, then at least in being Nisei. And in places where
Japanese Americans were concentrated, such as Hawai'i and parts of California,
the numbers of Nisei were large enough that the separate Nisei social world
seemed quite sufficient to most. The reader of Toshio Mori's stories of Nisei in
prewar San Francisco is struck by the fullness of the Nisei social universe. All
roles—from math whiz to track star, from model student to class bully, from
wallflower to prom queen—are played by Nisei. Whites and others exist in
Mori's stories, but they slide by on the margins and barely touch the Nisei at the
center.[33]

Japanese Americans created the full range of youth institutions for the Nisei.
As early as 1915, San Francisco's Japanese language school sponsored Troop 12,
an all-Nisei Boy Scout unit. In Los Angeles, the Japanese YMCA and YWCA provided facilities for play and meetings along with programs in athletics, sewing,
drama, and the like. The North American Buddhist Mission did its part, forming
Young Men's and Young Women's Buddhist Associations. Generally, the
Christian churches had more success than the Buddhists at attracting the Nisei,
for two reasons: the Christian religion was identified with the American culture
to which the Nisei aspired, and the Christian churches were more energetic and
flexible in courting youth. Japanese American churches were built with the

5.3   The 1935 L.A. Nippons. *Courtesy of Japanese American Museum.*

social needs of the community, and particularly of the children, in mind. Typically, a congregation's first building was a large, shedlike structure, with a high ceiling and a wood floor. On Sunday morning, it was used for worship services. Then the chairs and pulpit were carried away, and it became a social hall for congregational meetings and meals. Through most of the week, it was a community recreation center where neighborhood youngsters would come by to play basketball. Only years later, most frequently after World War II, did many Japanese churches add other buildings to hold offices, classrooms, and a separate formal sanctuary.

All these organizations sponsored Nisei baseball, basketball, football, and track teams. They held dances and ice cream socials. They went camping and to the beach. Mary Oyama Mittwer recalled the scene of the 1930s: "Li'l Tokyo was a busy, buzzing little place as the center of California's Southland for *Issei* and their *Nisei* offspring. The *Nisei* were already beginning to hold big-time dances with full orchestra, renting ballrooms with glass floors and fancy settings as contrasted with the more modest, small-scale dances in the later 1920s."[34] By the 1930s, the separate Nisei social world had spawned Nisei Week in Los Angeles and the Cherry Blossom Festival in San Francisco. These were partly attempts by the older generation to get their kids to come back to Little Tokyo, and partly Nisei-generated efforts to replicate mainstream American activities in their own ethnic context. Each sponsored a beauty contest; Nisei Week included a parade and essay contest as well. Margaret Nishikawa was the Nisei Week queen in 1938. She and a court of four kimono-clad princesses rode through

Little Tokyo in a convertible draped with the Stars and Stripes. Typically, the winning essay carefully danced the fence between Issei and Nisei sensibilities, advocating that the Nisei practice good American citizenship but remain true to their Japanese heritage and eschew further adoption of American mannerisms.[35]

All these events were recorded in the growing English-language sections of Japanese American newspapers and in a few specifically Nisei publications, such as *Current Life: The Magazine for the American Born Japanese* and the literary magazine *Leaves*. Few Nisei could read the complex characters in the Japanese-language sections of community newspapers, but they turned avidly to the pages printed in English. From *Rafu Shimpo* in Los Angeles to *Hokubei Mainichi* in San Francisco and the *Japanese American Courier* in Seattle, journalists like Togo Tanaka, Jimmie Sakamoto, and Bill Hosokawa wrote breathless accounts of ballgames and social events. In serious-minded editorials, they pondered the status and future of the Nisei. Creative writers like Hisaye Yamamoto and Toyo Sugemoto contributed fiction and poetry.

One of the most popular features of the Nisei press was the "I'm Telling You, Deirdre" advice column by Mary Oyama that appeared in the *New World Sun* from 1935 to 1941. According to the historian Valerie Matsumoto, "Her task was to provide the Nisei with guidelines to proper behavior that would enable them to navigate safely the social conventions of the white world as well as to meet the standards of their parents and the Japanese-American community."[36] Deirdre offered advice to the lovelorn and instructions as to the proper fork to choose at a formal dinner. One of the main topics over which Deirdre and her readers agonized was the question of arranged marriage versus love match. Deirdre and her readers were in favor of romance but recognized that their parents held just the opposite opinion. Most prewar Nisei marriages were in fact self-selected couples, especially in the cities. Farm Nisei sometimes knew only a small number of other Japanese Americans and so let their parents hire a marriage arranger to bring in suitable candidates. But even in the cities, some Nisei compromised to the extent that they allowed their parents to hire a go-between and went through all the rituals of an arranged marriage, with the stipulation that their partner in the end would be the spouse they had already chosen themselves. Deirdre also dispensed wisdom over how best to play the dating game and advice on interracial relationships. Deirdre, like many Nisei, favored platonic friendships and social intercourse with non-Japanese Americans. Unlike most Nisei, Deirdre also favored interracial dating and marriage.

Another topic taken up by the Nisei press in the late 1930s was the fate of the Nisei. Conscious of the Nisei's tenuous status—between countries, between cultures, and between generations—all manner of organizations, from the Young Men's Buddhist Association to the kenjinkai, also held special conclaves to take up the question of Nisei prospects. These gatherings brought together Nisei from different regions for the first time, and they found that they were not all alike. Stereotypes formed quickly. Californians derided Hawaiians as "Buddhaheads." The Hawaiians retorted that Californians were "kotonks"— after the sound their heads were supposed to make as they hit the floor in fights. Some Hawaiians thought the mainlanders too timid before Whites. Mainland Nisei thought the Hawaiians unsophisticated about American teen culture. Bill Hosokawa recalled some of the stereotypes: "Los Angeles *Nisei* were

5.4 The Nisei tendency to model on, but remain separate from, the general American social scene is epitomized by their all-Japanese dances. *Courtesy of Japanese American National Museum.*

said to be 'fast,' casual, interested in a good time. San Francisco *Nisei* were considered sophisticated, conservative, conscious of a need for good grooming and dressing well. Seattle *Nisei* had a reputation for being friendly but naive, unsophisticated."[37] The stereotypes were not completely off the mark: there were objective regional differences. California Nisei were more rural than northwesterners. More of the Nisei from Seattle and Portland had grown up among Whites than had those from Sacramento and Los Angeles. Northwestern Nisei were more likely to Christians, and Californians tended to be Buddhists. And so on.

Getting a Job

Part of the concern over the Nisei future was economic. For employment as for social life, as the Nisei came of age in the 1930s they were turned inward to the ethnic community. Issei parents and Nisei columnists exhorted the second generation to go to school, work hard, and seek middle-class jobs despite discrimination. Some Nisei approached these tasks with a brave attitude. One said: "Getting a white-collar job after graduating from college seems quite a proposition for me. But I shall never work at the kind of job with pick and shovel. Other difficulties may not affect me much, for I am an American citizen and have no fear for anything."[38]

Despite such bold intentions, most Nisei could not find places for themselves in the wider American economy in the 1930s. The combined effects of the Depression and White racism denied them the jobs for which they were qualified. Yuri Kochiyama recalled:

Back then, Japanese could not find jobs except in Japan Town and China Town. It seemed impossible to get an ordinary job in town. Even when I finished junior college, I was one of the only Japanese Americans who was working in San Pedro proper and I heard it was the first time that a five-and-dime store hired Japanese. Woolworth hired me where three other five-and-dime stores wouldn't even let me make out an application. Par for the course, for all Japanese were either working in a vegetable stand or doing domestic work.[39]

Taishi Matsumoto complained:

I am a fruitstand worker. It is not a very attractive nor distinguished occupation, and most certainly unappealing in print. I would much rather it were doctor or lawyer . . . but my aspirations of developing into such [were] frustrated long ago by circumstances, . . . [and] I am only what I am, a professional carrot washer. . . . The little optimism that is left in me goads me on with the hope that when I have a few shekels saved that I can call my own, and only God knows when that may be, I will invest it in an enterprise which will be, through habit and familiarity rather than choice, most likely another market.[40]

Kazuo Kawai described a situation from the era before the effects of the Depression were fully felt:

A few months ago I met an American-born Japanese fellow who had just been graduated with high honors in electrical engineering from a university in the Middle West. Every other member of his class had been offered a position before graduation, by electrical concerns near the university, and upon graduation they had stepped right into their professional field. But this one Japanese, simply because of his race, could not get a position. He had drifted to Los Angeles, still seeking work, and the last I heard of him was that he had finally secured a minor position in a little third-rate electrical shop in Honolulu, which offered practically no chance for advancement.

I know another American-born Japanese who was graduated after specializing in foreign trade in the college of commerce of the foremost university on the Pacific Coast. But no American firm would employ him as long as white applicants were available, although they might be not quite so capable as he, and no Japanese firm in America was doing enough business to need a specialist in foreign trade, so for months this man was without work. Finally, the manager of the San Francisco branch offices of the T.T.K. Steamship Line took pity on him and gave him a position as a clerk in his office, at seventy dollars a month.[41]

The plans and aspirations of the Nisei were being frustrated. Around 1930, Edward Strong and some Stanford colleagues surveyed 9,416 Japanese Californians, 5,362 of them Nisei. The survey revealed these preferences among the Nisei for their future occupations:

Table 5.2   *Nisei Occupational Preferences, California,* 1930 *(percentage)*

Farmer	15%
Engineer	13
Retailer or wholesaler	13
Physician	10
Skilled tradesperson	9
Dentist or pharmacist	7
General businessperson	7
Chemist, geologist, etc.	4
Aviation	3
Office worker	3
Architect	2
Lawyer	2
Others(each)	1 (or less)

SOURCE: Ichihashi, *Japanese in the United States,* 359; Strong, *Second-Generation Oriental,* 2.

That is, about 40 percent aspired to professional positions, 20 percent hoped for business careers, 15 percent intended to be farmers, and only very small numbers were looking toward other occupations.

A decade later, the Nisei had not begun to reach their professional goals. Admittedly, they were still a young group, and the majority were new to the job market. But in the city of Los Angeles in 1940, only 3 percent of Nisei men and 5 percent of Nisei women were professionals, most of them teachers. Another 12 percent of the men and 4 percent of the women owned or managed businesses. More than one-third of the Nisei, women and men, were working as clerks or salespeople. Twenty-six percent of the men and 9 percent of the women were laborers. Seven percent of the men and 39 percent of the women were domestic or other servants. Except for the domestics, only 5 percent of the Los Angeles Nisei worked for non-Japanese employers. In the rural parts of Los Angeles County, more than half of Nisei men and women worked in farm occupations, most as unpaid laborers on their families' farms (see appendix, table 17).[42]

A large part of the problem was the combined effect of discrimination and the Depression. But another factor was also at work. Nisei hopes for advancement were blocked by the Issei. The economic historian John Modell described the situation: "As the Nisei came of age, they found their progress blocked both by the caste line and by their fathers' successes. . . . In the Depression, Nisei needed employment by their parents' generation more than the latter needed Nisei employees; however, few independent sources of employment for Nisei were available."[43] With no capital of their own or the means of acquiring it, and with impressive educations that went unused for want of White employers who would hire them, the Nisei languished in economic subjection to their parents' generation.

A few Nisei who had professional aspirations tried to make something for themselves out of their ancestral connection to Japan. Bill Hosokawa and Clarke Kawakami wrote for Japanese news organizations. Charles Yoshii took his University of Oregon education to Tokyo and became a radio announcer. Monica

Sone's friend Dick Matsui was unable to do anything with his engineering degree more professional than sell vegetables at Seattle's Pike Place Market. Finally, in desperation, he landed a job with the Goto Company in Japan. Some Issei friends of his parents thought he was doing the right thing. Mr. Sakaguchi, one of his parents' friends, said:

> Dick's a smart lad to be going back to Japan! Where else could Dicku get a real man's job? Certainly not here! . . . Name me one young man who is now working in an American firm on equal terms with his white colleagues. Our Nisei engineers push lawn mowers. Men with degrees in chemistry and physics do research in the fruit stands of the public market. And they all rot away inside. . . . With his training and ability to use both the English and Japanese language, he'll probably be a big shot one of these days in the Orient.[44]

Such were the hopes of some. But other Issei had not yet given up on America, and they were reluctant in any case to break up their families. As for the Nisei, not many thought going back to Japan a good plan. Kazuo Kawai considered the Japanese alternative but abandoned it, lamenting: "The trouble with us is that we have been too thoroughly Americanized. We have attended American schools, we speak English exclusively, we know practically nothing of Japan except what an average American knows; our ideals, customs, mode of thinking, our whole psychology is American. Although physically we are Japanese, culturally we are American. We simply are not capable of fitting into Japanese society, so we are destined to remain here." Most Nisei shared Kawai's assessment. In the Stanford survey, less than 3 percent of the Nisei were looking to careers in Japan.[45] Sone summarized the most common Nisei reaction: "We had all felt as Dick had, one time or another. We had often felt despair and wondered if we must beat our heads against the wall of prejudice all our lives. In the privacy of our hearts, we had raged, we had cried against the injustices, but in the end, we had swallowed our pride and learned to endure. Even with all the mental anguish and struggle, an elemental instinct bound us to this soil. Here we were born; here we wanted to live."[46]

As a result of these difficulties, the Nisei experienced economic life as rejection from White Americans and domination by the Issei. Some Nisei took the situation as an opportunity to build their character. A young Nisei surveyed the job scene in the mid-1930s and struck a chord of hard work and determination that would echo through the Second World War:

> I used to wish that I were white and I used to be pessimistic because I was not, but now I'd rather be what I am. I think it is a privilege to be a Japanese in America, because we have to do much more than the average person to earn recognition. We have to equip ourselves better than the white Americans do. My father stressed this idea for a long time that a Japanese person must be above the average, and he has encouraged us to prepare ourselves well. I must not be so easily discouraged. Fighting against all odds makes the man. Fight! I shall fight until the very last.[47]

Other Nisei were less optimistic about their chances.

Twice Immigrants

One group of Nisei who seemed particularly lost were the *Kibei:* Japanese Americans who were born in the United States but taken to Japan as children and educated there, who then returned to the United States as teenagers and young adults (the Japanese characters for *kibei* mean "returned to America"). Sometimes they were eldest sons whose parents, expecting to return to Japan soon, sent them on ahead to get a Japanese education and prepare to lead their families. In other cases, Issei were working so hard in America, they sent their child back to Japan to be raised by relatives. Sometimes Issei who were not yet ready to return to Japan themselves placated their impatient parents by sending a grandchild or two back to the family home. Probably the largest number of Kibei were not sent, not separated from their parents, but accompanied back to Japan by parents who had given up on America.[48]

The practice of sending or taking Nisei to Japan reached its height during the early 1920s. About half the Japanese born in America were taken to Japan in those years, and most of them remained there. This movement of Nisei and their families continued through the early 1930s and then tapered off. Those Issei, and their American-born children, who remained that long in the United States had, like Kazuo Kawai's and Monica Sone's families, decided to stay and make America their home.

By the eve of World War II, about 50,000 Nisei had gone to Japan as children.[49] Close to 10,000 of them migrated across the Pacific a second time, back to the United States. Some Kibei left their immediate families in Japan to strike out on their own. Others chose to rejoin the families that sent them away and had since decided not to return to Japan after all. The Kibei who came back to America hoped and expected to be accorded positions of honor and respect in their families and in the Japanese American community. They were the ones who had been selected to provide the link between American Japanese and their cultural heritage. Many came to the United States expecting to become the new generation of community leaders, revered for their Japanese education and cultural knowledge, ready to instill proper attitudes and behavior in young Japanese Americans.

Theirs was a rude awakening. Far from being greeted with new honors and responsibilities, they found themselves disregarded by the Issei, who no longer had visions of a triumphal return to Japan, and disdained by the Nisei, who were more interested in bobby socks and ballgames than in things Japanese. Bradford Smith described the homecoming:

> They came back with manners that were Japanese—with the rather strained and tense sensitivity toward life, the earnestness, the quietness. The girls came back submissive and shy, the boys somewhat arrogant and expecting their superiority as males to be acknowledged. . . . American-raised girls would not stand being treated like Japanese women, and Nisei brothers found the returned brother a pain in the neck with his puritanical notions about jazz and dancing and movies, with his unflattering comparisons of America and Japan.[50]

Most Kibei managed, by dint of character and hard work, to make places for themselves in Japanese American communities. But some were not able, or were not allowed, to find a way to fit in. Generally speaking, it was harder for Kibei men than women. A Nisei wrote in his journal:

> There were a lot of Kibei working as farm hands in the Sacramento and San Joaquin Valleys before the war. I don't know why it was but the Nisei didn't like the Kibei, and the Kibei didn't like the Nisei. Every now and then there would be a gang fight between them on weekends when the farm workers came into town. Some Nisei would get the idea that they didn't like the Kibei so when they'd spot a group of Kibei boys they'd gang up on them and beat the tar out of them. Lots of times I think the Nisei beat up the Kibei just for the hell of it. I can't blame the Kibei for hating the Nisei the way they've been treated in the past.[51]

Conflicts such as these presaged bitter struggles between some Kibei and some Nisei during the war years.

The Nisei Underclass

Another group for whom things did not work out very well might be called the Nisei underclass. They were very few in number. The Nisei as a whole are well characterized by Bill Hosokawa's label, "the quiet people"—well-behaved, hardworking, patriotic, and intent upon assimilation. But there were a few others. They were people like Sus Kaminaka,* Rose Hayashi,* Harry Ando,* and their friends, who hung out in bars and on street corners in Los Angeles, Stockton, San Francisco, and other towns. The men wore zoot suits with broad-brimmed hats, padded shoulders, pleated pants that dropped to narrow cuffs, and floor-length chains hanging from their pockets. They ran with Whites, Chicanos, and Blacks as well as with other Nisei. Some hung out around Chinatown nightclubs like the Forbidden City in San Francisco. Many were school dropouts and not formally employed. Others worked as waitresses and laborers. Most were not criminal—Nisei crime and delinquency were the lowest of any ethnic group on the West Coast. They were just rowdy and tough. They brought their Chicano friends to Nisei dances and scandalized the other Japanese Americans by jitterbugging lewdly.[52]

The Japanese American Citizens League

At the opposite end of the respectability spectrum from the zoot-suiters were the clean-cut Nisei of the Japanese American Citizens League (JACL). They built an organization that was in some ways an institutional expression of the cultural imperatives of the Nisei: conservative, hardworking, devotedly pro-American, doggedly accepting of whatever crumbs White America offered, quietly persevering in the attempt to win a place for the Nisei in the United States.

The JACL had several beginnings. In the 1920s, there were lots of Nisei social clubs and sports leagues. As the first Nisei began to come of age, a few who had political interests started to meet and talk about their commonalities as American citizens and children of immigrants from Japan. In San Francisco, a Nisei dentist, Thomas T. Yatabe, organized the American Loyalty League in 1919. It died quickly but was resurrected in Fresno in 1923 and soon spawned 15 tiny chapters around California. In Santa Barbara, Yone Utsunomiya and Takasumi Asakura organized the ABC (American Born Citizens) Club. In Seattle, the attorney Clarence Arai and some friends in 1921 put together the short-lived Seattle Progressive Citizens League. None of these organizations had much to do, and none had more than a few dozen members.

These organizations avoided the word *Japanese* in their titles because they arose at a time when White Americans were trying forcibly to "Americanize" immigrants from all nations—to expunge all elements of foreign culture and affiliation—and were about to put a stop to Japanese immigration entirely. From the start, these progenitors of the JACL emphasized the American citizenship of the Nisei generation, loyalty to the United States, and disavowal of connections with Japan. They were, in fact, organizational manifestations of the second generation's sense of separation from their Issei parents. But at the time they were founded, few Nisei had reached adulthood, and even those who had were dependent on the Issei generation for their livelihood. They were unable to assert their independence effectively.

The younger generation was barely more independent by 1928, when Jimmie Sakamoto, a blind ex-prizefighter and pugnacious journalist, brought the Seattle Progressive Citizens League back to life. That same year, the San Francisco lawyer Saburo Kido founded the New American Citizens League. Representatives of these two clubs met and decided to form a loose federation called the National Council of Japanese-American Citizens Leagues and to hold a national meeting in Seattle in 1930. Thus, the JACL was born, though it barely survived infancy. The first national convention attracted only 100 Nisei, three-quarters of them from the Seattle area. The meeting consisted of little more than the flag salute and some patriotic speeches about the virtues of unhyphenated Americanism (the hyphen in "Japanese-American" was quickly dropped from the league's title). For the next decade, the JACL operated as a tiny, moderately right-wing civics club and was ignored by most Japanese Americans, who were bored by its political slant. It grew slowly but was not a force in Japanese communities before the 1940s. Some JACL members wanted to be leaders in their ethnic communities, but they, like other Nisei, were dominated by the immigrant generation.

All that changed with the coming of World War II. In 1941, with war imminent, the JACL hired its first full-time staffer, a bright, energetic young Nisei from Utah named Mike Masaoka. Together with Kido, who by now was league president, Masaoka undertook an aggressive campaign to recruit new members and publicize his generation's Americanism. He wrote and distributed widely the "Japanese American Creed," a paean to middle-class Americanism which read in part:

> I am proud that I am an American Citizen of Japanese Ancestry, for my very background makes me appreciate more fully the wonderful advantages of this nation. I believe in her institutions, ideals and traditions; I glory in her heritage; I boast of her history; I trust in her

future. She has granted me liberties and opportunities such as no individual enjoys in this world today. She has given me an education befitting kings. She has entrusted me with the responsibilities of the franchise. She has permitted me to build a home, to earn a livelihood, to worship, think, speak and act as I please. . . .

Although some individuals may discriminate against me, I shall never become bitter or lose faith. . . . I am firm in my belief that American sportsmanship and attitude of fair play will judge citizenship and patriotism on the basis of action and achievement, and not on the basis of physical characteristics.

Because I believe in America, and I trust she believes in me, and because I have received innumerable benefits from her, I pledge myself to do honor to her at all times . . . in the hope that I may become a better American in a greater America.[53]

When the war came, the JACL Nisei were ready to step in and take over the reins of leadership in Japanese American communities.

six

Refining Fire: Internment during World War II

War came to America on Sunday, 7 December 1941, when Japanese warplanes pounded Pearl Harbor. Caught unprepared, the island's defenders fired wildly. They brought down some Japanese attackers and also rained 39 antiaircraft shells on the city of Honolulu. James Koba, a promising young Nisei boxer, was weighing in for a Tuesday night fight at the Catholic Youth Organization gym when the bombing began. Stepping outside, he was killed instantly by an exploding shell whose high-altitude detonator had failed. Eight-year-old Masako Arakaki was blown apart when another shell hit her language school. Yoneto Hirasaki, also eight, fled the school unharmed. He died a few minutes later, along with his brother, sister, and several customers, at his mother's noodle stand. Sutematsu Kido and his son Kiichi died in a hail of machine-gun bullets from an American P-40 when they brought their fishing boat back to port later that day. Japanese Americans were losers in this war right from the start.[1]

Pearl Harbor changed Ken Moritomi's* life. He had dropped out of school ten years earlier to work the family potato farm in Idaho. When news of the war reached Pocatello, Ken and his brothers met to decide which of them would stay on the farm and which would act to salvage the image of Japanese Americans. Ken was elected to enlist.[2]

As soon as news of the attack reached the West Coast, police surrounded Japanese neighborhoods. Federal Bureau of Investigation (FBI) agents knocked on doors. On the first day, the FBI arrested 1,300 "dangerous aliens." By the end of December, they had jailed nearly 2,000 more. In March, the number surpassed 5,000. They took consular officials, executives of Japanese firms, leaders of the Japanese associations, Buddhist priests, newspaper people, Japanese language school teachers—all the Issei who looked like community leaders or had tangible connections with Japan. They arrested people whose only suspicious act had been visiting a relative in Japan or contributing money to the Japanese equivalent of the USO (United Service Organization). Japanese Americans were arrested, thrown into county jails, and then transported to detention centers run by the Immigration and Naturalization Service (INS). When Germany and Italy declared war on the United States, a few aliens from those countries were also rounded up, as were hundreds of Japanese on the East Coast.[3]

Many Japanese Americans were terrified and could not understand what was happening to them. They saw the FBI as acting like the Gestapo. A Nisei college student reported:

The strain and tension on the men in the community was terrific. Most of them had a little parcel of food, night shirt, etc., ready in case they were next on the list. It was pathetic to see their faces. It was as if they were awaiting an execution. . . .

Now came rumors that the FBI would ransack houses. Everyone became frantic. I think every family must have gone through their homes in search of incriminating articles. Of course most were harmless, yet the FBI agents had a funny way of interpreting innocent articles. We must have burned 50 or 75 books, merely because they were written in Japanese. I spied mother with tears burning pictures of her relatives back in Japan, looking at them one by one for the last time and burning them.[4]

Jeanne Wakatsuki recalled the FBI coming for her father:

They got him two weeks later, when we were staying overnight at Woody's place, on Terminal Island. Five hundred Japanese families lived there then, and FBI deputies had been questioning everyone, ransacking houses for anything that could conceivably be used for signaling planes or ships or that indicated loyalty to the Emperor. Most of the houses had radios with a short-wave band and a high aerial on the roof so that wives could make contact with the fishing boats during these long cruises. To the FBI every radio owner was a potential saboteur. The confiscators were often deputies sworn in hastily during the turbulent days right after Pearl Harbor, and these men seemed to be acting out the general panic, seeing sinister possibilities in the most ordinary household items: flashlights, kitchen knives, cameras, lanterns, toy swords. . . . [T]wo FBI men in fedora hats and trench coats—like out of a thirties movie—knocked on Woody's door, and when they left, Papa was between them. He didn't struggle. There was no point to it. He had become a man without a country. . . . About all he had left at this point was his tremendous dignity.[5]

Husbands and fathers were taken from their families suddenly, without explanation and without charge. Most did not see their families again until months later, when they were reunited behind barbed wire.

Japanese communities were immobilized by the FBI raids. They were left leaderless. The Issei who remained either lacked the skills to lead or refused to risk being arrested themselves. Issei organizations folded. Businesses closed or operated at a loss, with their owners jailed and all Issei assets frozen. Churches continued to hold services, although many leaders were gone. The institutional processes of Japanese American communities ground very nearly to a halt. The only Japanese American organization in a position to deal with the crisis was the Japanese American Citizens League.

6.1 "FBI Takes Father Away," watercolor by Gene Sogioka. *Courtesy of Cornell University Libraries.*

For over a year, the FBI and army and naval intelligence had been scouting West Coast Japanese neighborhoods, talking with people, reading Japanese newspapers, and compiling lists of individuals who would be arrested if war ever came. Among their informants were officers of the JACL. In San Francisco, FBI and naval intelligence regularly called on JACL President Saburo Kido to ask about the loyalties of specific Issei. He apparently hesitated to declare categorically that anyone was a spy, but he was not reluctant to pass on his suspicions. In Los Angeles, JACL leaders went further. National Vice President Ken Matsumoto developed "an intimate friendship" with a naval intelligence officer early in 1941. He and his colleagues invited intelligence agents to their prewar meetings and apparently contributed information that led to the arrests of people who were alleged to be Japanese spies. As Mike Masaoka put it, his organization passed on "facts or rumors relating to [various people's] ostensible business and sympathies, family relationships, and organizational ties."[6]

Masaoka, Matsumoto, and their JACL colleagues believed they were engaging in patriotic behavior by passing along information to U.S. officials, not spying on other Japanese Americans. Masaoka wrote: "The information asked for is not one which can be called 'spying' or 'informing.' You are merely asked to do what every other patriotic American may also be asked to do: Ferret out the bad in order to protect the rest of the community."[7] In fact, there was no network of spies in the Japanese American community, and no Japanese American was ever convicted of espionage. Yet that did not keep the U.S. government from fearing such a network, nor did it keep the FBI from arresting people, including those whose names they were fed by the JACL.[8]

The months between December 1941 and March 1942 were a time of rapid, enforced transition in the leadership of Japanese American communities. As the

Issei leaders were carted off, the intensely patriotic Nisei who ran the JACL stepped into their places. They censored Japanese community newspapers, closed down Japanese language schools, and intimidated Kibei and other potential community leaders from asserting themselves. The source of the JACL's power in those months was its relationship to the federal government—first to the FBI and naval intelligence, later to the War Relocation Authority (WRA), the keepers of the concentration camps. The former relationship came from the JACL's willingness to turn in Issei leaders, the latter from its help organizing the imprisonment of its own people.[9]

Jailing a People

Over those same months, it gradually became clear that non-Japanese Americans were going to put their Japanese American neighbors into concentration camps. After the immediate uproar over Pearl Harbor had died down, American society as a whole left Japanese Americans alone for a while as it geared up for war against the Axis powers. That did not last long. By the end of January 1942, politicians, newspapers, and patriotic groups had begun to call for punitive action against those Americans who shared ancestors with the enemy in Japan.

Secretary of the Navy Frank Knox made a quick trip to Hawai'i in December 1941 to survey the damage from the attack on Pearl Harbor and reported that "treachery" by Japanese Hawaiians, "the most effective fifth column work that's come out of this war, except in Norway," was responsible for the disaster. He knew he was lying—he knew the defeat was the result of unpreparedness and incompetence in the American command, as well as daring creativity on the part of Japanese strategists—but he lied anyway, and he was believed.[10] Others spread rumors that Japanese American farmworkers had mown huge arrows in the sugar cane fields to guide the Japanese planes—as if anyone in an airplane over the little island of Oahu needed to be told that the battleships they saw down in the harbor were indeed their target.

Beginning in December 1941 and increasingly throughout January and February 1942, newspapers, particularly the jingoistic Hearst chain, printed unfounded reports alleging fifth-column activity by Japanese Americans. Typical examples are these *Los Angeles Times* headlines from those months:

"Jap Boat Flashes Message Ashore"
"Two Japs with Maps and Alien Literature Seized"
"Caps on Japanese Tomato Plants Point to Air Base"
"Japanese Here Sent Vital Data to Tokyo"
"Map Reveals Jap Menace: Network of Alien Farms Covers Strategic Defense Areas over Southland"[11]

Demagogues found sinister intent in the location of many Japanese American houses near shipyards, factories, railroad lines, and airports—conveniently forgetting that the Japanese Americans lived there because those were the slums and marginal lands to which they had been segregated. California Attorney General Earl Warren (soon to be a candidate for governor and later chief justice of the Supreme Court) reasoned that the complete lack of spying by

Japanese Americans was proof positive that they were all involved in a carefully timed plot to destroy U.S. defenses by massive and simultaneous acts of sabotage. Others cited the Japanese dominance of the southern California truck garden industry as evidence of a plot to poison the non-Japanese population of Los Angeles.

By late January, the relatively calm attitude the U.S. public held initially toward Japanese Americans had turned into fear and hostility, and a kind of hysteria about Japanese Americans began to spread. It was not unrelated to the lightning advance of the Japanese army in the Philippines, Malaya, and Singapore, the sinking of the British Pacific fleet, and other military reverses for America's allies. Americans, stunned by Pearl Harbor, continued to reel. They were not sure when the Allied forces might begin to turn the tide. Many worried, quite unrealistically, about an imminent Japanese invasion of the West Coast (Japan never had such plans, nor had it such a capability, as U.S. military authorities well knew). Nonetheless, various people began to call for the removal of Japanese Americans from the western states.

Some had other reasons for wanting Japanese Americans removed. Japanese farmers had turned desert into some of the most fertile farmland in America in the Imperial and San Joaquin Valleys and built equally attractive enterprises elsewhere. Some of their neighbors coveted their farms. Austin Anson of the Grower-Shipper Association of Salinas, California, said, while lobbying in Washington for the mass incarceration of Japanese Americans, "We're charged with wanting to get rid of the Japs for selfish reasons. We might as well be honest. We do. It's a question of whether the white man lives on the Pacific Coast or the brown men. They came into this valley to work, and they stayed to take over."[12] The racism in this statement, and the resentment at Japanese Americans' refusal to stay in what Anson regarded as their proper place, are palpable. Floyd Oles of Yakima, Washington, testified before Congress, "The great cry of 'kick the Japanese out of the Yakima Valley' is not due to fear of sabotage; it is due to economic reasons."[13]

As the winter went on, Japanese Americans found themselves the objects of verbal and even physical harassment on the street. Miné Okubo came back from Europe, where she had been studying on an art scholarship, to find that her parents' home had been ransacked and her sketches destroyed. Those few Nisei who had found jobs with the state of California and various municipalities were discharged. Congress even debated a bill to deprive the Nisei of their citizenship.

The list of groups calling for ousting the Japanese Americans grew to include most of the farmers' associations on the West Coast, the chamber of commerce of nearly every West Coast city and town, anti-immigration organizations, the American Legion, the Native Sons and Daughters of the Golden West, and other patriotic and trade organizations. Henry McLemore of the *San Francisco Examiner* expressed the sentiments of such people on 29 January 1942: "I am for immediate removal of every Japanese on the West Coast to a point deep in the interior. I don't mean a nice part of the interior either. Herd 'em up, pack 'em off and give 'em the inside room in the badlands. Let 'em be pinched, hurt, hungry and dead up against it. . . . Let us have no patience with the enemy or with anyone whose veins carry his blood. . . . Personally, I hate the Japanese. And that goes for all of them."[14] Even a political liberal like California Governor Culbert Olson lent support: "You know, when I look out at a group of Americans of German or Italian descent, I can tell whether they're loyal or not. I can tell how they think and even perhaps what they are thinking. But it is impossible for me to do this with the inscrutable Orientals, and particularly the Japanese."[15]

Yet the decision to imprison the Japanese Americans was not made on the West Coast; it was made in Washington, D.C. There, western congressional members and their southern colleagues put pressure on the administration of Franklin Roosevelt to imprison Japanese Americans. The key role, however, was played by military leaders. The administration looked to its generals for guidance, and the generals said to jail the Japanese. Lieutenant General John L. DeWitt, whom the historian Roger Daniels has characterized as "a cautious, bigoted, indecisive sixty-one-year-old army bureaucrat," was in charge of the Western Defense Command, the military zone on the West Coast.[16] DeWitt said later, "A Jap's a Jap. They are a dangerous element, whether loyal or not. There is no way to determine their loyalty. . . . It makes no difference whether he is an American; theoretically he is still a Japanese, and you can't change him. . . . You can't change him by giving him a piece of paper."[17] Together with Major General Allen W. Gullion in Washington, the army's provost marshall general, and key underlings like Major Karl R. Bendetsen, DeWitt campaigned to remove the Japanese American population of his part of the country. The military chiefs claimed "military necessity," although they never demonstrated that such a necessity existed.

The higher-ups in Washington, busy with the war and guided by some racism of their own, bought the generals' argument. With only mild protests from people like Attorney General Francis Biddle and the FBI's J. Edgar Hoover—who argued that they had already jailed all the Japanese Americans who were dangerous—members of the Roosevelt administration supported the decision to remove the entire Japanese American population from the West Coast. On 19 February, President Roosevelt issued executive order 9066, which empowered Secretary of War Henry Stimson to designate "military areas" from which commanders could exclude anyone they chose. Despite the bland language, it was clear to everyone that the order was designed to exclude Japanese Americans from the West Coast.

On 2 March 1942, DeWitt divided Washington, Oregon, California, and Arizona into two military areas. Japanese Americans would be prohibited from the furthest western parts of the states (southern in the case of Arizona) and restricted to inland sections. Some Japanese Americans packed up their belongings, sold their homes and businesses, and headed for the interior. I. K. Ishimatsu moved a family of 24 from San Jose to Cedar City, Utah. He recalled later:

> When we arrived in Utah, we lived temporarily in a motel, but this man had lots of pressure from the local people to keep us moving. (There were so many caravans of Japanese carrying mattresses and household goods it reminded you of covered wagons passing through Cedar City which is located on the main highway east.) At the same time, there were rumors reaching Utah that some Japanese spies were running out of California. . . . Finally, the motel owner began to feel the pressure and asked us to find some other place to rent.

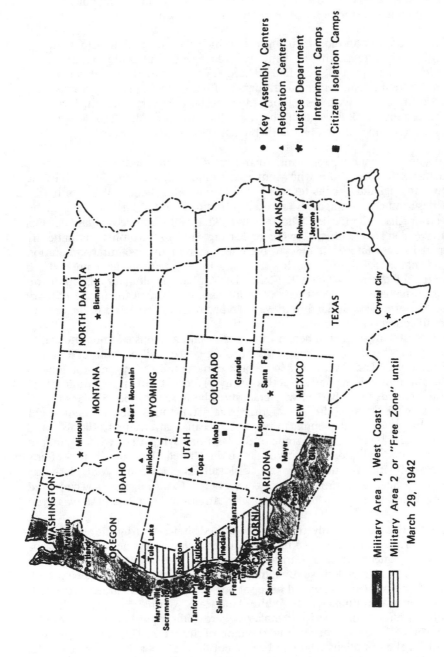

Figure 6.1 U.S. World War II assembly centers and relocation camps. Source: Michi Weglyn, *Years of Infamy: The Untold Story of America's Concentration Camps* (New York: Morrow, 1976)

The townspeople met and voted on whether to allow the Ishimatsu family to stay in Cedar City. After an impassioned plea from Mr. Ishimatsu ("the reason I want to stay here is to prove to you that I'm not a spy nor a dangerous alien"), they grudgingly agreed to make an exception for this one family.

> Later I found an old brick house to which we moved. I was told the price we were paying for rent was outrageous but I didn't have a choice. A couple times we had telephone calls during the night, apparently from a man under the influence of liquor, telling us to get out or they'd blast us with a shotgun. My wife became very nervous. I was scared too. . . . But we didn't bother calling the sheriff's office. We just sat there and waited. The man who threatened didn't come.[18]

For most Japanese Americans, such a move on short notice was impossible to achieve. Besides, those who went east found they were not very welcome anywhere. Vigilante groups formed in California's San Joaquin Valley to harass Japanese American migrants and keep them heading farther east. Idaho Governor Chase Clark said, "The Japs live like rats, breed like rats and act like rats. We don't want them buying or leasing land or becoming permanently located in our state."[19] It quickly became apparent that voluntary migration would not succeed in removing the Japanese American population from DeWitt's military areas. So on 27 March, DeWitt halted voluntary migration and put a curfew and travel restrictions on all Japanese Americans in the military zone. The army had decided to move everybody out by force and to incarcerate them in concentration camps.

This mass movement of people into concentration camps was not unusual in U.S. dealings with Native Americans—the Cherokee Trail of Tears in 1838–39 and the Navajo Long Walk in 1864 are just two examples. But the incarceration of Japanese Americans had no 20th-century precedent. An entire ethnic group was to be herded into barbed-wire enclosures because they looked like some of the people the United States was fighting against, because a few of them might think that other country ought to win, and because government officials could not tell the difference. Surely some of the Issei had sympathies with Japan, but there was no hard evidence of disloyalty to the United States on the part of any Japanese American—and in any case, disloyalty is not a crime. Much less was there any evidence of criminal activity or sabotage. Every Japanese spy convicted during World War II was a Caucasian. No American-born Japanese was even charged.

Japan was not the only country the United States was fighting against in World War II. What if the government had decided to apply the same standards to Italian Americans and German Americans that they did to Japanese Americans? Had they done so, Dwight Eisenhower, Joe DiMaggio, and New York Mayor Fiorello LaGuardia would have sat out the war behind barbed wire. Such a situation was unthinkable to White Americans. German Americans, in the minds of most White decision makers, were indistinguishable from Anglo-Americans. There was never any thought of interning German Americans, except for the few aliens who had been identified as probable Axis agents. The FBI did arrest some Italians thought to be dangerous, and it also restricted for a while the liberties of others who had never bothered to take out American citizenship papers. The administration relented, however, when it became clear that the Democrats would have a hard time carrying states like New York and Massachusetts without Italian American votes. It never considered taking action against American citizens of Italian ancestry.

It is revealing to note that in Hawai'i, the one place where Japanese Americans were a large enough group to do some damage if they really were conspiring—they made up more than one-third of the population—there was no call for internment. Japanese Hawaiians were too important to the Hawaiian economy for them to be scapegoated, as was happening on the mainland.

Almost no one spoke up for the Japanese Americans. Politicians, Democratic and Republican, howled for Japanese removal. So did newspaper people and civic leaders. Military people insisted on the existence of a military threat that they never could specify. Civil rights groups like the national American Civil Liberties Union did not speak out against the imprisonment. A few members of the Roosevelt administration, like the Justice Department official Edward Ennis, made ineffectual protests. The progressive journalist Carey McWilliams, the columnist Chester Rowell, and the labor leaders Harry Bridges and Louis Goldblatt spoke up, to no avail. Isolated individuals, some churches, and the American Friends Service Committee tried to help Japanese neighbors ease the transition. But no loud voice was raised in protest.

The Question of Resistance

The question remains, why didn't the Japanese Americans resist? Why did they go quietly off to concentration camps without putting up a fight? Some people have argued that Japanese Americans were passive by nature, that they were culturally predisposed to accept whatever came—*shikata ga nai*. Still, the Issei had been very active and resourceful (while remaining polite) in resisting previous attacks, such as the San Francisco schools crisis and the Alien Land Laws. Arguing the existence of a Japanese American cultural gene for passivity is not reasonable.

Mike Masaoka and other JACL leaders, looking back in later years, argued that the Japanese Americans were simply overwhelmed by the power of the U.S. government, which had more than two million soldiers in arms; any resistance would have been suicidal. Yet during those critical months in the winter of 1941–42, Masaoka and the JACL actively courted relationships with the U.S. government and proudly embraced the imprisonment of their people as their best chance to demonstrate their patriotism by doing whatever self-denigrating thing the White American populace asked of them. Mike Masaoka seems to have had a hand in planning the way the camps would be set up. After initially suggesting that only the Issei and not the Nisei be taken, he embraced the idea that all Japanese Americans would have to go. One must reluctantly conclude that the arrest of the Issei generation of leaders, and the wholehearted embrace of the U.S. government by those Nisei who stepped into their places, proved decisive in causing the Japanese Americans not to resist. Their natural leaders were gone, and the only leaders left—the JACL—told them to cooperate. Anti-incarceration and anti-JACL movements would later emerge, but only after everybody was inside a concentration camp.[20]

Some individuals protested what was being done to them, but their resistance emerged very late. Just as Japanese Americans were being carted off, a few individuals attempted to resist incarceration through legal action. Four such cases eventually reached the Supreme Court; the court in all four cases upheld the constitutionality of this patently illegal act.

Gordon Hirabayashi was a Nisei, a Quaker, a YMCA member, a Boy Scout leader, and a student at the University of Washington. On religious and moral grounds, he decided to stay near the campus in May 1942 when the other Seattle Nisei were joining their families and being shipped off to the Puyallup Fairgrounds. Then he went down to the Seattle office of the FBI and turned himself in for failing to report for imprisonment. The American Civil Liberties Union promised him legal help and then backed out. Hirabayashi spent five months in jail and was convicted of violating the government's curfew on people of Japanese ancestry. Then he was left to roam in eastern Washington, pending settlement of his appeal, while his family was in a concentration camp not far away. In June 1943 the Supreme Court decided in a 9–0 vote that the racially designated curfew was legal, and Hirabayashi was sentenced to another 90 days of work on a government road crew. The court's decision united such liberal justices as William O. Douglas and Frank Murphy with conservatives such as Harlan Stone. Douglas said, "We cannot sit in judgment on the military requirements of that hour," while Stone ventured the opinion that Japanese Americans constituted "a greater source of danger than those of a different ancestry."[21]

Min Yasui also was arrested for violating the curfew, but he did not wait for evacuation day. He was a Nisei from Hood River, Oregon, an officer in the army reserve, and a lawyer. Unable to find employment in Oregon, he had taken a job with the Japanese consul's office in Chicago. After Pearl Harbor, he reported to Fort Vancouver for active duty and was given command of a company, only to have it withdrawn and to be ordered off the base because he was a Japanese American. He then went to Portland to try to practice law. Like many other JACL Nisei, Yasui did not question the legality of instituting a curfew for the Issei, nor of putting them in concentration camps. Nonetheless, he stood up for his own rights as a U.S. citizen. When the curfew order came in March 1942, Yasui decided to challenge it:

I had my secretary call the police on March 28th, a Saturday night, and report that "There's a Japanese walking up and down the streets, arrest him." I had an awful time getting arrested. I was getting tired walking around town, and I approached a policeman at eleven o'clock at night. I pulled out this order that said all persons of Japanese ancestry must be in their place of abode, and I pulled out my birth certificate and said, "Look, I'm a person of Japanese ancestry, arrest me." And the policeman said, "Run along home, you'll get in trouble." I actually had to go down to the Second Avenue police station and talk to the sergeant and tell him what I wanted to do. He said, "Sure, we'll oblige you." So they threw me in the drunk tank until Monday morning, which was a miserable experience.[22]

At Yasui's trial, the judge held that the curfew did not apply to U.S. citizens, but that Min Yasui was no longer a U.S. citizen because he had gone to Japanese language school and had worked for the Japanese consulate. On appeal, the

Supreme Court did not rule on Yasui's case but ordered it returned to the lower court with a note calling on the judge to pay attention to the Hirabayashi ruling that the curfew was valid for U.S. citizens. Yasui spent a year in solitary confinement.

Fred Korematsu did not want to be anyone's test case. He just wanted to stay out of prison camp and get on with his life. He was a welder in San Leandro, California, who was engaged to Ida Boitano, a White woman who worked in a biscuit factory. Before the exclusion order, he decided to move to Arizona and marry his beloved. He contacted a shady San Francisco surgeon and had plastic surgery on his nose and eyelids in an attempt to look less Japanese. When the exclusion order came, Fred Korematsu was still in San Leandro, trying to pass himself off as a Spanish-Hawaiian named "Clyde Sarah." Someone informed police he was a Nisei, and he was arrested on 30 May. While he sat in the Tanforan Assembly Center awaiting trial, he received a letter from Boitano saying she wanted no further contact with him. Korematsu was contacted by Ernest Besig, a lawyer for the San Francisco ACLU who was looking for a test case. Korematsu proved willing and quietly stuck with the case until December 1944, when the Supreme Court ruled against him, this time in a split decision. In that decision, Justice Hugo Black wrote the most blatant of falsehoods: "Korematsu was not excluded from the Military Area because of hostility to him or to his race."[23]

In the Korematsu case, as with Hirabayashi and Yasui, government attorneys knowingly misled the Court by exaggerating the military's estimates of the security risk presented by Japanese Americans. That misconduct, together with their withholding of key documents, ultimately led to the overturning of the convictions—four decades later.

Mitsuye Endo's strategy was different. She complied with the imprisonment order and was interned at Tanforan. While there, she was contacted by James Purcell, a lawyer who convinced her to sue for habeas corpus. The other cases had challenged the military's curfews and exclusion orders. Endo's was the first case to challenge the concentration camps themselves. After more than two years behind barbed wire, during which time the United States and its allies had turned the tide of war and the Japanese Americans in concentration camps had become something of an embarrassment to the government, Endo was set free by a unanimous Supreme Court.

The JACL declared itself "unalterably opposed to test cases," even though two of the protesters, Min Yasui and Gordon Hirabayashi, were JACL members and Endo's lawyer had first been recruited by JACL President Saburo Kido. Mike Masaoka cited ten reasons for opposing Min Yasui's test case and any others like it:

1. cooperation in the war effort;
2. the JACL and its members had pledged total cooperation to the President;
3. cooperation with Federal Authorities will cause reciprocal cooperation;
4. our contribution to the war effort is to accept all army regulations and orders;
5. public opinion is opposed to any challenges of the Army and its authority;
6. we might win the case, but lose goodwill in the process;
7. any challenge might result in retaliation by the Army;

8. Attorney General Biddle said there was little chance the courts would challenge the military's authority;

9. the ACLU decided against a test case and they are the champions of civil liberties;

10. unfavorable publicity as seen in the headlines from the Yasui case.[24]

In any case, these were only isolated individuals, standing on various grounds of conscience against their personal imprisonment. There was no movement among Japanese Americans to resist until after they were all in camp.

Exodus

So it was that, in the end, 112,000 Japanese Americans were taken to concentration camps.[25] The first to be forced to abandon their homes were the fishing families of Terminal Island, next to the Port of Los Angeles. On 14 February the 500 Japanese American families on Terminal Island were notified they had a month to pack up and get out. They began to sell off their belongings and make plans to move in with friends or into temporary accommodations in other parts of southern California. On 25 February, new posters went up warning that they now had only 48 hours to leave. Panic-stricken, the Terminal Islanders sold their homes and belongings for a fraction of their worth or abandoned them altogether. Jeanne Wakatsuki wrote later:

> The secondhand dealers had been prowling around for weeks, like wolves, offering humiliating prices for goods and furniture they knew many of us would have to sell sooner or later. Mama had . . . one fine old set of china, blue and white porcelain, almost translucent. . . .
>
> One of the dealers offered her fifteen dollars for it. She said it was a full setting for twelve and worth at least two hundred. He said fifteen was his top price. Mama started to quiver. . . . She didn't say another word. She just glared at this man, all the rage and frustration channeled at him through her eyes.
>
> He watched her for a moment and said he was sure he couldn't pay more than seventeen fifty for that china. She reached into the red velvet case, took out a dinner plate and hurled it at the floor right in front of his feet.
>
> The man leaped back shouting, "Hey! Hey, don't do that! Those are valuable dishes!"
>
> Mama took out another dinner plate and hurled it at the floor, then another and another, never moving, never opening her mouth, just quivering and glaring at the retreating dealer, with tears streaming down her cheeks. He finally turned and scuttled out the door, heading for the next house. When he was gone she stood there smashing cups and bowls and platters until the whole set lay in scattered blue and white fragments across the wooden floor.[26]

Removal began in earnest on 30 March. The first to go were the Japanese American residents of Bainbridge Island, across Puget Sound from Seattle. They had only a week in which to settle their affairs. Throughout the spring, in one Japanese neighborhood after another, soldiers pasted up signs that read in part:

6.2 This family had to sign away most of their belongings and their farm near San Jose. *Courtesy of Bancroft Library.*

INSTRUCTIONS TO ALL PERSONS OF
JAPANESE ANCESTRY
LIVING IN THE FOLLOWING AREA:

. . . all persons of Japanese ancestry, both alien and non-alien, will be evacuated from the above area by 12 o'clock noon on. . . .

A responsible member of each family, preferably the head of the family, or the person in whose name most of the property is held, and each individual living alone, will report to the Civil Control Station to receive further instructions. This must be done between 8:00 A.M. and 5:00 P.M. on. . . . Evacuees must carry with them on departure for the Assembly Center, the following property:

a. Bedding and linens (no mattress) for each member of the family;
b. Toilet articles for each member of the family;
c. Extra clothing for each member of the family;
d. Sufficient knives, forks, spoons, plates, bowls and cups for each member of the family;

6.3   Child and soldier on moving day. *Courtesy of the National Archives.*

e. Essential personal effects for each member of the family.

All items carried will be securely packaged, tied and plainly marked with the name of the owner and numbered in accordance with instructions obtained at the Civil Control Station. The size and number of packages is limited to that which can be carried by the individual or family group.[27]

Each time posters went up in a new neighborhood, the vultures descended and a distress sale began. Some lucky families had non-Japanese neighbors whom they could trust to take care of their homes and belongings, even businesses, for the duration. But most simply lost everything.

When moving day arrived, Japanese American families gathered with their piles of belongings at government-designated locations. Miné Okubo and her brother arrived at First Congregational Church, the Civil Control Station for Berkeley, California, by 11:00 A.M. on 1 May, carrying duffle bags and wearing tags numbered 13660 tied to their buttons. At eleven-thirty, their number was called, and they were herded onto buses by armed soldiers. Paper covered the windows so they could not see out, nor could their fellow Americans see them being hauled away. An hour later, they debarked at Tanforan Assembly Center, a racetrack south of San Francisco that had been hastily converted for human occupants. They were stripped, searched for weapons, and given a medical examination, then led away to their new home.

The ground was wet from the downpour of the day before. Those who had come on that day were drenched and their baggage was soaked. . . .

6.4   Boarding the train for camp. *Courtesy of the National Archives.*

The guide left us at the door of Stall 50. We walked in and dropped our things inside the entrance. The place was in semidarkness; light barely came through the dirty window on either side of the entrance. A swinging half-door divided the 20 by 9 ft. stall into two rooms. The roof sloped down from a height of twelve feet in the rear room to seven feet in the front room; below the rafters an open space extended the full length of the stable. The rear room had housed the horse and the front room the fodder. Both rooms showed signs of a hurried whitewashing. Spider webs, horse hair, and hay had been white-washed with the walls. Huge spikes and nails stuck out all over the walls. A two-inch layer of dust covered the floor, but on removing it we discovered that linoleum the color of redwood had been placed over the rough manure-covered boards.

We opened the folded spring cots lying on the floor of the rear room and sat on them in the semidarkness. We heard someone crying in the next stall.[28]

The assembly centers were cramped and filthy. There was little privacy: more than one family often shared a single living space, separated only by sheets hung as partitions. Food was starchy and unappetizing but edible if one wanted to wait long enough in line at the mess hall. Medical care was rudimentary. Sanitary facilities were poor. Grace Fujimoto's grandmother had just undergone cancer surgery when the family received its notice to move. Desperately ill and weak, she was nonetheless moved to a hospital in San Mateo. Her family, incarcerated at Tanforan, was forbidden to visit. A week later, the government sent her to join her family in a horse stall amid the filth and cold and lack of sanitation. She died a month later.[29]

No one could go outside the barbed wire except for extreme medical emergencies, and then they went under guard. Friends could visit and sometimes did. Though the inmates' former homes might be only a few blocks or miles away, the guard towers, machine guns, guard dogs, searchlights, and fences reminded them that they were prisoners. The daily regimentation reinforced that awareness. There was a roll call in the mess hall each morning. At night there was a curfew, and the inmates were counted again.

Altogether there were 15 assembly centers, places like the Puyallup Fairgrounds near Seattle and the Santa Anita racetrack in Los Angeles. These were run by the Wartime Civil Control Commission, a branch of the army's Western Defense Command. They were temporary holding places while the government prepared ten permanent concentration camps. The permanent camps were run by a civilian agency, the War Relocation Authority. Eight of the ten WRA camps were located in remote, arid parts of the western states: Tule Lake and Manzanar in California, Poston and Gila River in Arizona, Topaz in Utah, Minidoka in Idaho, Heart Mountain in Wyoming, and Amache in Colorado. Two others, Rohwer and Jerome, were in the swamps of Arkansas. As those camps came open, inmates from the assembly centers were transferred.

The process of incarceration took several weeks to accomplish. By midsummer 1942, everyone was behind barbed wire. Ninety-two thousand of the inmates went first to assembly centers and then on to WRA camps; another 17,500 went directly from their homes to the custody of the WRA (see appendix, table 18). Miné Okubo described the transfer from Tanforan to Topaz in the early fall of 1942:

> The trip was a nightmare that lasted two nights and a day. The train creaked with age. It was covered with dust, and as the gaslights failed to function properly we traveled in complete darkness most of the night, reminding me of the blackout trains in Europe. All shades were drawn and we were not allowed to look out of the windows. . . . The first night was a novelty after four and a half months of internment. However, I could not sleep and I spent the entire night taking the chair apart and readjusting it. Many became train sick and vomited. The children cried from restlessness. At one point on the way, a brick was thrown into one of the cars. The journey was otherwise uneventful. In the daytime we saw only barren desert lands of Nevada and Utah. . . . The meals on the train were good after camp fare.[30]

Okubo and her brother transferred from train to bus at Ogden, Utah. There a small group of local Japanese Americans came out to wish the Bay Area deportees well. Then:

> We rode through seventeen miles of alfalfa fields and greasewood-covered desert. Half of the distance was made over rough, newly constructed dirt roads. We were all eyes, hoping to spot something interesting in the flat, dry land which extended for miles in all directions. Suddenly, the Central Utah Relocation Project was stretched out before us in a cloud of dust. It was a desolate scene. Hundreds of low black barracks covered with tarred paper were lined up row after row. A few

6.5   "Topaz, August 1943," watercolor by Suiko Mikami. *Courtesy of California First Bank.*

telephone poles stood like sentinels, and soldiers could be seen patrolling the grounds.[31]

There the exiles remade their lives yet again.

A word must be said about euphemisms. The Western Defense Command first used the term "evacuation" to describe the forcible and illegal removal of Japanese Americans from their homes. The term was later used by many people both inside and outside Japanese communities for many years. It conveys the impression that this was a rescue operation, that somehow the army was acting to save Japanese Americans and deliver them to higher ground, rather than to punish and imprison them for their race. The other euphemism, "relocation," is equally odious. It implies a moral neutrality—people were merely being moved from one place to another, with no adverse consequences. Hence, what were manifestly prison camps were referred to in WRA and JACL literature as "relocation centers"—such a nice term, and so irresponsible!

There is some controversy over the use of the term "concentration camp." The generation that grew up after World War II associates this term with Nazi death camps, and the U.S. camps for Japanese Americans were not designed for death (although some inmates did die there). Yet the term is technically correct and goes back to the concentration camps run by Britain in South Africa during the Boer War. Recent decades have witnessed similar instances of concentration camps for national minorities in several parts of the world. Another term, equally accurate, is "prison camps." The U.S. camps for Japanese Americans were indubitably prisons, although the inmates were never formally charged or convicted. James Purcell, Mitsuye Endo's lawyer, observed: "I grew up in Folsom prison. My father was a guard there. I know a prison when I see it, and

Tanforan was a prison with watch towers and guns. . . . Guards with machine guns stood at the gates."[32] Donald Hata once threatened to fight me because I used the term "prison camps," objecting that he was no jailbird. I mean no disrespect by using this term, nor by using terms like "inmates" and "prisoners" to describe the residents. Almost anyone can recognize that not everyone in a prison is a bad person or deserves to be there.

Life in Camp

The new prisons were large, empty spaces enclosed by high wire fences. Long rows of tar-paper barracks were broken at intervals by windswept streets—dusty in dry weather, vast pools of mud in the winter rains. Daily functions were performed in central mess halls, showers, and latrines. Outside the blocks of barracks, beyond the fences and guard towers, lay only the desert. Jeanne Wakatsuki Houston remembered Manzanar, in the desolate Owens Valley of eastern California: "Lovely as they were to look at, the Sierras were frightening to think about, an icy barricade. If you took off in the opposite direction and made it past the Inyos, you'd hit Death Valley, while to the south there loomed a range of brown, sculpted hills everyone said were full of rattlesnakes. Camp One was about as far as I cared to venture."[33] The fences were hardly necessary.

The inmates did what they could to make life in camp livable. They added bits of cloth for curtains and tacked up sheets for partitions to give the illusion of privacy. A few had brought radios or packs of cards. They stuffed government-issue sacks with straw to make mattresses, built shelves out of pilfered scraps of lumber, planted seeds when they could get them, and in general tried to make the barracks look like home. As in any prison, boredom and anomie overtook the inmates. Only a few had jobs, and there was little to do in camp but gossip, wait in lines for food or the shower or the toilet, read, or play cards.

One of the first casualties was family life. Before the war, the typical Issei father was a patriarch and the family a well-organized beehive of purposeful activity. Now there was little home life and no privacy. Often a family would be split between two different rooms; sometimes a non-family member was lodged in their midst. The father's strong position as the authority figure was the first to go, largely because he lost his economic function as primary provider. Charles Kikuchi wrote in his diary at Tanforan: "Made me feel sort of sorry for Pop tonight. He has his three electric clippers [he was a barber before the war] hung up on the wall and Tom has built him a barrel chair for the barber seat. It's a bit pathetic when he so tenderly cleans off the clippers after using them; oiling, brushing, and wrapping them up so carefully. He probably realizes that he no longer controls the family group and rarely exerts himself. . . . What a difference from . . . when I was a kid. He used to be a perfect terror and dictator."[34] Mothers did not always lose authority so completely. As Kikuchi wrote:

> The mother still has a role in the family life, because she still has to sew, to do the laundry, and look after the welfare of her children. The only thing she doesn't have to do is cooking! . . . Already Tom and Miyako [younger siblings] are getting much too sassy. It probably is our fault since we have practically taken all responsibilities away from

6.6   There were lines for everything. "Progress after One Year, the Mess Hall Line," water-color by Kango Takamura. *Courtesy of UCLA Department of Special Collections.*

Mom. She is fighting for her position although she does it in a quiet way. Pop bears the brunt of her suppressed feelings. This morning Mom told him to shut up and went out and slammed the door. . . . This evacuation is making a new life for Mom. For 28 years she has been restricted at home in Vallejo, raising children and doing the housework. Her social contacts have been extremely limited, and this has been hard for her because she is more the extrovert type of personality. Now she finds herself here with a lot of Japanese, and it has given her a great deal of pleasure to make all of these new social contacts. Pop on the other hand rarely leaves the house.[35]

Part of the problem was communal meals. Instead of providing each dwelling unit with kitchen facilities, the WRA had the inmates stand in line and eat in huge mess halls. Often fathers ate separately from the family, with their adult male friends. Teenagers congregated. Mothers ate with their younger children but had trouble controlling them amid the crush of people. A mother recalled:

My small daughter and I used to eat at a table where two little boys . . . ate with their mothers. They had become so uncontrollable that the mothers had given up, and let them eat as they pleased. They behaved so badly that I stopped eating there. . . . But my daughter was fascinated. They would come running into the mess hall, and the first thing both of them did was to take off their shoes and stockings and jump up and down on the seat. Then they would start yelling for their food. After they were given their food they wouldn't eat it, but would just play with it. . . . They would often bring toy automobiles and trains, etc., with them, making noises as they pushed the toys in and out of food that was spilled on the table. . . . Now these little boys had older brothers and sisters, and if they had eaten at one table with both parents, things like that couldn't have happened, for the older children would have protested out of pride, and the father probably would have forbidden it.[36]

Family unity and discipline were impossible to maintain under such circumstances.

Part of the problem was that the WRA preferred the Nisei to the Issei. Because they were American citizens, the WRA trusted them more and gave them more responsible jobs in the camps. All the functions involved in running the camps, except guarding the perimeter and making the top-level decisions, were placed in inmate hands. Japanese Americans were the camps' teachers, firefighters, nurses, and cooks. These better-paying jobs may have gone to Nisei more frequently than to Issei, but "better-paying" was a relative term. They paid only a nominal amount comparable to an army private's pay—$12, $16, or $19 per month, depending on the type of job. Some among the Nisei answered the call of WRA recruiters to go outside the camps temporarily and work in the fields. The war had drawn farmworkers away from the crops at the same time it had increased demand. Some Nisei, mostly men, went out in groups for a few weeks at a time in the summer and fall of 1942 to tend and harvest crops such as sugar beets in Utah and Idaho and cotton in Arizona. Work in the fields brought better pay and an element of freedom, but most Japanese Americans found themselves back in camp once the crops were harvested. As the camps became better established, some began agricultural enterprises of their own where inmates found work.

By the fall of 1942, the army had tired of interrogating innocent Issei like Ko Wakatsuki, a Terminal Island fisherman. After nine months in an alien enemy camp in North Dakota, Wakatsuki was sent to join his wife and ten children at Manzanar. A proud man before his arrest, he had become emotionally broken, by turns angry and depressed. To add to his torment, camp gossips whispered that the only reason he had been released was that he was an *inu*—a dog—who had informed on his fellow inmates in Bismarck. Ko Wakatsuki dissolved into a haze of drink and disconnectedness and never recovered.[37] Other Issei victims of the FBI raids were interned at Justice Department camps near Missoula, Montana; Crystal City, Texas; and Lordsburg, New Mexico.

The concentration camps held a few non-Japanese Americans. Elaine Black Yoneda, Estelle Ishigo, Hazel Araki, and Bernice Sugi were all White women who volunteered to go when their Nisei husbands were imprisoned. Ralph Lazo, a Mexican-Irish teenager, went off to camp simply because his Nisei friends were going and he did not want to be away from them.[38]

From very early in the war, the WRA and its JACL friends viewed the camps as an experiment in democracy. Mike Masaoka broached the subject on 6 April 1942, when he wrote Milton Eisenhower, the general's brother and the WRA's first director, with a plan for concentration camps as all-American communities. Masaoka described a vision of Norman Rockwell's America with everything but

6.7   Gerald Osamu and Mary Ann Tsuchi Sakamoto were a Seattle merchant couple before the war. At age 80, they celebrated their golden wedding anniversary behind barbed wire. *Courtesy of Bancroft Library.*

the picket fences: schools, movies, and baseball games; participatory self-government for the Nisei (but not their parents—there was some intergenerational striving here); and productive work and contribution to the war effort.

Eisenhower took the job as WRA head in obedience to his commander-in-chief, but he was pretty embarrassed to be the chief jailer for 112,000 people—two-thirds of them U.S. citizens—who, he well knew, had done nothing wrong. Eisenhower and his successor, Dillon Myer, quickly seized on the idea of demonstrating the ridiculousness of the imprisonment by exhibiting the Japanese American prisoners as paragons of small-town American virtues. In time, they hoped to convince other Americans to allow the Nisei and their parents back into society.

The camps did in fact perform many functions of small towns. They had schools for the children (and for many of the bored adults), with inmate teachers. They had dances and movies on the weekends and ballgames in the afternoons. Other recreational activities included a lot of gambling by Issei men, although it was frowned on by prison authorities. There were regular church services, although in some camps Christianity received preferential treatment over Buddhism, and organized expression of Shinto, the nationalistic Japanese religion, was forbidden. There were inmate fire departments, inmate newspapers—such as the *Heart Mountain Sentinel* and the *Rohwer Outpost*—elections, and town meetings. A riot of romantic activity occurred among the young people (there was not much else to do), and a rash of pregnancies occurred as well. Yoshiko Uchida described a wedding at Tanforan:

> One of the elementary school teachers was the first to be married at Tanforan. She wanted, understandably, to have the kind of wedding she would have had on the outside, and wore a beautiful white marquisette gown with a fingertip veil. For all of us who crowded into the church barrack that day, the wedding was a moment of extraordinary joy and brightness. We showered the couple with rice as they left, and they climbed into a borrowed car decorated with "just married" signs and a string of tin cans. They took several noisy turns around the racetrack in the car and then, after a reception in one of the recreation centers, began their married life in one of the horse stalls.[39]

But this portrait of prison camps as all-American communities can be overdone. Democracy in the WRA camps was a fraud. Although there were elections, at first only Nisei could participate. Even later, when all adults were allowed to take part, the people who were elected did not run their communities. They could make marginal decisions, such as which recreational events to schedule, but all their decisions were subject to WRA veto. And they could do nothing to undo the imprisonment of their people. The only inmates who had any real power were the block managers for each group of housing units, and they were appointed by the WRA.

The all-American image *was* overdone, purposely, by the WRA and many inmates. Eager to convince other Americans that Japanese Americans were benign, photographers such as Dorothea Lange and Ansel Adams recorded beauty, poignancy, and assimilationist striving in the inmates they photographed—but not much dirt, pain, or despair, and no anger at all. The same can be said of the anthropologists the WRA hired to study their charges. People

6.8   Not everything was dreary. Two small boys chat by the fence. *Courtesy of the Japanese American National Museum.*

like Edward Spicer and Katherine Luomala painted an academic picture of the camps that made the Japanese look like good Americans (which they were), but that also resolutely avoided the moral and legal implications of jailing an entire people on account of their race.[40] Nongovernmental researchers who invaded the camps, like Dorothy Thomas of the University of California and her squad of Nisei graduate student research assistants, did a little better: at least one of the books they wrote was about Japanese Americans who resisted their imprisonment.[41] But all the scholars who lined up to study this event were driven in greater or lesser degree by the same social engineering spirit that animated John McCloy, a War Department bureaucrat and one of the architects of the imprisonment:

> We would be missing a very big opportunity if we failed to study the Japanese in these camps at some length before they are dispersed. We have not done a very good job thus far in solving the Japanese problem in this country. I believe we have a great opportunity to give the thing intelligent thought now and to reach solid conclusions for the future. . . . We could find out what they are thinking about and we might very well influence their thinking in the right direction before they are again distributed into their communities.[42]

The Japanese Americans were a problem to be solved and a people to be molded, and the social scientists would do the solving and molding.

Protest and Accommodation

One thing neither the social scientists nor the WRA bureaucrats could solve was inmate resistance. Contrary to the image that the WRA and the JACL tried to project, camp life generated a lot of conflict. It began even in the assembly centers, where for the first time since the war began Japanese Americans could come together to protest their imprisonment. In the Santa Anita Assembly Center, a rumor spread that inmate policemen were seizing personal property for their own use. A couple of thousand inmates gathered to protest. Harry Kitano describes the scene: "[T]here were cries of '*Ko-ro-se!*' ('Kill them!') and '*Inu!*' ('Dog!'). A crowd of around 2,000 Japanese, including large numbers of teen-agers, ran aimlessly and wildly about, rumors flew, property was destroyed, and finally an accused policeman was set upon during the routine inspection and badly beaten. The incident was controlled through the intervention of 200 Army MPs, installation of martial law, and stricter security." A Santa Anita resident described the empowering effect of resistance on the inmates: "[T]he 'rioting' . . . seems to have raised their spirits in anticipation of brighter prospects to come. The residents now feel that they shouldn't allow themselves to be imposed upon too much, that occasionally they should assert their rights and not to lie supinely on their backs when injustice is being done."[43]

In November 1942, a strike rocked the Poston camp in Arizona. The camp was rife with suspicion that some inmates were acting as informers to the WRA and the FBI. On Saturday night, 14 November, someone beat up a 30-year-old Kibei man with a piece of pipe. Fifty inmates were arrested and questioned. Two, both Kibei in their twenties, were held in the camp jail pending the arrival of the FBI. Family and friends of the two men gathered support among the inmates and, on the 17th and 18th, sent delegations to protest their innocence and demand their release. When there was little response, a crowd of 2,500—half the camp's population—gathered in front of the jail at noon on the 18th. The elected Community Council passed a resolution demanding that the men be unconditionally released. The camp's administration rejected the resolution, whereupon the Community Council, the Issei Advisory Council, and the block managers all resigned.

By the next day, the entire camp was on strike except for such essential services as the hospital and fire department. Japanese music played loudly in the compound, and people whispered hatefully about *inu*. White camp administrators were split over whether to negotiate or call in troops to crush the rebellion. Meanwhile, the inmates' demands expanded to include meaningful self-government within the camp. By the 23rd, the camp administration decided to negotiate. They released one of the prisoners and arranged to have the other tried in camp by an inmate court. They gave recognition to the Emergency Executive Council that had been formed during the strike as the legitimate representative of the people. The strike leaders became the leaders of Poston. The compromise resulted in a working relationship that kept peace in the camp for the duration.

Only a few days later, on 5 December, Manzanar erupted. That night six men beat up Fred Tayama, a southern California JACL leader and reputed WRA stooge. It was never established that Tayama could identify any of his assailants, but three men were arrested and one, Harry Ueno, was taken out of camp and put in the county jail ten miles away. It was widely suspected that Ueno had been arrested because he was the aggressive leader of the Kitchen Workers Union, a mainly Kibei and Issei group that disliked the JACL and the WRA. He had recently accused the assistant camp director of stealing sugar and meat intended for inmates.

The next morning an emotional mass meeting drew up a blacklist of suspected inu and appointed a committee of five, headed by the World War I veteran Joe Kurihara, to present the administration with a demand for Ueno's return. They and 1,000 followers presented the demand, and Ralph Merritt, the camp director, complied, on the condition that there be no more protest meetings. Such a meeting took place anyway that night; in Michi Weglyn's words, it was "a mammoth rally of the more extremist element, whose long-pent-up thirst for revenge against fellow informers could no longer be contained, all of it exploding into a cry for immediate retribution and the rescue of Ueno from the center jail." The administration hid the injured Tayama and quickly removed from the camp all the JACL leaders and others thought at risk of attack. "[T]roops armed with submachine guns and rifles swarmed into the compound and surrounded the project jail. Riled by their failure to find their intended blacklisted victims, the angry crowd surged in a frenzy toward the camp jail, running head-on into the barricade of waiting troops."[44] The troops fired tear gas, the crowd surged, the troops opened fire. One inmate died instantly, another in the hospital afterward. Eight more were treated for gunshot wounds.

Kurihara and the inmate representatives were arrested. The inmates elected a new committee of six leaders, and they too were arrested. The camp was under martial law, ruled by soldiers, for two weeks. The soldiers were cleared of any wrongdoing. The alleged inu were given passes to stay outside the camp and not return. Ueno, Kurihara, and 14 others were taken under armed guard to a high-security camp near Moab, Utah. There they were joined by inmates from other camps who had engaged in work stoppages, spoken out against the WRA, or expressed bitterness at their incarceration. Not much is known about this isolation center except that it was hard, lonely prison time compared to the relative comfort of the WRA camps. There were no charges, no trials, no convictions. But there were fixed bayonets at the dinner table, in the shower, and in the toilet, and the military police had orders to shoot to kill. In April 1943, the Moab inmates were transferred to another, more stoutly built isolation center on the Navajo reservation near Leupp, Arizona. Many of them, including Joe Kurihara, ended up renouncing their American citizenship (or having it renounced for them) and going to Japan at the end of the war.

Two themes emerge from the conflicts in the WRA camps. One was that resentment for all the wrong that had been done to Japanese Americans coalesced and found a target in JACL members and other inmates who collaborated with the government. As the FBI investigator Myron Gurnea reported to WRA Director Dillon Myer: "One of the greatest causes for internal disorder has perhaps been the Japanese-American Citizens League. The members of the Japanese-American Citizens League have been very outspoken in proclaiming their loyalty to the United States. . . . It is the consensus of opinion among the Japanese that the Japanese-American Citizens League in collaboration with the United States Government, 'sold them out' and did not put up a fight to block relocation."[45] The other theme was the emergence of new leaders—Issei, Kibei, and less radically patriotic Nisei—to supplant the JACL as its brief moment of community leadership passed.

Dividing the Sheep from the Goats

The next big confrontation came over the question of loyalty to the United States. Had the U.S. government asked the Nisei prior to their imprisonment if they were loyal Americans who would willingly bear arms, the overwhelming response would have been "Yes!" Had the government asked if the Issei would refrain from acts against the United States, their answer would have been the same. But the hysteria of the winter of 1942 made that impossible; public opinion demanded that the Japanese Americans go to prison. A year later, however, Japanese Americans had passed from the consciousness of most other Americans. Dillon Myer, embarrassed to be the jailer of innocent American citizens and aliens being held without charge, much less conviction, began looking for a way to demonstrate to the American public that the Japanese Americans were good people who should be allowed back into society. At the same time, the JACL, eager to demonstrate its loyalty, wanted to get Nisei into the army. Finally, some camp administrators wanted to weed out people they regarded as troublemakers for harsher incarceration under tighter security. The result was the registration crisis of February 1943.

The WRA gave a questionnaire, the "Application for Leave Clearance," to all residents over the age of 18. If the respondent answered correctly, he or she became eligible to leave the prison camp and reenter society or to be drafted into the army; returning to the West Coast, however, was not an option. The questionnaires were poorly worded and clumsily administered. The parts that caused the most problems were questions 27 and 28:

> Question 27: Are you willing to serve in the armed forces of the United States on combat duty, wherever ordered? [This question was administered to male citizens only. Female citizens and male and female aliens were asked: "If the opportunity presents itself and you are found qualified, would you be willing to volunteer for the Army Nurse Corps or the WAAC?"]
>
> Question 28: Will you swear unqualified allegiance to the United States of America and faithfully defend the United States from any or all attack by foreign or domestic forces, and forswear any form of allegiance or obedience to the Japanese emperor, or any other foreign government, power, or organization? [The question for female citizens and male and female aliens omitted the "and faithfully defend . . ." clause].[46]

The WRA seems to have had no idea what a problem these questions posed for many inmates. Aside from the silliness of asking Issei men to enlist in the Women's Army Corps, the questions posed a dilemma for all Issei. If they answered no to question 28, they would be considered disloyal in the country where they had lived the majority of their adult lives as completely loyal and law-abiding members of society. But if they answered yes, they would have to forswear allegiance to Japan and, having been denied American citizenship because of their race, would thus become stateless. For the Nisei, American citizens most of whom had never even visited Japan, the implication that they had loyalties to a foreign power was added to the affront of being thrown into concentration camps. As a result, many answered no to question 28 out of bitterness.

The matter was complicated by the announcement that those declared disloyal on the basis of question 28 would be segregated from the rest of the inmates into camps of their own. In order to stay with their families, many declared themselves disloyal who would otherwise have answered the question in the affirmative. In addition, many felt that, no matter how one answered question 27, one would be drafted unless one declared oneself disloyal on question 28. So many did. One Manzanar man, at the time he decided to answer no to both questions, stood before a WRA interrogator, lips quivering, almost unable to speak. Informed that he was giving away his U.S. citizenship (which was not true), he nonetheless stuck by his decision:

> I thought that since there is a war on between Japan and America, since the people of this country have to be geared up to fight against Japan, they are taught to hate us. So they don't accept us. First I wanted to help this country, but they evacuated us instead of giving us a chance. Then I wanted to be neutral, but now that you force a decision, I have to say this. We have a Japanese face. Even if I try to be American I won't be entirely accepted. . . .
>
> I don't know Japan. I'm not interested in Japan. That's another thing that worries me. I don't know what will become of me and people like me if we have to go to Japan. The only thing that might save us is that most of us have our old parents still alive. If we were third generation and were entirely cut off from Japan we might not be able to make it. But if they are still alive we can go with our old parents. In Japan they respect the old people and, therefore, for their sake they may treat us well. There isn't much for us in Japan but at least there is something. . . .
>
> My dad is 58 years old now. He has been here 30 years at least. He came to this country with nothing but a bed roll. He worked on the railroads and he worked in the sugar beet fields. If I told you the hardships he had you wouldn't believe me. I owe a lot to my father. Everything I am I owe to him. All through his life he was working for me. During these last years he was happy because he thought he was coming to the place where his son would have a good life. I am the only son. I have to carry on the family name. . . .
>
> In order to go out prepared and willing to die, expecting to die, you have to believe in what you are fighting for. If I am going to end the family line, if my father is going to lose his only son, it should be for some cause we respect. I believe in democracy as I was taught in school. I would have been willing to go out forever before evacuation. It's not that I'm a coward or afraid to die. My father would have been willing to see me go out at one time. But my father can't feel the same after this evacuation and I can't either.[47]

For whatever reasons, about 12,000 inmates declared themselves "disloyal" to the United States. In September and October 1943, they were sent to the Tule Lake WRA camp in the wastes of northern California. They were predominately conservative people—Issei and Kibei, Buddhists, people from rural districts. City people, Nisei, and Christians mainly went to the other nine camps.[48] Thereafter, conflict declined in the other camps. It was not that the remaining inmates no longer had complaints against their captors, nor even that they were in fact more "loyal" to the United States. But they had begun to focus on new possibilities.

Accommodation

After the "no-noes" had been sent off to an uncertain future at Tule Lake (and the "yes-yeses" from Tule Lake had been distributed to other camps), the non-Tule Lake inmates were encouraged to either volunteer for the draft or resettle out of the camps. In fact, the first resettlers took off earlier than that. They were Nisei college students whose educations had been interrupted. Through the intervention of a number of West Coast university presidents, as early as September 1942 students began to venture eastward to complete their education. The West Coast was still closed to them, but they were allowed to go out of the camps to colleges and universities in the plains states, the Midwest, and the East.

The screening process for those first student resettlers was more cumbersome than the simple questionnaire that was used the following year. At first only a few left camp—not more than 250 by the end of 1942.[49] But the trickle turned to a stream, and then a flood by the fall semester of 1943. The WRA set up offices in several eastern and midwestern cities to facilitate the flow, including help with housing. The resettlers received more help from private individuals and church groups such as the American Friends Service Committee. They went by ones and twos to schools all over the map, from Wellesley, Smith, and Mount Holyoke Colleges in Massachusetts to the Universities of Nebraska, Utah, and Minnesota, to Grinnell College in Iowa, Earlham in Indiana, and Fisk in Tennessee. The WRA's strategy was to spread the Japanese Americans as widely as possible to avoid concentrations that might provoke White attack. The number of resettling students eventually totaled 4,300.[50]

The majority of other resettlers went not to school but into jobs. Some inmates had gone out temporarily to work on farms in the intermountain West, but those people had to return to camp after a specified time. After the leave clearance questionnaire settled the loyalty issue in the minds of the WRA bureaucrats, those who had declared their loyalty could go out to work permanently. Florence Sakada and her parents ran a restaurant in Denver. Rita Sano did domestic work in the same city. Several Nisei resumed prewar careers as chick sexers in Mankato, Minnesota. Hundreds worked under frankly exploitative conditions for Seabrook Farms, a New Jersey food company. Most resettlers held industrial or clerical jobs.[51]

Altogether, 35,989 Japanese American inmates left the concentration camps for points east before the end of 1944. The vast bulk of the resettlers—over 80 percent—were Nisei. Sixty percent were men.[52] Many of the Nisei were ambivalent about leaving their parents behind in camp. Kathy Ishikawa's hesitations kept her in Heart Mountain: "It's getting so more and more of the girls and boys are leaving camp, and I sure wish I could but mother's getting on and I just can't leave her."[53] Some Nisei like Ishikawa stayed in camp. Others went out with the intention of sending for their families later.

6.9   These Nisei left the camps to find jobs as stenographers in Washington, D.C. *Courtesy of Bancroft Library.*

They were tentative as they reentered the larger society and conscious that they had to put their best foot forward as representatives of their people. Monica Sone recalled: "In the beginning I worried a great deal about people's reactions to me. Before I left Camp Minidoka, I had been warned over and over again that once I was outside, I must behave as inconspicuously as possible so as not to offend the sensitive public eye. I made up my mind to make myself scarce and invisible."[54] Yoshiko Uchida voiced similar sentiments: "I left Topaz determined to work hard and prove I was as loyal as any other American. I felt a tremendous sense of responsibility to make good, not just for myself, but for all Japanese Americans. I felt I was representing all the Nisei, and it was sometimes an awesome burden to bear."[55] Miné Okubo spoke to the ambivalence as she recalled:

> The day of my departure arrived. I dashed to the block manager's office to turn in the blankets and other articles loaned to me, and went to the Administration Office to secure signatures on the various forms given me the day before. I received a train ticket and $25, plus $3 a day for meals while traveling. . . . I was now *free*. I looked at the crowd at the gate. Only the very old or very young were left. Here I was, alone, with no family responsibilities, and yet fear had chained me to the camp. I though, "My God! How do they expect those poor people to leave the one place they can call home." I swallowed a lump in my throat as I waved good-bye to them.[56]

The reception they met with was not always warm. In Cleveland and Minneapolis, White residents complained to the WRA about the resettling Japanese Americans. There was some staring, and some unkind words on the street, but the harassment was not as bad as it had been on the West Coast in the first months of the war. Most of the resettlers had a fairly positive experience.

Another 2,355 Nisei left camp to join the army.[57] Others enlisted after they left camp. They represented just a small fraction of the total Nisei enlistment. Nearly 20,000 Japanese Americans served in the U.S. Army in World War II; the majority of them came from Hawai'i. Hawaiian Japanese were less embittered than mainland Nisei; their families were not behind barbed wire. There were Nisei in uniform at the time the war began, but most were mustered out in the weeks that followed. Among the few exceptions were the 58 Nisei soldiers who were then in training at San Francisco's Presidio to serve in the Military Intelligence Service (MIS). Their number grew to 6,000 as the war progressed, and they served with distinction in every part of the Pacific. They worked as intelligence specialists not only with U.S. troops but with British, Canadian, Australian, Indian, Chinese, and New Zealand forces. They intercepted and translated Japanese communiqués, interrogated prisoners, and crept behind Japanese lines to perform deeds of heroism.

In addition to the MIS soldiers, there were the Nisei of the segregated 100th Infantry Battalion, a Hawaiian unit made up of Japanese American reservists, and its successor, the 442nd Regimental Combat Team, which included mainlanders as well. There were never as many mainland volunteers as the WRA and the JACL hoped for, but their numbers were considerable: 3,600 in all, split between the MIS and the 442nd. The Nisei soldiers volunteered from several motives, but all would have recognized Karl Yoneda's reasoning: "Enlisting was the best way to guarantee and protect our future."[58]

After training at Camp Shelby, Mississippi, the 100th/442nd shipped off to fight in the Allied invasion of Italy. Later the Nisei soldiers fought in France and Germany. Their motto, "Go for Broke," was reflected in their achievements. They compiled a record of heroism unparalleled in the history of American warfare: 15,513 medals and 9,486 enemy casualties for a unit of 3,000 men.[59] In so doing, they earned a place in history and, they hoped, a measure of legitimacy for their people. In the Vosges Forest in France, they were sent on what was thought to be a suicide mission, rescuing what became known as the Lost Battalion and earning honorary Texas citizenship for their heroism. In Germany, they liberated the prisoners in a Nazi concentration camp. One among the many heroes in the 100th and 442nd, Daniel Inouye, lost an arm on Mount Nebbione in Italy, won a Distinguished Service Cross and Bronze Star for heroism, and later served more than three decades in the U.S. Senate.[60]

Resistance Again

Of course, only a small number of the Nisei men volunteered for the draft. There were many individuals in the camps who declined to serve. Quite a number of the Nisei who registered their American patriotism by answering "yes-yes" nonetheless refused to be drafted while they and their families were still in concentration camps. The strongest draft resistance movement took place at Heart Mountain. There, Kiyoshi Okamoto, Frank Emi, and other con-

6.10   Nisei soldiers in France. *Courtesy of the Japanese American National Museum.*

stitutionally minded Nisei formed the Fair Play Committee in late 1943. They said:

> We . . . are not afraid to go to war. We are not afraid to risk our lives for our country. We would gladly sacrifice our lives to protect and uphold the principles and ideals of our country as set forth in the Constitution and Bill of Rights . . . freedom, liberty, justice and protection of all peoples, including Japanese Americans and all other minority groups.
>
> But have we been given such freedom, such liberty, such justice, such protection? No. Without any hearing, without due process of law . . . without any charges filed against us, without any evidence of wrongdoing on our part, 110,000 innocent people were kicked out of their homes . . . and herded like dangerous criminals into concentration camps. . . .
>
> Then, without rectification of this injustice committed against us, without restoration of our rights . . . we are ordered to join the Army through discriminatory procedures into a segregated combat unit. Is that the American way? No. . . .
>
> Therefore, we members of the Fair Play Committee hereby refuse to go to the physical examination or to the induction . . . in order to contest the issue.[61]

6.11   Draft resisters being counted in prison. *Photo by Carl Mydans,* Life *magazine,* © *Time Inc.*

The JACL sent Min Yasui (who had earlier protested his people's imprisonment by violating the curfew) and Joe Grant Masaoka (Mike's brother) to try to talk the men out of their position. When they failed, the JACL attacked the Fair Play Committee as un-American—a position supported by the American Civil Liberties Union, among others.

At a June 1944 trial, 85 Heart Mountain inmates were convicted of draft evasion and sentenced to federal prison. Their convictions were later upheld, and they each served about two years. Seven top leaders of the Fair Play Committee were indicted for conspiracy, along with Jimmie Omura, a Nisei journalist from Denver who had not been imprisoned, because he lived outside the exclusion zone, but who publicized the draft resisters' statements in his newspaper. Omura was acquitted on First Amendment grounds, but the others were convicted. They had served 18 months before an appeals court reversed their conviction. In 1947 President Harry Truman pardoned all the Heart Mountain draft resisters, along with 230 resisters from other camps. The entire incident so divided Japanese Americans that it was buried, unmentioned in Japanese communities for 40 years, and still caused intense conflict between community groups as late as the 1990s.

The other group of inmates who chose resistance rather than accommodation were the 12,000 "disloyals" who were segregated at Tule Lake.[62] There they joined about 6,000 "Old Tuleans," people who had declared their loyalty but who for one reason or another did not want to leave the camp. Political life at Tule Lake was intense from the fall of 1943 to the end of the war. There were strikes, threats, and violence right from the start. Inmates protested their imprisonment, the food, working conditions, the fact that expressions of Japanese culture were forbidden, the presence of people who were not patriotic Japanese, and other oppressions. The WRA had martial law declared, and the camp was taken over by federal troops for two months beginning in November 1943. Leaders of a dissident group, Daihyo Sha Kai, were picked up in the middle of the night, beaten, and put in solitary confinement. There they started a hunger strike. Their demands became more extreme, and the camp was split down the middle. On one side was an increasingly militant pro-Japanese group; on the other side were the majority of camp residents who, though they may have answered "no-no," did not have the political enthusiasm for extreme measures. The Daihyo Sha Kai became more extreme over the following year, to the point of demanding that they be separated from the other Tule Lake inmates and immediately sent to Japan. In the end, many of them were granted that wish.

In the early phase of resistance we noted two themes: the coalescing of resentments against the inu, and the rise of alternative leaders. In Tule Lake, a third theme emerged: cultural resistance. Some such resistance was religious, an expression of Buddhist and Shinto imperatives as opposed to the Christian principles that tended to operate in other camps.[63] Some of it proceeded on more generally cultural lines and was mediated through institutions such as the Sokoku Kenkyu Seinen-dan (Young Men's Association for the Study of the Mother Country). Sokoku sought to make good Japanese out of the Nisei in Tule Lake on the theory that they were going to the land of their ancestors pretty soon and their American ways were going to have to be expunged. Taeko Okamura described what it was like to be a child in Tule Lake at this time:

> My sister and I were enrolled in a Japanese school in preparation for our eventual expatriation to Japan. Our teachers were generally pro-Japan and taught us not only how to read and write in Japanese but also to be proud as Japanese. Their goals were to teach us to be good Japanese so that we would not be embarrassed when we got to Japan.
>
> We were often asked to wear red or white headbands and do marching exercises. We were awakened early, hurriedly got dressed and gathered at one end of the block where a leader led us in traditional Japanese calisthenics. As the sun rose, we bowed our heads to the east. This was to show our respect to the Emperor. . . .
>
> The double barbed wire fence was just beyond the next barrack from our compartment. A guard tower with uniformed men and weapons were in view at all times. Search lights were beamed onto the camp grounds at night. Uniformed men with weapons driving around in jeeps was a common sight. As a result of this experience, I used to be afraid of any white adult male for a very long time.
>
> Demonstrations in protest of one thing or other were frequent. We very often locked ourselves in our room to avoid participating in these demonstrations. Physical violence and verbal abuses were common at these demonstrations where feelings ran high. And whenever a large demonstration took place, we could always expect the camp authorities to send soldiers to search our rooms for contraband. These searches were very thorough and everything was ransacked.[64]

Tule Lake politics led inexorably to the renunciation of American citizenship by those who had it and their expatriation (repatriation for their parents) to

6.12   Some Japanese Americans renounced their U.S. citizenship after World War II. These renunciants are boarding a ship bound for Japan.

Japan. In 1944 the inmates formed the Sokuji Kikoku Hoshi-dan (Organization to Return Immediately to the Homeland to Serve). About 2,000 Japanese nationals had been repatriated to Japan earlier in the war in a prisoner exchange aboard the neutral Swedish liner *Gripsholm*. Most were diplomats and Issei from the INS camps, although a few came from the WRA concentration camps. At the height of the tension in Tule Lake, 5,766 Nisei formally renounced their U.S. citizenship and requested expatriation. They were joined by about 15,000 Issei. But as the war wound down, Tule Lake politics lost steam, and some people began to rethink their earlier decision. Through heroic efforts by the San Francisco civil rights lawyer Wayne Collins, most of these were able to rescind their renunciation and remain in the United States. In the end, 4,724 Japanese Americans left the WRA camps and went to Japan: 1,659 Issei, 1,949 Nisei who were minors and presumably accompanied their parents, and 1,116 adult Nisei.[65]

Perhaps the most prominent Nisei renunciant was Joe Kurihara, the Manzanar inmate leader. Kurihara was born in Hawai'i in 1895, had never visited Japan, and did not speak much Japanese. He moved to California in 1915, harvested crops, went to school, and enlisted in the army in World War I. After service in Germany, he returned to California and finished an accounting course in college. Then he worked in a number of businesses in southern California. When Pearl Harbor was attacked, he was a navigator on a San Diego tuna boat. He tried to reenlist, but at 46 he was too old for the army. Intensely patriotic, he assumed the U.S. government would not intern loyal Japanese Americans, certainly not those who had proved their patriotism by fighting in World War I. His incarceration and his experiences at Manzanar, Moab, and Leupp left him deeply embittered. After two years at Tule Lake, he renounced his U.S. citizenship and sailed to Japan in February 1946. On that occasion he wrote: "It is my sincere desire to get over there as soon as possible to help rebuild Japan politically and economically. The American Democracy with which I was infused in my childhood is still unshaken. My life is dedicated to Japan with Democracy as my goal."[66]

An End—And a Beginning?

As late as January 1945, there were still nearly 75,000 Japanese Americans in WRA custody. Where were they to go? The Supreme Court's decision in the Endo case in December 1944 reopened the West Coast to Japanese Americans, and about two-thirds of the remaining inmates went there. That was a smaller percentage than the nearly 90 percent who had lived in California, Washington, and Oregon before the war, but it was still a substantially higher concentration than the WRA wanted. The WRA had in mind spreading the Japanese Americans thinly over the landscape so that they would not attract harassment from other Americans. Their hopes were not realized, as most Japanese Americans, quite reasonably, hoped to return to whatever was left of their homes.

They trickled back at first. By April 1945, no more than 1,300 had returned to California. Part of the problem was fear of their former neighbors. In the first six months of 1945, there were more than 40 incidents of violence or intimidation against returning Japanese Americans up and down the West Coast. Assailants shot into Japanese American homes. Fires were started. In Hood River, Oregon, the American Legion post painted over the names of Nisei soldiers on their roll of honor, including those who had been decorated and given their lives in Europe and the Pacific. In Brawley, a town in the heart of California's Imperial Valley—which before the war had been prime Japanese American farming country—3,500 people attended an anti-Japanese rally on a high school athletic field.[67] On his return from Europe, Dan Inouye went into a barbershop in his army uniform, his right sleeve dangling empty for want of the arm he had lost in Italy.

> I had been discharged from Percy Jones General Hospital in Battle Creek and was on my way home for good. Naturally I wanted to look my spruced-up best and a day or so before the troopship left, I went to this barbershop in one of the towns ringing San Francisco—and got as far as the door.
> "Are you Chinese?" the man said to me.
> I looked past him at the three empty chairs, the other two barbers watching us closely. "I'm an American," I said.
> "Are you Chinese?"
> "I think what you want to know is where my father was born. My father was born in Japan. I'm an American." Deep in my gut I knew what was coming.
> "Don't give me that American stuff," he said swiftly. "You're a Jap and we don't cut Jap hair."

AMERICAN
FARMER

JAPS OR HINDUS NOT
WANTED
Anti-Alien Ass'n

6.13   Many West Coast whites made it clear they did not want their Japanese American neighbors back. *Courtesy of the National Archives.*

I wanted to hit him. I could see myself—it was as though I were standing in front of a mirror. There I stood, in full uniform, the new captain's bars bright on my shoulders, four rows of ribbons on my chest, the combat infantry badge, the distinguished unit citations—and a hook where my hand was supposed to be. And he didn't cut Jap hair. To think that I had gone through a war to save his skin—and he didn't cut Jap hair.

I said, "I'm sorry. I'm sorry for you and the likes of you." And I went back to my ship.[68]

Fearing reactions such as these, as late as August 1945, 44,000 people still had not left the WRA camps.

The end of the war came as an anticlimax to most Nisei, since it had been apparent for some time that the United States was going to win. They had almost all favored the American side—even the draft resisters. But at the same time, they recognized an affinity for Japan and knew their parents had relatives there. They heard of great devastation in the land of their ancestors, and they feared for their own futures. Most Issei shared the ambivalence. Shoichi Fukuda felt intense pain at Japan's loss even though he had chosen to remain in America, had left the concentration camp, and was back in California long before V-J Day: "I felt that Japan would never be conquered. The next day factories were blowing their sirens and cars were honking their horns. They said, 'Japan is conquered! Japan is conquered!' I was very shocked and felt *nasakenai* [it is a shameful situation]. I just did not want to talk to anyone, but I could not take a day off. Tears were rolling down my face. I did not want to see anybody at work, and I did not want to talk to my wife either. I walked to the warehouse and worked silently."[69] He did not want to live in Japan—he was committed to America—but he hurt for the land of his birth.

Ko Wakatsuki was one who decided to keep his family in Manzanar as long as he could. His daughter recalled:

> Then the word went out that the entire camp would close without fail by December 1. Those who did not choose to leave voluntarily would be scheduled for resettlement in weekly quotas. Once you were sched-uled, you could choose a place—a state, a city, a town—and the gov-ernment would pay your way there. If you didn't choose, they'd send you back to the community you lived in before you were evacuated.
>
> Papa gave himself up to the schedule. The government had put him here, he reasoned, the government could arrange his departure. What could he lose by waiting? Outside he had no job to go back to. A California law passed in 1943 made it illegal now for Issei to hold com-mercial fishing licenses. And his boats and nets were gone, he knew—confiscated or stolen. Here in camp he had shelter. The women and children still with him had enough to eat. He decided to sit it out as long as he could. . . .
>
> Every day busloads left from the main gate, heading south with their quotas, filled with Mamas and Papas and Grannies who had postponed movement as long as possible, and soldiers' wives like Chizu, and children like Kiyo and May and me, too young yet to be out on our own. Some of the older folks resisted leaving right up to the end and had to have their bags packed for them and be physically lifted and shoved onto the buses. When our day finally arrived, in early October, there were maybe 2,000 people still living out there, waiting their turn and hoping it wouldn't come.[70]

All the camps except Tule Lake were closed by December 1945. Tule Lake pushed out its last inmate in March 1946. Their war over at last, Japanese Americans were left to rebuild their lives with worn-out tools.

Counting the Cost

The true cost of the incarceration of the Japanese American people—in dol-lars, in lives wasted—cannot be calculated, but one can point toward some of the elements in such an accounting. First would be the workers lost to the American war effort: roughly 75,000 Japanese American adults times an aver-age of three years behind barbed wire equals 225,000 person-years wasted. America could ill afford such a waste of workers in wartime.

The inmates' economic losses are possible to assess roughly. The best esti-mate of the U.S. Commission on the Wartime Relocation and Internment of Civilians was that the prisoners had suffered about $370 million in direct prop-erty losses, which the commission converted to between $1 billion and $3 billion in 1983 dollars.[71] That figure did not include lost income or opportunities—only property that was stolen, destroyed, confiscated, or sold under duress at less than fair value.

There were substantial costs to Americans' constitutional liberties as well. Not until the 1980s were the Hirabayashi and Korematsu cases overturned. For 40 years, law students learned in their constitutional law classes that in wartime, as these cases demonstrated, the guarantees of due process in the Constitution amount only to paper promises. If the government can claim military necessity, the government can do anything it wants. Several times in those decades government figures such as the FBI's J. Edgar Hoover contemplated another concentration camp episode—for Chinese Americans during the Korean War, for African American militants in the 1960s.

Japanese American families and communities lost the most. The decline of parental authority and family cohesion engendered by camp life was never quite made up in the years after the war. The episode dispersed the Japanese American population over the entire country. People came back only slowly to the cities and rural enclaves of the three West Coast states, and never in the numbers of the prewar years. Seattle was particularly hard hit; one of the foremost centers of Japanese American population before the war, it never regained that status. Within the communities, the institutions of Issei authority had been destroyed but not replaced. The JACL stepped forward briefly in the war's early months, but it was soon discredited. It took nearly a generation for Japanese American communities to build strong community institutions again.

And then there were the psychological costs. Several researchers have begun to assess this dimension in recent years. Why is it that the Nisei typically said little or nothing about their concentration camp experiences to their Sansei children? Jeanne Wakatsuki Houston wrote:

> As I came to understand what Manzanar had meant, it gradually filled me with shame for being a person guilty of something enormous enough to deserve that kind of treatment. In order to please my accusers, I tried . . . to become someone acceptable. . . . [A]s I sought for ways to live agreeably in Anglo-American society, my memories of Manzanar, for many years, lived far below the surface. . . . I half-suspected that the place did not exist. So few people I met in those years had even heard of it, and those who had knew so little about it, sometimes I imagined I had made the whole thing up, dreamed it. Even among my brothers and sisters, we seldom discussed the internment. If we spoke of it at all, we joked. . . . It stayed alive in our separate memories, but it was too painful to call out into the open.[72]

Some observers have seen a desperate striving for acceptance, a hyper-assimilationist impulse, in the Nisei generation, based on their sense of rejection by White America during the war.[73] Amy Iwasaki Mass believes that the camp experience deeply and negatively affected the self-esteem of the Nisei generation:

> To admit that we were hated, as if we were the enemy, by the America we tried so hard to be a part of, was so painfully unacceptable to us, we denied the harsh facts even as we were going through the actual experience of evacuation and rejection.

6.14   Charles Iwasaki brought his family back to their farm near Reedley, California, in the spring of 1945. Levi Multanen fired several shotgun blasts into their house. Mrs. Iwasaki is pictured here with her daughter Amy and a neighbor, Annie Torosian. *Courtesy of Bancroft Library.*

It was obvious we were interned because of our race. Being from a country that was a wartime enemy was not the only reason. . . . [T]here was the unspoken assumption that there was something wrong with us because we were Japanese. Along with this was the hope that if we were more like white Americans, less obviously Japanese in our habits, manners, and customs, we would be more acceptable to other Americans. We tried to be quiet and hardworking, drawing as little attention to our being Japanese as possible. We tried to prove we were 110% patriotic Americans. . . .

The problem is that acceptance by accommodation exacts a high price. It is at the expense of the individual's sense of true self-worth. What is sacrificed is the individual's own self-acceptance. It places an exaggerated emphasis on surface qualities like a pleasant non-offensive manner, neat grooming and appearance, nice homes, new cars, well-behaved children. Though we may be seen by others as model Americans, we have paid a tremendous price for this acceptance. . . . It has left a permanent scar.[74]

Donna Nagata's research suggests that the concentration camps' effects have been passed on to the Sansei generation as well.[75]

Japanese American Ethnicity in the Early Second Generation

The early years of the second generation, 1930 to 1945, were characterized by generational and cultural conflict between the Issei and Nisei.[76] This was a time when institutions remained strong. The Japanese associations and the Issei economic and religious organizations maintained complete control of their communities during the Depression. When those organizations were attacked by U.S. government authorities at the start of World War II (their leaders were carried off to prison camps several months in advance of the rest of the Japanese American population), another organization, the Japanese American Citizens League, leaped in to take their place.

Common interests were also strong. The first challenge was to survive the Depression at a time when no Japanese could expect much help from White America. In many ways, the economic solidarity of Japanese Americans was enhanced by the fact that even college-educated Nisei could not get jobs outside the Japanese community in the 1930s. The second task was to pull together to survive imprisonment and group character assassination during World War II.

But with the generations diverging in language and worldview, shared culture stood at perhaps only about the midpoint on the continuum. Two examples will illustrate the beginnings of divergence here. Most members of the Nisei generation, now reaching adulthood, could not speak Japanese with the fluency of their parents, and few Issei parents could speak English as well as their children. Religiously, about 80 percent of the Issei were Buddhists; only about 50 percent of the Nisei were Buddhists. The breakup of cultural uniformity was not complete, however. The generations still held many aspects of culture in common.[77]

Table 6.1   Japanese American Ethnicity in the Early Second Generation, 1930–1945

Interests	low	medium	**high**
Culture	low	**medium**	high
Institutions	low	medium	**high**

seven

Since World War II

Japanese Americans emerged from World War II a disorganized and demoralized people. As outlined toward the end of the last chapter, the concentration camp episode had led to a precipitous decline in Issei power and authority, with few members of the next generation ready to take over; dissolution of community institutions; economic disarray; and psychic damage to the Nisei generation.

Initial Adjustment

It took several years to begin rebuilding. Just keeping body and soul together was a big job, and community rebuilding had to wait. Gene Oishi's parents had been prosperous farmers and his father a community leader. After the war, they could not find a way to support the family other than as field laborers. In late middle age, they had to go back to where they had started 40 years before.[1] Masao Hirata recalled:

> When we got out of the camp, they gave each of us only twenty-five dollars per person. I experienced unspeakable hardships to support all my family. I will never forget it. When we returned to California, we didn't have a place to live. One of my friends leased me this small house. The next problem was that I couldn't start my work. I didn't have a car or anything. My farm had not been touched for five years, and I didn't even have any tools to cut down the tall weeds on the land. But I had to work to support my family; so I borrowed old tools and worked on my farm. Every Japanese person had to start again from the beginning.

Such a transition was too much for many Issei. Some lucky ones had it easier. Tokushiga Kizuka had non-Japanese friends in Watsonville from before the war who gave his family a place to stay and leased him some land to plant strawberries. The family built a house using the lumber and nails from an old barn and set to work on the land.[2]

The prewar Issei secular institutions, such as the Japanese associations, never regained prominence. The JACL was the most widespread Nisei organization, and its institutional hagiographer refers to this period as "the golden era." Yet its membership in each area was small, and its activities were irrelevant to the lives of most Japanese Americans for at least a decade after the war's end.[3] The first community institutions to start rebuilding and organizing the lives of the people were churches, Buddhist and Christian. The Buddhist Church in Del Rey, California, began to hold worship services shortly after the Japanese returned to town. The Young Buddhist League was soon holding basketball competitions, and the Buddhist Sunday School started classes for Nisei and Sansei youngsters in 1952. A host of community activities revolved around the Buddhist Church.[4]

We do not know what we should about the emotions of the members of the Issei generation in the years after World War II. The existing accounts emphasize *gaman,* endurance, and hard work in the face of daunting obstacles, but we do not know much about what went on beneath the stoic exterior.

About the Nisei we know a bit more. The Nisei suffered a lingering shame that it took decades to overcome. As David Mura noted, "Each Japanese American was imprisoned not for any particular act, but simply by the fact of their race. An equation was set up then between being Japanese and being bad." Michi Weglyn described her generation as suffering "psychic damage . . . 'castration': a deep consciousness of personal inferiority, a proclivity to noncommunication and inarticulateness, evidenced in a shying away from exposure which might subject them to further hurt." Edison Uno said: "We were like the victims of rape. We felt shamed. We could not bear to speak of the assault." Fred Korematsu's son Kenneth had to learn about his father's resistance to imprisonment in a high school civics class—the elder Korematsu had never told him. Like many Nisei, he found himself simply unable to talk about it for two or three decades.[5]

There was also lingering social opprobrium. One soldier recalled, "When I came back from the service in 1945, people would spit at me and push me off the road. We don't tend to tell our kids that, we try to forget and look at how good things are now."[6] To pursue a career in stand-up comedy and acting, Jack Suzuki had to take the name Jack Soo and pretend to be Chinese or Korean; he could not find work as a Japanese American. At Seattle's Garfield High School in the late 1940s, University of Washington researchers found Japanese Americans the least popular with their classmates in a student body that included large numbers of African Americans, Whites, and Chinese.[7]

At Long Beach Polytechnic, Jeanne Wakatsuki found her social life thwarted by her Japaneseness. When her White friend Radine joined a high school sorority, "[t]he question of whether or not I should be asked was never even raised. The boys I had crushes on would not ask me out. They would flirt with me in the hallways or meet me after school, but they would ask Radine to the dances, or someone like Radine, someone they could safely be *seen* with. . . . This sort of treatment did not discourage me. I was used to it. I expected it, a condition of life. . . . I never wanted to change my face or to be someone other than myself. What I wanted was the kind of acceptance that seemed to come so easily to Radine." Wakatsuki in later years understood her striving for acceptance by Whites not only as a normal adolescent preoccupation but as a reaction to her imprisonment and continuing rejection: "As I came to understand what Manzanar [and later incidents] had meant, it gradually filled me with shame for being a person guilty of something enormous enough to deserve that kind of treatment. In order to please my accusers, I tried, for the first few years after our release, to become someone acceptable."[8]

Yet despite starting the 1950s poor, demoralized, and scattered, within a generation most Japanese Americans had joined the middle class economically and integrated themselves into mainstream American society to a significant degree. This achievement had its limitations and costs but remains nonetheless one of the more remarkable turnarounds in American history in the last half-century.

The Japanese Americans of Hawai'i pointed the way. Hawai'i's Japanese had gone through World War II not in the isolation of prison camps but amid a whirlwind of exposure to new people and possibilities. Tens of thousands of GIs came through Hawai'i on their way to war and turned upside down the insular social and economic life of the islands. Young women from the plantation in Waipahu were working for the navy and dating sailors from Tennessee. At the same time, the young men of the 100th and 442nd were rambling across the European countryside, killing Germans and making friends with the French. In the two decades after the war, Japanese Hawaiians, who constituted about one-third of the islands' population, moved toward the mainstream of Hawaiian economic and political life. Some young Hawaiian Japanese went off in search of their fortunes: Tetsuo Najita left Hilo High to go to college in the early 1950s; by the 1980s, he was a professor at the University of Chicago and one of the most honored historians in the United States. Wally Yonamine left Honolulu's Farrington High for the army, then signed on to play halfback for the San Francisco 49ers. Later he had an all-star career in the Japanese baseball leagues as a centerfielder for the Yomiuri Giants.[9]

More Japanese Hawaiians made their mark at home. Certain segments of the economy, such as the teaching profession, came to be dominated by Nisei and their children, the third-generation Sansei. As statehood approached in the 1950s, a new Democratic Party made up largely of Nisei veterans of World War II captured territorial politics from the Republican old guard; they have held control of island politics ever since. Their Japanese American-dominated political coalition has now entered its second generation: Matt Matsunaga, the son of the Nisei war veteran and U.S. senator Spark Matsunaga, is at this writing one of the bright young lights of island politics. Not that there have been no racial problems in Hawai'i; there have been many. But in the generation after World War II, Japanese Hawaiians moved from the fringes to the center of civic life.

Where They Went

Things proceeded much more slowly on the mainland. Gradually in the late 1940s and 1950s, some of the Japanese Americans who had moved east made their way back to the Pacific Coast. By 1950 the Japanese American populations of Los Angeles and San Francisco had returned to prewar levels, but it took another decade for the Seattle Japanese population to be restored (see appendix, table 10). The rural communities never returned to their prewar size. The result was that, although the total West Coast Japanese American population continued to rise in absolute numbers each decade, the percentage of Japanese Americans who lived on the West Coast steadily declined after

Table 7.1   Regional Japanese American Population (*excluding Hawai'i*),
1930–1990 (*percentage*)

Census Year Region	1930	1940	1950	1960	1970	1980	1990
Pacific Coast	86.7	88.6	69.4	68.8	65.0	64.2	60.2
Mountain West	8.3	6.8	10.0	6.7	5.5	6.2	5.7
North Central	1.5	1.2	13.2	11.3	11.5	9.7	10.5
South	0.8	0.8	2.2	6.2	7.7	10.0	11.2
Northeast	2.8	2.6	5.2	3.1	10.3	9.8	12.4

SOURCE: See appendix, table 2.

World War II (see table 7.1). The war caused a net migration in percentage terms out of the West and into the Northeast, Midwest, and South.

Japanese Americans did not just move away from the West Coast. Within the West, they moved from farm to city. In western cities, they also moved out of the inner-city ghettos to more suburban, racially mixed neighborhoods. Figures 7.1 and 7.2 show the spatial distribution of the Seattle Japanese population in 1920 and 1960. In 1920, Japanese Seattle fit the description in chapter 5: tightly concentrated in and around Chinatown and extending eastward through the area south of Yesler Way up to about 16th Avenue; only a few families were scattered in other parts of the city. When the Japanese Americans first came back to Seattle after World War II, they clustered in the old neighborhood. But by 1960 they had begun to spread east toward Lake Washington, north onto Capitol Hill, south onto Beacon Hill, and southeast down Rainier Valley. A similar map drawn in 1980 would show an almost random scattering of dots across the city map and no clusters. By that time, one could hardly find two Seattle Japanese American families living near each other (see appendix, table 14).

The pattern in other cities was similar. In Los Angeles before the war, nearly all Japanese Americans lived in or near Little Tokyo, with small outlying clusters on Boyle Heights, in Hollywood, on the West Side near 36th Street, and around Olympic Boulevard and Tenth Street. After the war, the population became much more dispersed. There were new concentrations of Japanese Angelenos farther out: in Crenshaw to the west; in the Sawtelle neighborhood even farther west near Santa Monica; to the south in semirural Gardena; and out the freeway to the east in Monterey Park. But by the 1960s most Japanese Americans in southern California did not live in any of these clusters; they lived near no other Japanese at all.[10]

Some Japanese Americans, smaller numbers of them, did go back to farm country in the West. Most of the Japanese families who had lived in Cortez in the San Joaquin Valley returned after the war. They had leased their farms to White tenants. Valerie Matsumoto told of their return:

> In their first months back, the Cortez families lived communally as they had in camp. While they waited for their tenants' leases to expire in November [1945], most camped in rented army tents around the Gakuen building which also housed the Buddhist Church. "We used to

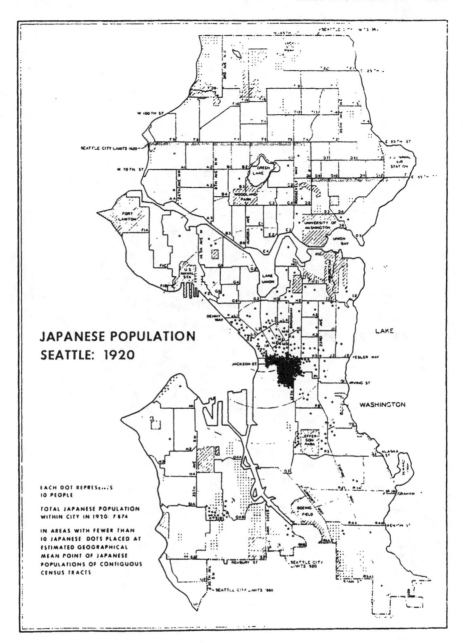

**JAPANESE POPULATION
SEATTLE: 1920**

EACH DOT REPRESENTS
10 PEOPLE

TOTAL JAPANESE POPULATION
WITHIN CITY IN 1920: 7 874

IN AREAS WITH FEWER THAN
10 JAPANESE DOTS PLACED AT
ESTIMATED GEOGRAPHICAL
MEAN POINT OF JAPANESE
POPULATIONS OF CONTIGUOUS
CENSUS TRACTS

Figure 7.1   SOURCE: Calvin F. Schmid, Charles E. Nobbe, and Arlene E. Mitchell, *Nonwhite Races, State of Washington* (Olympia; Washington State Planning and Community Affairs Agency, 1968), 63.

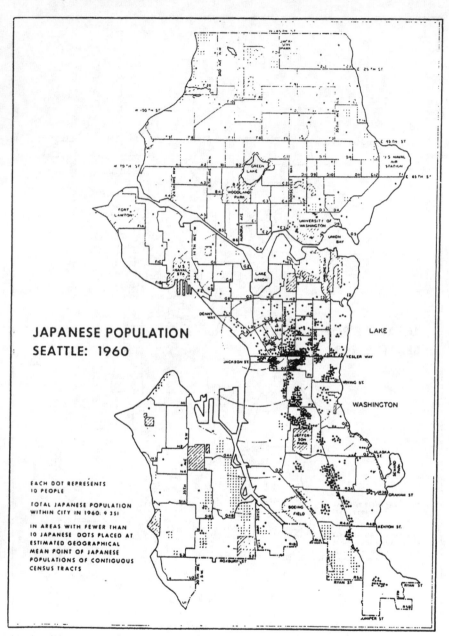

Figure 7.2   SOURCE: Calvin Schmid, et al, *Nonwhite Races*, p. 64.

take Japanese baths in the tents over here," Mae Taniguchi Kajioka recalled. . . . The women did all the cooking outside in large pots, and everyone ate together. The men went out every day, according to a schedule, to help their tenants with the grape harvest. Gradually as the tenants left, the Japanese Americans moved back into their own homes.

The condition of their farms and houses varied according to the skill—and good will—of the tenants. The few who had had friends running their farms found their belongings intact and their lands well kept. Many, however, were less pleased about the conditions to which they returned. The Taniguchis, for example, had to fumigate their house before moving in, and the weeds outside had grown taller than the windows; in addition, the locks had been jimmied and many of the family's possessions taken.

Some neighbors were friendly and others let their hostility show. One woman said, "I guess we tried to associate with the ones that we knew were happy to see us and we just shied away from where there was a question mark. We were a little careful." Some White children acted out their parents' prejudices by calling the returning younger Nisei and Sansei "Japs" and demanding to know why they dared to return to Cortez. The results, predictably, were hurt feelings and fistfights.[11]

Family life in postwar Cortez was different. Many of the Nisei had married during the war; many daughters did not return with their families but went to live elsewhere with their husbands. And a lot of Nisei men brought back to Cortez their brides from towns, cities, and other rural areas. Soon they had children of their own, and three generations lived under one roof. The Sansei experienced something their parents had never known: grandparents. The two generations often had difficulty conversing: the Issei's rudimentary English matched the Sansei's Japanese. But there passed between them that special kind of love that exists only between grandparent and grandchild, something the Nisei had missed.

Many of those who went east during and after the war never came back to the West Coast. Denver's Japanese population grew tenfold, from 323 in 1940 to 3,329 in 1950. New York City's went from 2,000 in 1940 to 16,000 in 1970 (see appendix, table 10). The New York community was large enough to support its own newspaper, the *New York Nichibei*, starting in November 1945. Chicago had fewer than 400 Japanese American residents in 1940; a decade later, it had more than 11,000, the largest Japanese American population in the·Midwest or East. Chicago's fairly strong Japanese community supported ethnic institutions that drew people together. Japanese Americans who came there during the war to take jobs founded a strong chapter of the JACL, three Buddhist temples, and a newspaper, the *Chicago Shimpo*. Other urban Japanese American communities, such as in Minneapolis-St. Paul and Cleveland, were not as institutionally connected. Although New York had a large Japanese American population, they were scattered across the city and did not form a community.

In most of the eastern two-thirds of the United States, Japanese Americans lived separated from one another amid a sea of White faces. That isolation, and the Americanist stance of many of the Nisei who went east, were reflected in a high degree of assimilation. Joy Nakano* grew up in Brooklyn, the daughter of a Jewish mother and a Nisei father. As a child, all her ethnic connections, as well as her identity, were Jewish. It was only in college in the 1970s that she began to get in touch with the Japanese side of her heritage. Her father had never denied he was Japanese, but he had never made things Japanese American a part of the daily experience of his family. Thus it was for many Japanese Americans who lived in the eastern parts of the United States.

Pursuing the American Dream

Once the initial postwar adjustments had been made, most of the members of the Nisei generation embarked on a relentless pursuit of middle-class status. Harry Kitano summarized the case:

> In 1940 more than a quarter of all Japanese males were laborers, while in the 1960s, the proportion had dwindled to about 5 percent. In 1960, 15 percent of Japanese males were classified as professional, the same proportion as in white groups, and a proportion that can be compared with a figure of 5 percent for Negroes. Yet in 1940, only 3.8 percent of Japanese had been professionals. Income, too, has risen beyond that of other groups. A recent [1963] survey of employees in the California State Civil Service reported in a Japanese-American newspaper reveals that the modal civil service income for Oriental employees (primarily Japanese) was $7,400 a year, nearly $3,000 more than that of other minority groups in the Civil Service.[12]

Kitano saw the wartime experience as driving the Nisei out of the prewar ethnic economy that had bound them and giving them a chance to learn to succeed in the wider economy.

A study of Japanese American education, occupation, and income levels in Washington State in 1960 (see figure 7.3) revealed both the extent of Japanese American economic achievements and the limits placed on their upward mobility. It found that Japanese Americans had by far the highest educational level of any ethnic group in the state, including Whites, Chinese, African Americans, Filipinos, and Native Americans. In occupational categories, Japanese and Chinese ranked together, just a bit above Whites. But in income, Whites enjoyed a large edge over Japanese Americans. Japanese Americans in the second generation had achieved a lot, but they were not yet receiving rewards commensurate with their achievements.

It was a rare group of Nisei who openly engaged in partisan politics in the 1940s and 1950s, but during this period Japanese Americans did begin to make some tentative forays into politics—the one area in which the JACL provided leadership. One group that called itself "Nisei for Wallace" rallied in Los Angeles for the Progressive presidential candidate Henry Wallace in 1948 under banners that read "No More Hiroshimas" and "Citizenship for Our Parents."[13] The latter concern was one of the primary goals of the JACL's Mike Masaoka, who spent most of the four decades from the end of the war until his death working as a lobbyist in Washington, D.C. He and other Japanese Americans were instrumen-

7.1 Middle-class family life was the postwar ideal. *Courtesy of Japanese American National Museum.*

tal in having the Alien Land Laws overturned in the courts in 1950 and in securing passage of the McCarran-Walter Act of 1952. The latter made racist quotas central to U.S. immigration policy, but it did make it possible for the Issei to acquire U.S. citizenship at last.

As the postwar decades proceeded, the Nisei generation moved into the comfortable, relatively apolitical middle class. They spread across the country and into the suburbs on the West Coast. They wanted nothing to do with the memory of their imprisonment. They just wanted to be left alone and accorded the status of ordinary Americans.

War Brides

A new set of Japanese immigrants came to the United States in the 1950s: the brides of U.S. soldiers who had served in Japan during the American occupation and in the Korean War. Several tens of thousands of Japanese war brides accompanied their husbands when they returned from overseas duty. They were scattered over the country, but an especially large number settled in the South. Theirs tended to be an isolated existence. Seldom did these women connect with Japanese American individuals or communities. These marriages helped establish the stereotype held by many White Americans about the ideal coupling of Asian women with White men and a host of other exotic stereotypes that plague relations between Whites and Asians to this day.[14]

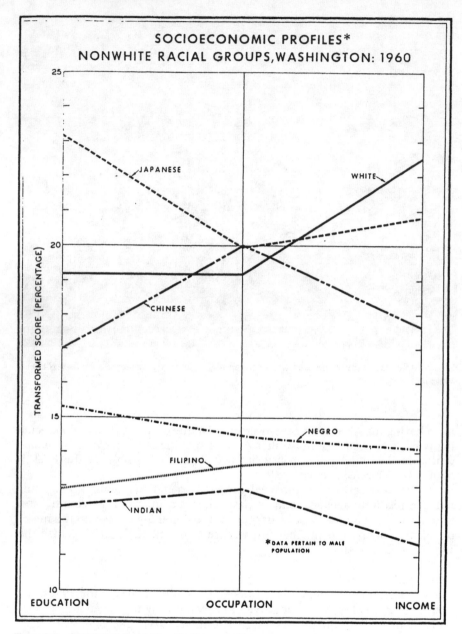

SOCIOECONOMIC PROFILES*
NONWHITE RACIAL GROUPS, WASHINGTON: 1960

Figure 7.3   SOURCE: Schmid, *Nonwhite Races*, p. 128.

Table 7.2   *Japanese American Ethnicity in the Late Second Generation,*
1945–1965

Interests	**low**	medium	high
Culture	low	**medium**	high
Institutions	low	**medium**	high

Ethnicity in the Late Second Generation

In the later years of the second generation, from 1945 to perhaps 1965, all three bases of ethnic group bonding declined. Shared culture was no higher than the midpoint. Participation in ethnic institutions was middling at best. Although churches re-formed after the war, the Issei economic and social organizations never regained anything like their prewar vitality. JACL membership dropped drastically during the war and did not rebound until many years later. Shared interests were extremely low as class differences among the Nisei emerged and formerly ghettoized Japanese Americans moved to the suburbs and spread across the country. Japanese American ethnicity was weaker than it had been at any time since the frontier period.

Compared to the second generation of White immigrant groups, such as Italians and Jews, the postwar Nisei were equally acculturated to American norms but less integrated into mainstream institutions and social life. Compared to the second generation of the other main Asian group, the Chinese, Japanese Americans were substantially more acculturated, more integrated, and more assimilationist in their outlook.

The Third Generation and Beyond

The third-generation Sansei continued the economic trends of their parents' generation. Where the typical Issei had primary education and a bit of secondary, and the average Nisei had completed high school and attended college for a while, the average Sansei had graduated from college and done some graduate work.[15] Not only were Japanese Americans going to college and staying there longer, they were going to the best schools in the land. In the 1980s, Sansei and Yonsei (the fourth generation) figured prominently among the Asians who made up roughly one-quarter of the students at Stanford and one-third of those at Berkeley.

More education translated into higher-status occupations with better pay. There was a decided shift from the Nisei to the Sansei generation: out of agriculture, the trades, and service industries and into professional, technical, and managerial employment (see appendix, table 19). Some middle-class Nisei had joined the professions but more worked for large employers like state governments and banks; moreover, a significant minority ran their own small businesses. The Sansei generation created a professional class of Japanese Americans—lawyers, doctors, architects, engineers, and the like, as well as the teachers and civil servants who had been more common in their parents' generation. A 1974 survey of Sansei students found that three-quarters of the men intended to enter professional fields—between one-third and one-half chose engineering and science—and that Sansei women favored teaching, a profession with a softer image.[16]

Not all Sansei, however, were members of the middle class. For one thing, the disparity between educational achievement and income for the Nisei continued to exist for their children. Average Japanese American *family* income was higher than the average income of White families, but more Japanese Americans worked in the average family; individuals continued not to earn as much as their educational level would have brought Whites.[17] In addition, considerable evidence emerged in the Sansei generation of a greater division between the middle and working classes than had existed at any previous time in Japanese American history.

Examples abound of Sansei achievement, which runs the gamut of occupations. Len Sakata played major league baseball, and Kristi Yamaguchi won an Olympic gold medal in figure skating. Steven Okazaki won an Oscar in 1991 for his documentary film *Days of Waiting*, and Richard Sakai produced hit movies and the television series *The Simpsons*. Ellison Onizuka was an astronaut. Robert Nakasone was president of the toymaker Toys R Us. Lance Ito was the judge in the murder trial of O. J. Simpson.

Achievement and the Model Minority Myth

Sansei upward mobility began to give rise in the 1960s to a stereotype in the White popular mind: the myth of the model minority. First applied to Japanese Americans and later generalized to all Asians, the myth was that by dint of quiet hard work and good values, Japanese Americans and other Asians had become what other, darker, seemingly more threatening minorities had not: successful members of the American middle class. The sociologist William Petersen stated the case in the *New York Times* in 1966: "By any criterion of good citizenship that we choose, the Japanese Americans are better than any other group in our society, including native-born whites. They have established this remarkable record, moreover, by their own almost totally unaided effort. Every attempt to hamper their progress resulted only in enhancing their determination to succeed. Even in a country whose patron saint is the Horatio Alger hero, there is no parallel to this success story."[18]

Some of the feelings and actions of Japanese Americans themselves reinforced the model minority idea. Jeanne Wakatsuki Houston described the Nisei generation's repression of the prison camp experience and their striving for middle-class respectability: "To come out of prison, having been put there because of race . . . the only way to survive was to assimilate and prove our American-ness as a 'model minority.'"[19]

While it is true that average Nisei and Sansei achievement was high, the average did not apply to everyone. There is good evidence that Japanese American abilities and virtues were spread across the bell curve in patterns similar to those of other ethnic groups. The model minority myth hid from public view those Japanese Americans who were poor or socially disadvantaged. The myth also put unfair pressure on those who did not fit the stereotype. Teachers, for example, would expect every Sansei child to be good at math and none to be gifted at acting or football. They would expect every Japanese American to be excruciatingly well behaved and would be offended if a Sansei child acted as rowdy as her Caucasian peers.

The stereotype likewise tended to diminish others' appreciation of Sansei individuals' real accomplishments. Recently I commented to a White chemistry professor that his student, a Yonsei, or fourth-generation Japanese American, had done something remarkable: achieved a perfect score on a chemistry test. His response was simply, "What do you expect? She's Japanese."

The model minority myth fed into a lack of recognition of the limits that American society put on Japanese American achievement. Many community observers testified that there appeared to be a glass ceiling on Japanese American careers; that Nisei and Sansei managers could aspire to make vice president for technical services but not president; that Japanese American men in particular were not perceived as having the dynamic qualities needed for top positions.[20] As late as the 1970s, this assessment was certainly accurate. In the 1990s, however, the glass ceiling may be disappearing: Japanese Americans have taken top leadership positions in a variety of fields, including those that require emotional or athletic expression. A level of achievement that was not generally available to the Nisei seems to be opening up for their children.

Perhaps the most pernicious aspect of the model minority myth was its use as a bludgeon to punish other people of color. A 1966 *U.S. News and World Report* article recounted the words of a White Los Angeles social worker: "[I]t must be recognized that the Chinese and other Orientals in California were faced with even more prejudice than faces the Negro today. We haven't stuck Negroes in concentration camps, for instance, as we did the Japanese in World War II. The Orientals came back, and today they have established themselves as strong contributors to the health of the whole community."[21] The comparative judgment was that African Americans, if they would just apply themselves as the Asians had, would prosper and cease to be a bothersome social burden on White Americans. It was a way for White Americans to avoid dealing with the real problems of racial hierarchy in the United States.

Decline of Community

Like the drive to achieve, a second development in the Sansei generation, a decreasing connection to Japanese American social institutions, was also a continuation of Nisei trends. Just as Nisei were more likely than Issei to live in non-Japanese neighborhoods and to interact socially with non-Japanese Americans, so Sansei were more likely than their parents to operate outside a Japanese American sphere. Some of this shift was related to their educational and job choices. As the sociologists Darrel Montero and Gene Levine noted, members of the Sansei generation "tend to choose fields that would separate them from the immediate confines of a local Japanese American community . . . like engineering, science, and professorships. Requirements of the labor market would willy-nilly cause their dispersal over the land to locales devoid of Japanese Americans."[22]

Even for those who remained near other Japanese Americans, involvement in Japanese community institutions became, for most Sansei, a weekend activity at best. San Francisco's Nihonmachi and Los Angeles' Little Tokyo ceased to function as authentic ethnic communities and became instead tourist attractions for out-of-town visitors in search of ethnic flavor. Some Japanese American institutions endured, as did certain ritual occasions like the Cherry Blossom Festival and Nisei Week. But the Sansei lived their daily lives far away.

Commenting on the change from Nisei to Sansei community life, San Francisco's Rita Takahashi said: "Japanese American orientations are more individualistic today than they were in the past. Group unity and aggregate spirits are less prevalent."[23] One young Los Angeles Sansei testified to her lack of connectedness, even though she went to church with other Japanese Americans:

> I was never close to the people at church, you know. I went because at first I was forced to, told to, and I never really liked it. I know when I was little, I really disliked going because I didn't know anybody. Like we lived on the other side of the city. The Japanese were kind of centered on one part of the city and we were away on the other side so I never went to any of the schools; and when I went to church, I was always like an outsider. So I was always uncomfortable and I really didn't have any friends.

Other Sansei who were more connected to the Japanese community still had ethnically mixed circles of friends: "My best friend would be Asian but then another circle of friends would be mostly white with a few Asians. . . . I would go to an all white high school during the week and hang around with white friends, and on weekends I would hang around with mostly Asian friends."[24]

Another reflection of declining connectedness was the sharp increase in out-marriage by members of the Sansei generation. Only a tiny number of Issei married non-Japanese. For all their assimilationist zeal, less than 10 percent of the Nisei generation intermarried (partly because they came of marriageable age during the 1940s, when they were forcibly separated from non-Japanese people). But in the 1960s, with the coming of age of the older Sansei, the rate of out-marriage began to climb; it topped 50 percent in the 1980s. While it is true that marrying someone who is not Japanese does not make one less Japanese American oneself, nonetheless, to marry someone outside the group does create intimate social connectedness with at least one person from another ethnic group.

Interracial romance and marriage was a steady theme of community debate from the 1960s on. Much of the concern centered around the gender differential in interracial romance: far more Sansei women than men dated and married non-Japanese, at least as late as the 1970s. The complex chords of conflict that resulted are suggested by the words of the Asian activist Jan Masaoka:

> I guess that one of the most difficult things for me to understand is how to relate to my boyfriend who is white. Sometimes I flash back on all the ideas my parents taught me such as the idea that to marry a white man was to sort of degrade myself, and it's really hard to know how to deal with these kinds of feelings.
>
> I once read this poem by an Asian woman where she said that after looking into blue eyes for so long she forgot hers were black. I really feel this, and it's hard to understand: I identify so strongly with this man I love and that's inevitably tied up somewhat to the way he looks, which conflicts with me and my background and the way I look.
>
> So I look at him and all the feelings I have get mixed up and make me upset and dizzy: loving him, hating myself for loving a white man,

hating him because he's white, hating white people in general, feeling underneath that I'm superior to white people, and even deeper underneath that I'm inferior to white people, especially men, feeling guilty for not having an Asian boyfriend, feeling that I'm taking unfair advantage of my social and sexual mobility racially when Asian men don't have that mobility, and being afraid of what other people think about my going with a white man—it's just really frightening.[25]

Despite community disputes and personal internal conflicts, intermarriage continued apace. Most Japanese American families quickly made their peace with intermarriage, although there was a decided Nisei preference that their children choose White or other Asian mates over African Americans or Latinos. By the 1980s Japanese American communities were accepting the mixed children of intermarried couples into their midst. Some of this acceptance was based on what Cynthia Nakashima calls the "claim-us-if-we're-famous" principle.[26] Rex Walters would probably not have been written about as a Japanese American in the pages of community newspapers had he not been an all-American basketball player. But by the 1980s the high level of acceptance of mixed children was certainly based as well on the high rate of intermarriage—almost every extended family had at least one set of children resulting from such a marriage.[27]

Other developments contributed to the declining sense of community in the prime of the Sansei generation. One was simply the aging of those people who had done the most to maintain community connectedness. In 1949, Hitoshi and Taeko Taniguchi, both Nisei, began to manage the Publix Hotel in Seattle's International District. It catered to young Filipino working men, then to elderly Chinese and Japanese, many of whom spent their last years in the hotel. After 41 years, the Taniguchis themselves finally reached retirement in 1990. The passing of the Issei and the aging of the Nisei meant the loss of most of the people who had known Japan, who had felt most deeply its cultural imperatives, who spoke Japanese, and who were most deeply enmeshed in the web of Japanese American community. Some of them maintained community in old age, in places like the Keiro Nursing Home, not far from the Publix Hotel. But the same commitment to community was not felt by the next generation.[28]

One aspect of the decline of community was the parallel decline of a shared and distinctive Japanese American culture. Some older Sansei learned some Japanese as children, and others studied it in college, but few ever learned it well enough to communicate well with their grandparents. They knew some Japanese foods and festivals and had been told how Japanese people were supposed to behave, but little more. Jane Muramoto Yung talked about Japanese holidays: "As for customs and practices, New Year's has always been big for me, more so than Christmas. It's a time when I feel very Japanese. As a kid we'd always go to Bachan's [Grandma's] for family and Japanese 'soul food.' Now we always go to my folks. We didn't celebrate other Japanese holidays or speak Japanese because my grandparents died early. I know the camp experience made my folks minimize Japanese customs in our house."[29]

The daily cultural expressions of most Sansei and Yonsei did not in fact diverge much from those of non-Japanese Americans. Almost nowhere was there a thoroughly separate Sansei social scene, like the one the Nisei had created, where such shared culture could be mediated. From the 1960s on, non-Japanese Americans were almost always involved in Sansei-generation activities, and a lot of Sansei spent most of their time absorbed in non-Japanese American social networks.

Asian Power

Despite the centrifugal forces of economic and geographical mobility and of generational change, Japanese Americans could still act powerfully as a group on occasion. For example, in 1989, Don Nakanishi was granted tenure—a permanent professor's job—at UCLA after a three-year battle. During the struggle, Nakanishi and his lawyer, Dale Minami, called on the JACL and a host of other community organizations and individuals to put pressure on the university. The pressure worked to overcome what many regarded as a biased first reading of Nakanishi's credentials. When tenure was granted, Nakanishi's supporters held a large community victory party.[30]

Yet Nakanishi's victory was not just an example of the Japanese community at work. It was an expression of a wider movement of Asian Americans, irrespective of national origin, which was itself an outgrowth of the youth and Black power movements of the late 1960s. Amy Uyematsu stated the case for Asian power in 1969:

> Asian Americans can no longer afford to watch the black-and-white struggle from the sidelines. They have their own cause to fight, since they are also victims—with less visible scars—of the white institutionalized racism. A yellow movement has been set into motion by the black power movement. Addressing itself to the unique problems of Asian Americans, this "yellow power" movement is relevant to the black power movement in that both are part of the Third World struggle to liberate all colored people. . . .
>
> The yellow power movement has been motivated largely by the problem of self-identity in Asian Americans. The psychological focus of this movement is vital, for Asian Americans suffer the critical mental crises of having "integrated" into American society. [In *Black Power,* Stokely Carmichael and Charles V. Hamilton write,] "No person can be healthy, complete, and mature if he must deny a part of himself; this is what 'integration' has required so far."
>
> The Asian Americans' current position in America is not viewed as a social problem. Having achieved middle-class incomes while presenting no real threat in numbers to the white majority, the main body of Asian Americans (namely, the Japanese and the Chinese) have received the token acceptance of white America.
>
> Precisely because Asian Americans have become economically secure, do they face serious identity problems. Fully committed to a system that subordinates them on the basis of non-whiteness, Asian Americans still try to gain complete acceptance by denying their yellowness. They have become white in every respect but color. . . .
>
> Mentally, they have adjusted to the white man's culture by giving up their own languages, customs, histories, and cultural values. . . .
> Next, they have rejected their physical heritages, resulting in extreme

self-hatred. Yellow people share with blacks the desire to look white. Just as blacks wish to be light-complected with thin lips and unkinky hair, "yellows" want to be tall with long legs and large eyes.

Uyemura continued by calling on Asian Americans to stop seeking acceptance from White America, to establish alternative Asian models of beauty and accomplishment, to build separate Asian community institutions and culture, to create programs to study Asian American history and culture, to protest discrimination against Asians, and to join with other people of color in common cause.[31]

The events that spurred the Asian power movement were the 1969 Third World student strikes at San Francisco State University and the University of California in nearby Berkeley. The strikers' goal was to establish programs of ethnic studies at the two universities. The historian of that movement, William Wei, described the strikers' plans:

[T]hey went on strike to achieve self-determination for themselves and their communities and to eradicate individual and institutional racism. . . . Ethnic Studies was to be open to all students of color who wanted a higher education. Its central purpose was to imbue them with the knowledge, understanding, and commitment needed to solve the problems of their communities. It would increase the diversity of the student body and faculty at San Francisco State and the University of California, Berkeley, making them more representative of the society they served and less exclusively European American. It was deemed necessary because conventional educational institutions offered a curriculum that was said to be irrelevant to the experiences of people of color. University courses, the striker claimed, suppressed the social and political consciousness of students of color by denying or distorting their historical experience and by promoting a Eurocentric ideology that denigrated other cultures.[32]

Ironically, it was a Nisei, San Francisco State President S. I. Hayakawa, who became the most visible symbol of opposition to Asian power. His resolute stand against the younger generation of his own ethnic group and their colleagues earned him headlines and a place in the U.S. Senate, though little affection among Japanese Americans.

There were two elements to the ideology that propelled the Asian power movement: cultural nationalism and pan-Asian ethnicity. Both were new for most Japanese Americans. Most Nisei had subscribed to some version of the American melting pot myth—that people would come to America from all over the earth, share equally what they brought with them, and gradually and benignly be transformed into a new people, unhyphenated Americans. Those Sansei who were active in the Asian power movement radically rejected this assimilationist (they would say hegemonic) vision and called for enduring ethnic subcultures, with a reapportionment of power away from White America and to the subcultures.

The pan-Asian idea put a new limit on ethnic particularity. There had been little love lost between the Issei and other Asian peoples in America—in fact, there was a lot of animosity between Chinese and Japanese Americans from early in the century up through World War II. Yet the Sansei had grown up in a period when tensions between Asian ethnic groups were waning. Often they grew up in the same parts of town as Chinese Americans and went to the same schools. Most non-Asian Americans could not tell Chinese and Japanese apart and applied the same stereotypes to both. At the same time, Japanese Americans were a tiny and relatively powerless minority. Considering that they got along fairly well with Chinese Americans, the White majority lumped them together anyway, and they could build a more effective lobby by increasing the size of their bloc, it made sense to create a larger ethnic entity. Thus began a very conscious attempt to build a pan-Asian ethnic group.

In the heat of student activism and community service, the pan-Asian idea took on a life of its own and was pursued to its logical extreme. The Asian group grew, in the eyes of activists, to include first Chinese and Japanese; then Filipinos; then the Koreans and Vietnamese, whose presence in the United States was growing in the 1970s and 1980s; then other Southeast Asians and Asian Indians. Some Asian activists even extended the idea to include Samoans, Hawaiians, and other Pacific Islanders and considered including Persians and Arabs. Asian American studies programs, Asian American legal agencies, and Asian American health clinics tried to include and to serve all these diverse con-stituencies. They generally did a better job with their core constituencies—Chinese, Japanese, Filipino, Korean, Vietnamese—than with the outliers.

The Asian idea did take hold among the Sansei population. Most saw them-selves as Asians at the same time they saw themselves as Japanese. Sometimes pan-Asianism took forms that must have appalled the movement's founders. Most Asian activists were also supporters of feminism and doubtless regarded beauty contests as thinly veiled abuse of women. Yet one expression of the pan-Asian perspective in the late 1980s and 1990s was the Miss Asian America beauty contest. Japanese Americans, Chinese, Filipinos, and all the rest saw themselves as Asians in some sense, even as they did not give up their separate identities related to national origin.

More typically, and more importantly, pan-Asian sentiments brought the resources of the Japanese American community to the service of other Asians, in fact to other peoples of color. Thus, the JACL fought alongside the Organization of Chinese Americans and the Asian Pacific American Labor Alliance to halt a congressional bill that would have limited the rights of immigrants, even though there were no longer a lot of Japanese immigrants.[33] Thus, too, the Nakanishi tenure case, while its main actors were Japanese Americans, was pur-sued as an Asian, not a Japanese, issue. Some attempts have been made to cre-ate a pan-Asian culture, but none have yielded much fruit. Several of the Asian groups have drawn on a common cultural base in Confucianism, but others have not. There has been a lot of mutual appreciation of each other's culture, but it is a long way from political coalition to the creation of a common, pan-Asian culture.

The Asian American movement was both a success and a failure. It created institutions such as the San Francisco Asian American Mental Health Training Center and the UCLA Asian American Studies Program. It stirred purely Japanese community institutions to new life. It gave voice to long-suppressed grievances. It both reflected the sense of commonality that was developing among Japanese and Chinese Americans in the 1950s and 1960s and gave it a distinctive ideological foundation. Yet, although the Asian American movement strengthened the community in many ways and helped many Japanese Americans stay in touch with their ethnic identity, the majority of Sansei were never more than marginally involved.

Just Like Other Americans

The story of the Sansei generation was in many ways the story of an ethnic minority becoming ever more like other Americans, while not losing entirely its distinctive ethnic identity. The ways in which Japanese Americans came to resemble the general American population were neither political nor economic but more generally cultural. Japanese American artists, like the singer Sadao Watanabe with the 1990 hit song "Any Other Fool," came close to the core of American popular culture. In the 1980s and 1990s, some Japanese American lesbians and gay men began coming out of the closet, and even the conservative JACL voted to support laws allowing same-sex marriage. Life in the suburbs led to Japanese American mall crawlers, valley girls, and the non-ethnic fiction of the teenage novelist Holly Uyemoto, author of *Rebel without a Clue.*[34]

One of the dubious achievements of the Sansei and Yonsei was a crime rate that, starting in the 1970s, began to approach equality with that of the rest of American society (see appendix, table 13). Belatedly, Japanese Americans began in the 1990s to talk about the domestic violence that had long existed in their community. In 1992 a community newspaper dubbed Greg Nishinaka "Southern California's most prolific bank robber": he was charged with 45 heists.[35] In the mid-1970s, a Japanese American woman, Wendy Yoshimura, was among the Symbionese Liberation Army captors of the newspaper-heiress-turned-radical-bank-robber Patricia Hearst. Both Yoshimura and Hearst served time in federal penitentiaries. That a Japanese American would be deeply involved in left fringe politics is testimony to the degree to which Japanese Americans had entered the American mainstream. That the conservative northern California Japanese American community would rally around Yoshimura and provide her with an excellent legal defense team is testimony to a level of community resources and self-confidence in the face of potential criticism that had not existed before the 1960s.

New Immigrants

Even as the Sansei generation supplanted the Nisei, new Japanese immigrants began to arrive in the United States. The number coming swelled from about 4,000 a year in the early 1970s to about 25,000 a year by the late 1980s. Some were students like Jinei Yamaguchi, who came to MIT's Sloan School of Management in the late 1980s. His goal was to earn an M.B.A. and to learn about how Americans think, as preparation for a career in international business. He said that business school "is more to learn about America than to learn about net present value." Other students had a deeper interest in academics for its own sake, particularly the large number pursuing Ph.D.s. Altogether, about 40,000 Japanese were studying in the United States in 1992.[36]

Other immigrants were businesspeople employed by Japanese corporations abroad, people like the father of Mariko*, mentioned in chapter 1. Still others were artists and professionals. Two hundred thousand strong by 1990, they led upper-middle-class lives in American suburbs and frequently had little to do with American-born Japanese. They were very concerned with corporate culture and with how to reintegrate themselves into Japan once their overseas tours of duty were finished. Some of the businesspeople, and some of the students, liked America so much, or found it so profitable, that they did not want to return. One was Sam Kusumoto, who first came to America in the 1950s as a Minolta camera salesman on a third-class ticket. By 1990 he was president of Minolta's American subsidiary and a permanent resident, jetting back and forth across the Pacific doing deals. Another was the Boston Symphony Orchestra conductor Seiji Ozawa, who also guest-directed a number of other American orchestras as well as symphonies around the world. Others who came to America found that they were changed so much in their time abroad that they could not comfortably go back. But far more did eventually return to Japan.[37]

In numerical terms, the new wave of Japanese immigrants was not as important as the migrations of some of the other Asian groups who flocked to America in the late twentieth century, although their significance for international trade was immense. In social-class terms, the new middle-class immigrants were a far cry from the laborers who had entered the United States at the turn of the twentieth century. But in other ways, they were similar to the Issei. Most writers on Japanese Americans and other ethnic groups employ old ideas about immigration. They posit a one-way flow: people leaving the old country and coming to the new. Yet as we saw in chapters 3 and 4, Japanese American migration has always had a two-way quality, out from Japan and back across the Pacific. Over time, the Nisei and Sansei lost the trans-Pacific mentality of the Issei, although the resurgence of ethnic interest in the Sansei generation included an element of interest in Japan. The new immigrants of the 1980s and 1990s were again *dekasegi-nin*—people who went out to work, with the expectation of returning to Japan—just like the Issei nearly a century before.

Politics: Entering the Mainstream

Politically, Japanese Americans outside Hawai'i were almost invisible up to the 1960s. After all, the Issei could not be citizens, and there was not much the Nisei could do from prison camps during World War II. Slowly after the war, and with increasing momentum after 1960, Japanese Americans made their way into mainstream politics, by several channels. The first was through lobbying in Washington, D.C., by the JACL's Mike Masaoka and several associates. Masaoka had not been much of a community defender during the war, but he proved himself a dynamic advocate for three decades thereafter. He first worked for the JACL and then opened up a private lobbying firm. He was instrumental in gaining citizenship rights for the Issei, an end to the Alien Land Laws, token reparations for a small portion of the financial losses suffered by the concentration camp inmates, a small quota for Japanese immigrants, and entry into American markets for several Japanese businesses.

Other Japanese Americans involved themselves in the political process through labor unions. Karl Yoneda, for example, was for decades a legendary organizer of Japanese workers on behalf of a number of different unions. There were antilabor leaders as well, among them the Nisei Farmers League, one of the most vocal opponents of the United Farm Workers Union in its organizing drives of the 1970s.

Despite their history, the Nisei had believed in American democratic institutions and always voted—with a higher rate of participation, in fact, than the White population. They were split politically: urban Nisei tended to be Democrats, while rural people divided about equally between Democrats and Republicans. Even though they voted, however, fewer Nisei and Sansei participated personally in politics than was the case for other groups.[38]

Japanese Hawaiians led the way to more active participation. Beginning as campaign workers in the statehood movement of the 1950s, and continuing into elected office in the 1960s and beyond, a string of Nisei and Sansei took center stage in island politics. Among them were U.S. Senators Daniel Inouye and Spark Matsunaga, Congresswoman Patsy Mink, and Governor George Ariyoshi, all Democrats. On the mainland, by contrast, the very conservative S. I. Hayakawa was the first Japanese American to rise to political prominence by becoming a Republican U.S. senator from California in 1976. In that same period, the Democrats Robert Matsui and Norman Mineta became multiterm members of Congress. Their high visibility on many issues, including civil rights, and their ability to build coalitions with White liberals and other people of color, made them effective and widely respected legislators.

In the 1990s, many Japanese American candidates have run for office all over the country: Al Sugiyama for the Seattle School Board, Warren Furutani for a similar post in Los Angeles, Glenn Sugiyama running for Congress in Illinois. They have also been elected as state senators, mayors, and county sheriffs. In a parallel to American developments, Alberto Fujimori became the president of Peru in 1990 and proceeded to take his nation down a controversial path, teetering on the knife edge between democracy and dictatorship.

Sansei-era politicians ranged not just all over the map but all over the political spectrum. Though most Sansei were Democrats, there were articulate conservatives as well, and it was useful to both parties to be able to claim Japanese American support. Hawai'i's Pat Saiki and Eunice Sato of Long Beach spoke clearly on behalf of the policies of Presidents Reagan and Bush. So did Francis Fukuyama, a planner in the Reagan-Bush State Department and a darling of the hard right. Fukuyama wrote a book and essay, "The End of History," that proclaimed the triumph of American values over all others for all time.[39] On the other side of the ledger were all the Democrats mentioned earlier, plus several members of the Clinton administration and a host of workers in local races. A bit further to the left, Trisha Murakawa served as president of the southern California chapter of the American Civil Liberties Union. It is clear that the Sansei generation has been vigorously involved in American politics.

The War That Would Not Go Away

Among Sansei political involvements, three issues from the World War II era continued to occupy the community throughout the 1970s, 1980s, and 1990s.

Redress

One issue was the campaign to secure some measure of redress from the U.S. government for the suffering the Japanese American inmates endured during the war. The token compensation the federal government appropriated in 1948 did not begin to cover actual inmate financial losses, much less compensate for the pain, humiliation, and lost opportunities. In 1976, under pressure from a wide range of Japanese American community and political leaders, President Gerald Ford repealed Roosevelt's executive order 9066 and issued a sort of apology: "An honest reckoning, however, must include a recognition of our national mistakes as well as our national achievements. . . . We now know what we should have known then—not only was the evacuation wrong, but Japanese Americans were and are loyal Americans."[40]

The pressure on Ford was part of a movement that was gathering momentum to secure not only such half-hearted apologies but also reparations from the U.S. government. The JACL had spent the generation after World War II trying, quite successfully, to get White America to recognize the Nisei's loyalty and remove the limitations placed on Japanese American citizenship. A new generation of Japanese American activists emerged from the 1960s with a pushier agenda. The 1970s were a decade of controversy within the organization, as Mike Masaoka's generation faded from power and a younger group took over. They were still middle-of-the-roaders, not radicals, but they were willing in 1978 to call on Congress to make a formal apology and a reparations payment of $25,000 to each former inmate. Some conservative Japanese Americans like S. I. Hayakawa were outraged that their people's most prominent organization was abandoning its accommodationist stance (Hayakawa had been in college in Chicago, after all, and had not been interned). Others were just as outraged that the JACL was asking for so little. Most White American opinion makers were willing to support an apology but thought financial redress was asking too much.

William Hohri and a group of Seattle Japanese Americans forced the issue by talking Washington Congressman Mike Lowry into introducing a redress bill that would give $25,000 to each former internee or that person's heirs. They provided the outside pressure. Inside pressure came from the JACL and the seven Japanese American members of Congress from Hawai'i and California, who sought to buy time and build support for redress by assigning a congressional commission to study the internment.

Central to the redress movement were the 1981 hearings of the Commission on the Wartime Relocation and Internment of Civilians. Over 750 witnesses testified, including former government officials and scholars, but most importantly, former inmates. The hearings were a cathartic event for Japanese Americans across the country, as many were moved to tell of their experiences in public for the first time; countless others followed the proceedings with avid interest. A key role was played by a Sansei grass-roots group, the National Coalition for Redress/Reparations (NCRR), which mobilized Japanese Americans to speak out about what they had suffered. In the end, the commission published a volume on the concentration camp episode and recommended:

1. a formal apology from the U.S. government;
2. pardons for those who had resisted the draft or violated the curfew;
3. reinstatement of veterans' benefits and honorable discharges for those who had been summarily dismissed from the military in the war's first weeks;

4. funding for a foundation to study and educate the public about the concentration camps; and

5. a tax-free payment of $20,000 to each former inmate who was still alive.

The commission's activities created enough national awareness of the World War II injustices that most Americans began to favor redress payments, despite last-ditch opposition campaigns by people like John McCloy and Karl Bendetsen, two of the architects of internment.

The Reagan administration was intransigent, but more pressure was applied from outside again. William Hohri and the National Council for Japanese American Redress (NCJAR) attacked the JACL for continuing in its former collaborationist ways. NCJAR celebrated the wartime actions of Joe Kurihara at Tule Lake and of the Heart Mountain draft resisters. In 1983 the group brought a class-action suit on behalf of all the former inmates and their heirs, demanding $25.2 billion in reparations ($210,000 for each victim). The suit was dismissed and refiled several times.

The NCJAR pressure, together with heavy lobbying by all three groups (JACL, NCRR, and NCJAR) and skillful work by the Japanese American congressional delegation, brought the commission's recommendations to the floor of Congress in 1988. President Reagan reversed his former opposition and the Civil Rights Act of 1988 completed the preparation for redress. It then took more than two years to get Congress to appropriate, and the Bush administration to release, money to begin paying the former inmates, the oldest ones first. The Office of Redress Administration (ORA) was created to arrange the payments. Community organizations and newspapers mobilized Japanese Americans and disseminated the information needed to comply with government regulations. The first checks were mailed on 9 October 1990. The ORA made the last payments in 1994.

The redress movement revitalized the Japanese American community and provided an occasion for many Nisei to speak of their concentration camp experiences for the first time. James Okutsu wrote, "The congressional hearings on the wartime internment in 1981 became the cathartic event which released the anger suppressed for years, and. . . . Nisei testified and spoke of the humiliating and degrading treatment experienced by these American citizens simply because of their race."[41] The day-by-day accounts in community newspapers of the progress of the redress proposal—congressional approval, the presidential signature, the appropriation of funds, locating former inmates, and disbursing the checks—brought the prison camp experience to the forefront of community consciousness and held it there for many months. Many Nisei began for the first time to talk about that which they had avoided for many years.

The Nisei reawakening to their own past quickly extended beyond the simple issue of redress. Sansei activists and a few Nisei had been making pilgrimages since the early 1970s to Manzanar and some of the other concentration camp sites. In the 1980s, Nisei began to go along, then to organize their own remembrances. The pace of remembrance picked up in the 1990s with the arrival of the 50th anniversaries of World War II events. The Nisei generation, newly retired and with the leisure to reflect, published a spate of books on the concentration camps. They traveled to all the camps and put together museum exhibits. Sansei organized and Nisei and Sansei groups and individuals funded a growing number of museums and cultural organizations, like the Japanese American National Museum in Los Angeles, to celebrate and preserve the Japanese American legacy.

The redress campaign brought the generations together. Many Sansei activists worked in the redress campaigns and cultural exhibitions, and their parents' newfound ability to talk about redress brought other Sansei back in touch with their ethnic communities for the first time in years. The talking between the generations was helpful, too, in reducing the intensity of what the Sansei psychologist Donna Nagata called "the transgenerational consequences of traumatic stress."[42]

The redress movement also tied Japanese Americans to non-Japanese. Some Sansei activists began to reach out to other people who had been or might be interned—Navajos, Iranians, and Arabs.[43] Some Whites groused about the payments at first, but most Americans joined with Japanese Americans in remembering their experience and honoring their struggle. Several of the concentration camps were named national or state historical sites, and the Smithsonian put on a concentration camp exhibit. A memorial to the Nisei soldiers of World War II was designed. The movement for Japanese American redress brought unity and healing both within the Japanese American community and between Japanese Americans and their fellow citizens of other races.

The Cases

A second lingering issue from World War II continued to bother Japanese Americans four decades after Hiroshima: the Supreme Court decisions that had validated their imprisonment. In 1981, Peter Irons, a Massachusetts legal scholar, found some documents in federal archives that he believed proved government lawyers had lied to the courts and suppressed evidence that would have kept Gordon Hirabayashi, Min Yasui, and Fred Korematsu out of jail. He took his evidence to the three men and to a group of Japanese American lawyers led by the Bay Area activist Dale Minami. Minami, Rod Kawakami, and the other lawyers brought cases on behalf of all three men in federal courts in San Francisco, Portland, and Seattle under an obscure legal doctrine called *coram nobis*. The government countered by asking the courts to vacate the three men's convictions but refrain from ruling on the central issues of racism and government misconduct in the internment cases.

The government won in Min Yasui's case, and Yasui died before he could complete appeals. Korematsu and Hirabayashi, on the other hand, were vindicated. Korematsu, a shy man, nonetheless spoke up to Judge Marilyn Patel: "Your Honor, I still remember forty years ago when I was handcuffed and arrested as a criminal here in San Francisco. . . . As long as my record stands in federal court, any American citizen can be held in prison or concentration camps without a trial or a hearing. . . . I would like to see the government admit that they were wrong and do something about it so this will never happen again to any American citizen of any race, creed or color." Hirabayashi, blunter and more ebullient, said to reporters, "Ancestry is not a crime." Seattle Judge Donald Voorhees, in ruling for Hirabayashi, wrote: "It is now conceded by almost everyone that the internment of Japanese Americans during World War II was simply a tragic mistake for which American society as a whole must accept responsibility. If, in the future, this country should find itself in a comparable national emergency, the sacrifices made by Gordon Hirabayashi, Fred Korematsu, and Minoru Yasui may, it is hoped, stay the hand of a government again tempted to imprison a defenseless minority without trial and for no offense."[44] The case was finally closed.

The JACL

One of the corollaries to the redress movement was the renewed controversy in the 1980s over the role the JACL had played during the war. There had always been grumbling in the community, and JACL's power and purpose had always been greater outside the community than within it. The JACL was caught behind the curve on the movement for reparations; indeed, some of its prominent leaders never endorsed redress. However, playing catchup and using their formidable organizational experience and Washington connections, the new generation of JACL leaders took on an important role in the redress struggle. They also reached beyond the Japanese American community on occasion—for example, in opposing immigration restriction laws.

Yet the JACL remained unable to overcome its past. At the group's 1988 convention in Seattle, some members called for the league to acknowledge and apologize for opposing the draft resisters during the war and engaging in other acts of collaboration with the U.S. government's imprisonment of Japanese Americans. No action was immediately forthcoming, but the league did hire a researcher, Deborah Lim, to gather information. Two years later, the organization managed a backhanded acknowledgment of the draft resisters. In the meantime, the journalist James Omura and the draft resisters, like Hirabayashi and Korematsu, had become community celebrities. But the Lim report that the JACL finally issued to its membership was sanitized and stripped of its most damning evidence of wartime collaboration. Much to the dismay of some JACL advocates, copies of the complete draft report circulated widely nonetheless.[45]

Japanese Americans and White Attitudes toward Japan

Most White Americans were fairly positive about Japanese Americans in the Sansei era. They admired the achievement and family values they perceived to be Japanese American traits, and they frequently seemed to regard Japanese Americans as "honorary Whites." As Whites became more aware of the World War II concentration camps and of the principled response of Japanese Americans like Gordon Hirabayashi and William Hohri, they seemed willing to apologize on behalf of their own ancestors and to make amends. Hirabayashi and Korematsu were honored for their stands by legal and educational institutions. The University of California and many West Coast high schools marked the 50th anniversary of the imprisonment by inviting back those who would have graduated in June 1942 for much-belated commencement ceremonies. The *San Francisco Examiner* chose the anniversary to apologize for its support of internment.

On the other hand, the 1980s and 1990s have witnessed a dark undercurrent of animosity against Japan, a current that has occasionally burst forth into public acts against Japanese Americans. This animosity resulted not from domestic politics but from international economics. Americans have felt increasingly insecure about their ability to compete in a global marketplace. There have been strong calls for protectionist legislation against Japanese goods and investments—though not, significantly, against the larger quantities of goods and investments that flow from Europe. There was a great hue and cry when Japanese businesspeople bought Rockefeller Center and the Seattle Mariners baseball team, but not when British businesspeople bought Holiday Inn, which constitutes a much larger chunk of the American economy. Japanese auto manufacturers have been a particular target of protectionist, even xenophobic sentiment, and Japan-bashing a staple of editorial pages and late-night talk-show comedy.

Occasionally, all the talk has burst into action directed against Asian Americans. On 19 June 1982, a young Chinese American named Vincent Chin was celebrating his upcoming wedding in a Detroit bar. Two unemployed White autoworkers harassed Chin, called him a "Jap," and blamed him for the state of the U.S. auto industry and for their joblessness. They followed Chin out of the bar and beat him with a baseball bat, causing injuries from which he died four days later. The murderers—there is no other word for them—pleaded guilty to manslaughter and were sentenced to probation and a small fine. Among the grounds on which they claimed mitigating circumstances was the fact that they had thought Chin was a Japanese American.[46]

Crude hate letters were sent to Mary Tsukamoto, an elderly redress leader in Florin, California, as well as to the JACL's San Francisco office. Other community leaders received threatening letters and phone calls. On the 50th anniversary of Pearl Harbor, three Molotov cocktails were thrown at the home of an elderly Japanese American couple in San Leandro, California. The Pearl Harbor anniversary also sparked a rash of anti-Japanese remarks by local and national political figures, from a supervisor in Imperial County, California, to Michigan's U.S. Senator Donald Riegle. In February 1992, the businessman Yasuo Kato was found stabbed to death in his home, days after two White men tried to force their way into his house, screaming that he was Japanese and the Japanese were hurting the American economy. Japanese American Girl Scouts in Los Angeles approached several White potential customers, only to be told that they would only buy from Americans.

Later that year, on 17 October, the exchange student Yoshihiro Hattori and a friend, Webb Haymaker, rang the doorbell of the home of Rodney Peairs in Baton Rouge, Louisiana. They were looking for a Halloween party. According to a newspaper account based on Haymaker's testimony: "They rang the doorbell at the wrong house. When a woman answered the door, Webb Haymaker, realizing the mistake, said, 'Excuse me,' and the boys started walking away from the house, according to Richard Haymaker [Webb's father]. Moments later, as the boys had reached the end of an alley, a man appeared from the side door and asked the boys to come back, said Haymaker. When they did, a shot rang out and Hattori fell to the ground."[47] Hattori died; Peairs admitted pulling the trigger but was acquitted of any wrongdoing.

These are just a few of the many incidents of discrimination, threats, and violence directed against Japanese and other Asian Americans in the 1980s and 1990s. These incidents did not change the place Japanese Americans have made for themselves in the United States in the decades following World War II. They did not change the high level of Sansei achievement and integration into American society. They did not reduce the spread of Japanese Americans across the land. But they did threaten Japanese American self-confidence. Ron Wakabayashi of the Los Angeles County Human Relations Commission said in February 1992, before the Hattori slaying: "I see so many members of the Japanese-American community fearful once again. I didn't think that would happen again [after the success of the redress movement]. I thought we turned the corner, and I was wrong. You know, I can't tell you how sad I am that I'm wrong."[48]

Shall I Be Japanese American? Identity at the Close of the Twentieth Century

What, then, is the fate of Japanese American identity in the last years of the twentieth century? One might suppose that Japanese American ethnicity is about to disappear. The third generation, coming of age after 1965, has found itself low in all three areas affecting ethnic group cohesion: interests, institutions, and culture. The cultural connection to things Japanese has all but disappeared. Few Sansei speak Japanese or observe the nuances of interpersonal behavior that their parents recognized and their grandparents had valued. Sansei who live in a few heavily Japanese American places such as Honolulu and Gardena, California, speak among themselves an informal language whose codes tend to separate them from mainstream Americans. But most Sansei across the country have entered more or less fully into mainstream American cultural life and modes of expression.

Japanese American institutions do not organize people's lives very much anymore. To be sure, there continue to be Japanese community baseball leagues in some areas, and the San Francisco Cherry Blossom Festival has never quite died out. Some institutions—churches and the JACL—are as strong as ever, but they mobilize a shrinking percentage of the people. With 40 percent of the mainland Japanese population located east of the Rocky Mountains and most of the rest living in White suburbs on the West Coast, many Japanese Americans are connected to Japanese community institutions by little more than sporadic ritual behavior. Finally, it seems that the Sansei and Yonsei are so scattered and diverse that they share virtually no common interests.

Some observers might predict that Japanese Americans are on a straight-line train for ethnic oblivion. Yet in the 1970s, 1980s, and 1990s, ethnic interests began to reemerge. A remnant of Sansei became ethnic activists and central players in the Asian American movement. They worked self-consciously both to enhance the salience of Japanese American ethnicity and to broaden it to encompass a wider pan-Asian identity. There was a modest uptick of Japanese American ethnicity, based on two renewed common interests: (1) the successful movement to gain redress from the U.S. government for the wrongs of the World War II concentration camps, and (2) fear that Japan-bashing would increase hostility against and harassment of Japanese Americans. As the century approaches its close, it may be that these interests will prove strong enough to revivify Japanese American institutions and especially Japanese American culture, or it may be that other common interests will emerge. The tasks for

Table 7.3   *Japanese Americans in the Third Generation, 1965–*

Interests	low	**medium**	high
Culture	**low**	medium	high
Institutions	**low**	medium	high

those who would strengthen Japanese American ethnicity are: (1) to find ways to include the outlying members of their population—suburbanites, nonpartici-pants in community institutions, intermarriers and their children—in Japanese American culture, interests, and institutions, and (2) to identify new interests that may bind the group together.

Appendix

Tables

Table 1   Japanese Immigration to the United States, 1861–1990

1861–1870	186
1871–1880	149
1881–1890	2,270
1891–1900	25,942
1901–1910	129,797
1911–1920	83,837
1921–1930	33,462
1931–1940	1,948
1941–1950	1,555
1951–1960	46,250
1961–1970	39,988
1971–1980	49,775
1981–1990	47,085

SOURCE: U.S. Immigration and Naturalization Service, *Statistical Yearbook of the Immigration and Naturalization Service* (Washington: Government Printing Office, 1993), 26–28.

Table 2   Japanese American Population by State and Region, 1880–1990

Region or State	1880	1890	1900	1910	1920	1930	1940	1950	1960	1970	1980	1990
Total US (incl. Hawaii)	256	14,637	85,393	151,705	220,122	277,943	284,731	326,276	463,568	587,246	716,331	847,562
Hawaii	116ᵃ	12,610	61,111	79,675	109,274	139,631	157,905	184,598	203,455	217,175	239,734	247,486
Pacific Coast	88	1,532	18,269	57,703	93,490	119,892	112,353	98,310	178,985	240,532	306,328	361,217
Alaskaᵇ										854	1,545	2,066
California	86	1,147	10,151	41,356	71,952	97,456	93,717	84,956	157,317	213,277	268,814	312,989
Oregon	2	25	2,501	3,418	4,151	4,598	4,071	3,660	5,016	6,213	8,580	11,796
Washington	1	360	5,617	12,929	17,387	17,838	14,565	9,694	16,652	20,188	27,389	34,366
Mountain West	5	26	5,107	10,447	10,792	11,418	8,574	14,231	17,549	20,318	29,471	34,254
Arizona	2	1	281	371	550	879	632	780	1,501	2,530	4,629	6,302
Colorado		10	48	2,300	2,464	3,213	2,734	5,412	6,846	7,861	10,841	11,402
Idaho			1,291	1,363	1,569	1,421	1,191	1,980	2,254	2,012	3,102	2,719
Montana		6	2,441	1,585	1,074	753	508	524	589	613	803	829
Nevada	3	3	228	864	754	608	470	382	544	1,046	2,478	4,024
New Mexico		2	8	258	251	249	186	251	930	937	1,353	1,895
Utah		4	417	2,110	2,936	3,269	2,210	4,452	4,371	4,862	5,508	6,500
Wyoming			393	1,596	1,194	1,026	643	450	514	457	757	583
North Central	8	117	349	1,482	2,142	2,205	1,571	18,734	29,318	42,670	46,254	63,210
Illinois	3	14	80	285	472	564	462	11,646	14,074	17,645	18,432	21,831
Indiana		18	5	38	81	71	29	318	1,093	2,100	2,503	4,715
Iowa		1	7	36	29	19	29	310	599	733	1,024	1,619
Kansas		4	4	107	52	37	19	116	1,362	1,566	1,611	2,037
Michigan		38	9	49	184	176	139	1,517	3,211	5,464	6,460	10,681
Minnesota	1	2	51	67	85	69	51	1,049	1,726	2,693	3,191	3,581
Missouri	1	6	9	99	135	94	74	527	1,473	2,320	2,897	3,391
Nebraska		2	3	590	804	674	480	619	905	1,253	1,212	1,574
North Dakota		1		59	72	91	83	61	127	312	225	245
Ohio	3	22	148	76	130	187	163	1,986	3,135	5,896	6,271	10,485
South Dakota			1	42	38	19	19	56	188	199	305	286
Wisconsin		9	5	34	60	24	23	529	1,425	2,449	2,123	2,765

South	5	116	66	610	973	1,126	1,049	3,055	16,245	28,504	47,631	67,193
Alabama		3	3	4	18	25	21	88	500	1,043	1,427	2,028
Arkansas			1	9	5	12	3	113	237	588	697	957
Delaware		1	7	4	8	8	22	14	152	432	412	690
Dist. of Columbia	4	14	1	47	103	78	68	353	900	716	808	1,029
Florida		5	1	50	106	153	154	238	1,315	3,968	5,667	8,505
Georgia		3		4	9	32	31	128	885	1,334	3,596	6,372
Kentucky		39		12	9	9	9	74	774	920	1,170	2,513
Louisiana		7	17	31	57	52	46	127	519	876	1,671	1,526
Maryland		7	9	24	29	38	36	289	1,842	3,637	4,656	6,617
Mississippi	1			2	1	1	1	62	178	378	583	700
North Carolina	1			2	24	17	21	98	1,265	2,088	3,594	5,040
Oklahoma				48	67	104	57	137	749	1,214	2,249	2,385
South Carolina					8	15	33	34	460	675	1,584	1,885
Tennessee	6	4		8	8	11	12	104	507	857	1,752	3,440
Texas	3	13		340	449	519	458	957	4,053	6,216	12,084	14,795
Virginia		16	14	14	56	43	74	193	1,733	3,296	5,173	7,931
West Virginia	3	3	10	3	10	9	3	46	176	266	508	780
Northeast	33	236	491	1,788	3,451	3,851	3,279	7,348	18,016	38,047	47,913	74,202
Connecticut	6	18	18	71	102	130	164	254	653	1,517	1,841	3,811
Maine		1	4	13	7	3	5	30	343	215	302	590
Massachusetts		7	9	24	29	38	36	289	1,842	3,637	4,290	8,784
New Hampshire		2	1	1	8		5	30	343	252	356	747
New Jersey	2	22	52	206	325	439	298	1,784	3,514	6,344	10,263	17,253
New York	17	148	354	1,247	2,686	2,930	2,538	3,893	8,702	19,794	24,754	35,281
Pennsylvania	8	32	40	190	255	293	224	1,029	2,348	5,417	4,422	6,613
Rhode Island		5	13	33	35	17	6	25	192	744	464	750
Vermont	1			3	4	1	3	14	79	73	221	373

[a] 1884.

[b] Not separately available before 1970.

SOURCES: Harry H. L. Kitano, *Japanese Americans*, 2nd ed. (Englewood Cliff, N.J.: Prentice-Hall, 1976), 210–11; Andrew Lind, *Hawaii's People* (Honolulu: University of Hawaii Press, 1955); Yamato Ichihashi, *Japanese Immigration* (San Francisco: 1915); 18; William Petersen, *Japanese Americans* (New York: Random House, 1971), 22; U.S. Bureau of the Census, *Nonwhite Population by Race*, Subject Report PC2–1C (Washington, D.C.: Government Printing Office, 1963); U.S. Bureau of the Census, *Japanese, Chinese, and Filipinos in the United States*, Subject Report PC2–1G (Washington, D.C.: Government Printing Office, 1973); U.S. Bureau of the Census, *Asian and Pacific Islander Population by State: 1980*, Supplementary Report PC80-S1–12 (Washington, D.C.: Government Printing Office, December 1983), 12; "Census Bureau Releases 1990 Census Counts on Specific Racial Groups," *U.S. Department of Commerce News* (12 June 1991).

Table 3   Japanese Aliens Admitted to and Departed from the United States, 1891–1942

Year/ Decade	Issei Admitted	Issei Departed[a]	Year/ Decade	Issei Admitted	Issei Departed
1891	1,136		1921	10,615	11,638
1892	1,498		1922	8,981	11,173
1893	1,380		1923	8,055	8,393
1894	1,931		1924	11,526	9,248
1895	1,150		1925	3,222	7,265
1896	1,110		1926	4,652	7,751
1897	1,526		1927	5,477	8,192
1898	2,230		1928	5,935	8,016
1899	3,395		1929	6,293	7,281
1900	12,628		1930	6,274	7,490
1891–1900	27,984		1921–30	71,030	86,447
1901	4,911		1931	5,810	7,124
1902	5,330		1932	4,137	6,138
1903	6,996		1933	3,065	6,225
1904	7,792		1934	2,927	5,368
1905	4,329		1935	3,483	5,333
1906	5,192		1936	3,719	4,855
1907	9,959		1937	4,254	5,140
1908	9,544	4,796	1938	3,908	4,610
1909	2,432	5,004	1939	3,200	4,265
1910	2,698	5,024	1940	2,942	4,206
1900–10	59,083		1931–40	37,445	53,264
1911	4,282	5,869	1941	2,642	4,974
1912	5,358	5,437	1942	480	1,600
1913	6,771	5,647			
1914	8,462	6,300			
1915	9,029	5,967			
1916	9,100	6,922			
1917	9,159	6,581			
1918	11,143	7,691			
1919	11,404	8,328			
1920	12,868	11,662			
1911–20	87,516	70,404			

a. Figures for Issei departures not available before fiscal 1908.

SOURCE: Dorothy S. Thomas, Charles Kikuchi, and James Sakoda, *The Salvage* (Berkeley: University of California Press, 1952), 573.

Table 4   Percentage of Males Among Japanese Emigrants to U.S.

Year	Percent Male
1898	83.8
1900	91.4[a]
1907	77.8[b]
1911	51.6
1919	60.5[c]
1924	60.2

a. Japanese government limits labor immigration.
b. Gentlemen's agreement.
c. Japanese government bans picture brides.
SOURCE: Tomonori Ishikawa, "A Statistical Analysis of Japanese Emigrants,"
Geographical Science, 11 (May 1969), cited in Yasuo Wakatsuki, "Japanese Emigration to the
United States, 1866–1924," *Perspectives in American History,* 12 (1979), 513.

Table 5   Issei Characteristics by Arrival before or after Gentlemen's Agreement

Characteristic	Arrived before Gentlemen's Agreement (to 1907)	Arrived after Gentlemen's Agreement (1909 or later)
Median age on arrival	19.0	17.5
Socioeconomic level of parents in Japan		
Low	6%	11%
Medium	53	57
High	41	32
Father's occupation in Japan		
Farm proprietor	49%	45%
Farm laborer	25	27
Nonagricultural	26	28
Student in Japan		
Yes	41%	80%
No	59	20
Relatives in United States at arrival		
Yes	41%	60%
No	59	40
Parents in United States at arrival		
Yes	5%	58%
No	95	42
Intended upon arrival to stay in United States permanently		
Yes	15%	36%
No	85	64
Total number of cases in survey	336	348

SOURCE: John Modell, "Tradition and Opportunity: The Japanese Immigrant in America," *Pacific Historical Review* (1973): 166.

Table 6   Age, Sex, and Generational Group of Japanese American
Concentration Camp Inmates, 1942

| | | Males | | | Females | |
Age	Issei	Kibei	Nisei	Issei	Kibei	Nisei
0–4	18		4,165	13		3,860
5–9	25		3,584	34		3,520
10–14	36	27	4,737	41	28	4,626
15–19	68	525	7,379	64	346	7,387
20–24	120	1,848	6,069	139	1,348	6,601
25–29	147	1,755	3,116	129	1,503	3,265
30–34	303	911	2,667	274	703	1,240
35–39	1,652	405	706	1,625	211	125
40–44	2,812	127	302	3,336	61	125
45–49	1,896	37	93	3,792	21	59
50–54	3,415	25	25	2,725	7	14
55–59	4,851	2	5	1,529		6
60–64	4,339	1	3	960		1
65–69	2,429			464		
70–74	810		4	130	1	8
75+	290			54		
Total	23,211	5,663	31,640	15,309	4,229	31,118

SOURCE: Dorothy S. Thomas, Charles Kikuchi, and James Sakoda, *The Salvage* (Berkeley: University of California Press, 1952), 580.

Table 7 Ratio of Men to Women Emigrants From Wakayama to the United States,[a]
1898–1924

Year	Males	Females	Females per 100 Males
1898	291	1	0.3
1899	1,769	56	3.2
1900	534	0	0.0
1901	181	6	3.3
1902	407	14	3.4
1903	685	44	6.4
1904	883	59	6.7
1905	606	62	10.2
1906	1,225	91	7.4
1907	794	113	14.2
1908	235	116	49.4
1909	86	91	105.8
1910	149	156	104.7
1911	0	0	0
1912	122	148	121.3
1913	381	310	81.4
1914	508	381	75.0
1915	577	352	61.0
1916	549	374	68.1
1917	568	483	85.0
1918	567	520	91.7
1919	567	520	91.7
1920	482	500	103.7
1921	544	368	67.6
1922	461	347	75.3
1923	416	276	66.3
1924	512	357	69.7

a. Includes Hawaii.

SOURCE: Yasuo Wakatsuki, "Japanese Emigration to the United States, 1866–1924," *Perspectives in American History,* 12 (1979): 514.

Table 8 First and Second Jobs and Principal Occupations of Issei in the United States[a]

Job Category	First Job	Second Job	Principal Occupation
Professional and technical	2%	1%	4%
Farmer	42	42	45
Manager, official, proprietor	3	12	28
Clerical and sales	3	5	2
Craftsperson, foreman	1	3	4
Operative	7	8	4
Private household service	20	15	5
Labor (nonfarm)	20	14	10

a. Survey of 901 Issei in the 1960s.

SOURCE: Gene N. Levine and R. Colbert Rhodes, "Japanese Community: Persistence and Transformation over Three Generations" (unpublished manuscript, 1977), 50.

Table 9 Japanese American Landholdings in California, 1905–1925 *(in acres)*

Year	Contract	Type of Landholding Share Lease	Cash Lease	Owned	Total
1905	4,775	19,573	35,258	2,442	61,858
1906	22,100	24,826	41,855	8,671	97,452
1907	13,359	48,228	56,889	13,815	131,292
1908	26,128	57,578	55,971	15,114	155,581
1909	42,276	57,001	80,232	16,449	195,958
1910	37,898	50,399	89,464	16,980	194,742
1911	49,443	62,070	110,442	17,765	239,720
1912	38,473	56,053	124,656	26,571	245,753
1913	48,997	50,495	155,488	26,707	281,687
1914	41,300	72,040	155,206	31,828	300,474
1918	23,608	336,721		30,306	390,635
1920	70,137	121,000	192,150	74,769	458,056
1922		279,511		50,542	330,653
1925		263,058		41,898	304,966

SOURCES: Yuji Ichioka, *Issei* (New York: Free Press, 1988), 150,155; Yamato Ichihashi, *Japanese in the United States* (Stanford, Calif.: Stanford University Press, 1932), 193.

Table 10   Japanese American Populations of Selected Cities, 1910–1970

City	1910	1920	1930	1940	1950[a]	1960[a]	1970[a]
Chicago				390	11,233	12,907	15,732
Denver				323	3,329	4,816	5,635
Honolulu						150,570	169,025
Los Angeles	4,238	11,618	21,081	23,321	37,809	82,261	104,994
New York				2,087	3,716	7,818	16,630
Oakland[b]	1,520	2,709	2,137	1,790			
Portland				1,680		2,963	
Sacramento	1,437	1,976	3,347	2,879	5,288	8,374	11,958
San Diego				828		5,164	7,621
San Francisco	4,518	5,358	6,250	5,280	13,762	24,444	33,587
San Jose					5,979	10,326	15,177
Seattle				6,975	6,837	10,982	14,079

a. Standard Metropolitan Statistical Areas (SMSAs).
b. Oakland subsumed under San Francisco SMSA after 1950.

SOURCES: U.S. Bureau of the Census, *Sixteenth Census of the United States: 1940. Population. Characteristics of the Nonwhite Population by Race*, (Washington, D.C.: Government Printing Office, 1943), 6; idem., *U.S. Census of Population: 1950. Nonwhite Population by Race*, Special Report P-E, No. 3B (Washington, D.C.: Government Printing Office, 1953), 63; idem., *U.S. Census of Population: 1960. Nonwhite Population by Race*, Subject Report PC[2]-1C (Washington, D.C.: Government Printing Office, 1963), 214; idem., *1970 Census of Population. Japanese, Chinese, and Filipinos in the United States*, Subject Report PC[2]-1G (Washington, D.C.: Government Printing Office, 1973), 50–51; Yamato Ichihashi, *Japanese in the United States* (Stanford, Calif.: Stanford University Press, 1932), 100.

Table 11 Occupations of Employed Japanese Americans, 1900–1940

	Men			
Occupation	1900	1920	1930	1940
Agriculture, forestry, animal husbandry	5,345	23,860	22,454	17,733
Extraction of minerals	168	1,119	680	
Manufacturing	826	6,424	3,508	3,962[a]
Transportation	6,277	4,273	2,290	
Trade and clerical	198	5,306	7,476	9,125
Public service		119	89	
Professional	132	1,150	1,641	1,254
Domestic and personal services	9,058	10,363	9,351	4,491
Nonfarm labor				4,499
Other	336			258
Total	22,340	52,614	47,489	41,322

	Women			
Occupation	1900	1920	1930	1940
Agriculture, forestry, animal husbandry	13	1,797	2,041	2,525
Domestic and personal services	208	2,360	2,658	2,269
Trade and clerical	9	444	1,217	683
Manufacturing	31	502	468	801
Professional	5	145	329	214
Other		41	27	201
Total	266	5,289	6,741	6,693

a. Includes workers in transportation and extraction of materials.

SOURCE: Evelyn Nakano Glenn, *Issei, Nisei, War Bride* (Philadelphia: Temple University Press, 1986), 70–73.

Table 12   Japanese American Religious Affiliations

Place/Group	Year	Buddhist	Christian	Shinto	Sample Total
Los Angeles[a]	1924	3,140	972	780	4,892
California	1930	3,525	1,294		4,819
Issei		3,000	681		3,681
Nisei		525	613		1,138
Seattle[a]	1936	800	1,200	120	2,120
Tule Lake[b]	1943	7,197	2,469		9,666
Former North-					
west residents					
Total		2,360	1,096		3,456
Issei		1,364	335		1,699
Kibei		271	69		340
Nisei		725	692		1,417
Former Cali-					
fornia residents					
Total		4,837	1,373		6,210
Issei		2,360	452		2,812
Kibei		753	97		850
Nisei		1,724	824		2,548

a. Only the Los Angeles and Seattle studies included a separate category for Shinto. Presumably, Shintoists are to be found among the Buddhists in the other studies.

b. The Tule Lake study also included a category for "secularists" which has been eliminated here.

SOURCES: Gretchen Tuthill, "A Study of the Japanese in the City of Los Angeles" (M.A. thesis, University of Southern California, 1924), 66–67; Edward K. Strong, *Japanese in California* (Stanford, Calif.: Stanford University Press, 1933), 168; S. Frank Miyamoto, *Social Solidarity among the Japanese in Seattle*, rev. ed. (1939; Seattle: University of Washington Press, 1984), 45; Dorothy S. Thomas, Charles Kikuchi, and James Sakoda, *The Salvage* (Berkeley: University of California Press, 1952), 607.

Table 13 Arrest Rates for Selected Ethnic Groups, Honolulu, 1902–1970

Ethnic Group	1902	1940	1950	1960	1970
Japanese	1.1%	3.5%	2.1%	1.9%	6.6%
Chinese	3.0	13.3	7.2	8.7	5.9
White	5.3	3.7	4.3	14.6	24.6
Hawaiian	6.1				
Black		13.3	13.7	56.4	74.8
Native American		10.9	21.4	136.9	165.2

SOURCES: William Petersen, *Japanese Americans* (New York: Random House, 1971), 135; Harry H. L. Kitano, *Japanese Americans*, 2nd ed. (Englewood Cliffs, N.J.: Prentice-Hall, 1976), 145.

Table 14 Changes in Nisei Neighborhood Ethnicity, 1915–1967

Year	Japanese American	Mixed	Non-Japanese American	Sample Total
1915	30%	33%	37%	183
1920	22	38	39	566
1925	21	41	39	1,151
1930	19	43	38	1,550
1935	19	44	38	1,801
1940	17	45	38	1,952
1945	13	36	51	1,882
1950	10	44	47	2,241
1955	6	44	50	2,243
1960	5	43	52	2,261
1965	4	41	55	2,279
1967	4	38	58	2,295

SOURCE: UCLA Japanese American Research Project, reported in Darrel Montero, *Japanese Americans: Changing Patterns of Ethnic Affiliation over Three Generations* (Boulder, Colo.: Westview, 1980), 39; Gene N. Levine and Colbert Rhodes, *The Japanese American Community* (New York: Praeger, 1981), 46.

Table 15   Nisei Education Compared with Non-Japanese American Education

Years of School Completed	Males Nisei[a]	Males Non-Japanese[b]	Females Nisei[a]	Females Non-Japanese[b]
None	81	63	100	31
Grade School				
1–4	174	195	126	90
5–6	198	280	185	147
7–8	1,223	1,396	957	774
High School				
1–3	1,040	1,501	740	1,110
4	2,557	1,833	2,036	1,678
College				
1–3	680	728	310	544
4 or more	605	566	242	331
No report	64	61	33	24
Total	6,622	6,622	4,729	4,729

a. The Japanese American sample included former residents of California and Washington in WRA camps in 1942, aged 25 and over, and indicated their educational levels as of 1940.

b. The non-Japanese numbers represent a sample of the same size allocated according to norms derived from the 1940 census.

SOURCE: Dorothy S. Thomas, Charles Kikuchi, and James Sakoda, *The Salvage* (Berkeley: University of California Press, 1952), 611.

Table 16   Issei versus Nisei Educational Attainments, 1930

Age 1930	Issei Mean School Grade Completed Males	Issei Mean School Grade Completed Females	Nisei Mean School Grade Completed Males	Nisei Mean School Grade Completed Females
7–13	4.5	3.6	3.6	3.6
14–20	9.9	9.4	9.5	9.4
21–27	11.0	8.9	12.5	12.0
28–34	9.7	8.6	12.3	11.3
35–41	9.5	7.6	*	*
42–48	8.8	6.5	*	*
49–55	7.2	5.2	*	*
56–62	6.9	4.2	*	*
63+	6.0	*	*	*
Number of cases	2,349	1,843	1,820	1,685

*Too few cases to report means.

SOURCE: Edward K. Strong, *The Second-Generation Japanese Problem* (Stanford, Calif.: Stanford University Press, 1934; New York: Arno, 1970), 186.

Table 17   Occupations of Employed Nisei, Los Angeles, 1940

| | Los Angeles City | | Rest of Los Angeles County | |
Occupation	Males	Females	Males	Females
Professional, semiprofessional	3%	5%	1%	2%
Proprietor, manager, official	12	4	8	2
Clerical, sales	37	35	19	22
Craftsperson, foreman, operative	13	12	5	2
Nonfarm laborer	20	2	6	*

* Less than 0.5 percent.
SOURCE: John Modell, *The Economics and Politics of Racial Accommodation* (Urbana: University of Illinois Press, 1977), 130.

Table 18   Sources and Destinations of Inmates of
War Relocation Authority Camps, 1942–1946

From		To	
WCCA assembly centers:	90,491	Returned to West Coast:	54,127
Directly imprisoned:	17,491	Resettled to interior:	52,798
Born in camp:	5,918	Japan:	4,724
INS internment camps:	1,735	INS internment camps:	3,121
Seasonal workers (furloughed from assembly centers to work in agriculture, then to WRA):	1,579	Armed forces:	2,355
		Died:	1,862
		To institutions:	1,322
		Unauthorized departures:	4
Penal and medical institutions:	1,275		
Hawaii:	1,118		
Voluntary inmates (mainly non-Japanese spouses):	219		
Total population ever under WRA control:	120,313	Total:	120,313

SOURCE: Roger Daniels, "The Forced Migrations of West Coast Japanese Americans, 1942–1946: A Quantitative Note," in *Japanese Americans: From Evacuation to Redress,* Roger Daniels, Sandra C. Taylor, and Harry H. L. Kitano, ed. (Salt Lake City: University of Utah Press, 1986), 72–74.

Table 19   Occupations of Nisei and Sansei Men, 1979–1980

Occupation	Nisei Not Self-Employed	Nisei Self-Employed	Sansei Not Self-Employed	Sansei Self-Employed
Professional and technical	39.4%	23.7%	46.8%	55.2%
Managerial	10.1	9.3	14.1	4.9
Clerical and sales	16.0	9.3	21.8	13.1
Service	8.0	1.7	4.0	1.6
Agriculture, fishing, forestry	5.3	45.8	4.8	23.0
Trades	19.7	9.3	8.5	1.6
Miscellaneous	1.6	0.8	0.0	0.0

Sample total: 615

SOURCE: Stephen S. Fugita and David J. O'Brien, *Japanese American Ethnicity* (Seattle: University of Washington Press, 1991), 127.

Bibliographic Essay:
The State of Japanese American History

The study of Japanese American history has at last approached maturity as a field of study.[1] It was once a lonely field; only a few people toiled on projects that seemed most important to them. These days, a bustling, jostling crowd of scholars must clamor to make their individual voices heard. Once scholars in the field had very few arguments, for seldom did two people attack the same issue around the same time; when they did, they seem to have been so glad of each other's company that they muted their disagreements. Nowadays they have fights, at least occasionally, and have begun to express genuinely revisionist views. Yet for all the activity, it is curious that one topic, Japanese American imprisonment in the World War II concentration camps, has commanded so much attention, that there are still so many topics left almost untouched, and that the range of theoretical perspectives among students of Japanese American history has been so limited. Clearly, there is still a great deal of work to be done.

In the first four decades of this century, a number of people wrote about Japanese Americans, but almost none of them wrote history. These early students may be gathered in two groups. First were the sociologists and economists who sought simply to describe the social and economic conditions of Japanese immigration and life in America. Foremost among these was Yamato Ichihashi, whose *Japanese Immigration: Its Status in California* (1915) and *Japanese in the United States* (1932) remain the most comprehensive studies of the early years of the Issei generation. S. Frank Miyamoto added a particularly sensitive community study in 1939: *Social Solidarity among the Japanese in Seattle*. These scholars' efforts were echoed by a number of valuable social surveys of West Coast Japanese communities, most undertaken as graduate theses during the 1920s and 1930s.[2]

The other major group of writings on Japanese Americans consisted of spirited defenses of the Issei against those who wanted to bar them from the country. The most prominent of these writers was Kiyoshi Karl Kawakami, a suave gentleman and prolific author whose books and articles on both sides of the Pacific sought to interpret Japan and Japanese Americans to other Americans, and also America to the Japanese. Although some of the writers in this vein were professional academics, these were not scholarly analyses but rhetorical tracts designed to achieve the political end of defending Japanese Americans against their detractors.[3]

The writing about Japanese Americans continued to be dominated by social scientists through the 1940s and 1950s. During those decades, the Nisei generation came of age and the Japanese American people suffered what, to judge from the scholarship at least, was their formative experience: mass imprisonment during World War II. The writings of this period can also be divided into two categories. The smaller amount of work was devoted to describing the adjustment of second-generation Japanese Americans to life in White America. One particular focus here was cultural and personal conflict between the Nisei and their immigrant parents. Edward Strong heralded this trend by publishing *The Second-Generation Japanese Problem,* mainly a statistical study, in 1934. Emory Bogardus and Robert Ross weighed in with "The Second-Generation Race Relations Cycle" (1940), and Jitsuichi Masuoka wrote about "Race Relations and Nisei Problems" (1946). Other writers contributed accounts of Nisei culture and Issei-Nisei conflict, such as John Okada's powerful novel *No-No Boy* (1957) and two memoirs, Daisuke Kitagawa's *Issei and Nisei* (1967) and *Nisei Daughter* by Monica Sone (1953).[4]

By far the largest volume of writing by and about Japanese Americans has focused on the group's prison camp experience during World War II. With a couple of notable exceptions, most of the best work in this area was done by sociologists writing within a few years of the events. Yet people have continued to write about the camp episode for more than four decades. It has now become one of the most frequently described subjects in American history.

An excellent start on this subject—although controversial in its methodology—was made in the three volumes published by the University of California's Japanese American Evacuation and Resettlement Study. Dorothy Thomas and Richard Nishimoto focused on the camp experience itself, chronicling the tragic events at Tule Lake in *The Spoilage* (1946). Thomas, Charles Kikuchi, and James Sakoda followed up in 1952 with *The Salvage,* which reproduced large numbers of social statistics and many of Kikuchi's excellent interviews with Nisei who left the camps and settled in the Midwest. Two years later, the series was completed with a more interpretive study, *Prejudice, War, and the Constitution,* written by Jacobus tenBroek, Edward Barnhart, and Floyd Matson. This third book detailed the background of anti-Japanese prejudice, the social and ideological forces that led to imprisonment, and the implications of the episode for American constitutional guarantees. In decades since, other authors have added many important details and interpretations, but they have not revised the outlines set forth in this trilogy. That first generation of studies also included important reports by Leonard Broom, John Kitsuse, Ruth Riemer, Morton Grodzins, and Eugene Rostow.[5]

The federal government conducted the Japanese American imprisonment and also wrote a great deal about it. The government's published reports constitute an important source of raw data about the entire episode, although they seldom feature scholarly analysis and are open to the charge of special pleading. The most useful volumes for later scholars have been the *Final Report* of the army's Western Defense Command (1943); the *Hearings* conducted by the House Select Committee Investigating National Defense Migration—a euphemism for imprisonment—in 1942; and a statistical volume titled *The Evacuated People.*[6]

People have continued to write about the World War II camps down to this day. Many of these books and articles are interesting, challenging, heart-rending, uplifting. Some look at topics that the early writers neglected to explore. Only a few offer major new insights or interpretations. A chronological catalog of books that tell the old story well but add nothing new includes the following: Mine Okubo, *Citizen 13660* (1946—cartoons); Allan Bosworth, *America's Concentration Camps* (1967); Edward Spicer et al., *Impounded People: Japanese Americans in Relocation Centers* (1969, an expansion of a 1946 WRA publication); Audrie Girdner and Anne Loftis, *The Great Betrayal* (1969); Maisie and Richard Conrat, a photo-essay entitled *Executive Order 9066* (1972); Jeanne Wakatsuki Houston and James D. Houston, *Farewell to Manzanar* (1973); Michi Weglyn, *Years of Infamy* (1976); and Sandra Taylor, *Jewel of the Desert* (1993). Although most of these books are not written by professional historians, they constitute the first body of literature on Japanese Americans to reflect a historical viewpoint.[7]

One book that stands in this mainstream tradition yet has considerable interpretive edge is Roger Daniels's *Concentration Camps U.S.A.* (1971). This is the most widely read book on the World War II era, and the best treatment of the political aspects of the incarceration. Daniels offers clear ideas, pungent prose, and important revisions of Grodzins and tenBroek. He not only differs from all other writers in his detailed mining of government documents to understand the forces that caused the imprisonment but departs from earlier scholars in assigning blame for the episode. Grodzins credited West Coast pressure groups with forcing the evacuation. TenBroek and his colleagues blamed Lieutenant General John L. DeWitt, head of the army's Western Defense Command, as well as a pervasive White racism and fear-mongering. Grodzins believed that West Coast politicians could share the blame. On the basis of more thorough research in government documents, Daniels points to specific government officials: Colonel Karl R. Bendetsen, Provost Marshall General Allen W. Gullion, and ultimately, President Franklin Roosevelt himself. Daniels's book does not purport to be a study of the social dynamics attendant upon the camp experience; it is mainly a political study, and an excellent one. Daniels updated his book with postwar developments related to the incarceration in *Prisoners without Trial* (1993).[8]

Most of the books written on the war episode between 1955 and 1980 (Daniels excepted) embody some form of what Raymond Okamura calls the "WRA-JACL viewpoint." Okamura is speaking of the wartime collaboration between the Japanese American Citizens League and the War Relocation Authority. The WRA-JACL argument is that the imprisonment was an unfortunate situation but was overcome by Japanese American patriotism, virtue, and hard work and by sympathetic understanding from the WRA; that the human suffering involved was not very intense; and that there is no one to blame (except possibly General DeWitt or miscellaneous public opinion). This argument would have us forget about the bad parts and concentrate on the theme of people acting nobly under pressure. Even the books in this tradition that focus on the enormity of the wrongs done to Japanese Americans portray them as helpless victims, not self-conscious actors. Okamura argues that Weglyn departs from the WRA-JACL tradition in that she pictures some active resistance to imprisonment. But, as Gary Okihiro points out, Weglyn is still more interested in warning Americans about the potential loss of their civil liberties than she is in portraying the subtleties of Japanese American community culture or the underlying causes of resistance.[9]

Okihiro's writing constitutes a new point of departure for study of the prison camps. In several articles and reviews, beginning in the 1970s, Okihiro has contributed subtle analysis of Japanese American political culture. Where earlier authors (Thomas excepted) portrayed Japanese Americans merely as victims and noble sufferers, Okihiro depicted actors with clear motives for resistance to their imprisonment. My own work in this area shares some of Okihiro's point of view and delineates the cultural and political divisions in the early months of the war that crucially shaped the prison camp experience and postwar Japanese American society. *Views from Within*, a recent (1989) conference volume of uneven quality, brought the Japanese American Evacuation and Resettlement Study under scrutiny from a similar perspective.[10]

Since the late 1970s, a new group of studies has gone back to depicting Japanese Americans as victims, but with a new, activist twist. Indignant Japanese Americans have brought considerable political pressure to bear on Congress, the courts, and public opinion to redress the wrongs of the World War II era. Highlights of this trend have been the JACL's 1978 call for redress; the 1982 report of the Commission on Wartime Relocation and Internment of Civilians, emphatically titled *Personal Justice Denied;* Peter Irons's influential legal study, *Justice at War* (1983); John Tateishi's collection of interviews, *And Justice for All* (1984); *Japanese Americans: From Relocation to Redress* (1986; rev. 1991), a collection of essays edited by Roger Daniels, Sandra Taylor, and Harry Kitano; the activist William Hohri's *Repairing America* (1988); and Leslie Hatamiya's legislative account, *Righting a Wrong* (1993).[11]

The renewal of interest among Japanese Americans about the wartime incarceration has been paralleled by activity north of the border. The most complete book is a history of Japanese Canadians by the journalist Ken Adachi, *The Enemy That Never Was* (1976). Joy Kogawa's first novel, *Obasan* (1981), is the lyrical telling of the cruel Canadian camp experience from the point of view of a small girl.[12]

Starting in the 1960s, historians began to contribute as much as social scientists to the study of Japanese Americans. Many concentrated on the World War II concentration camps, but other topics captured their attention as well. Studies of Japanese Americans written by the generation that fought World War II can be divided into three types: (1) those that attack anti-Japanese bigotry; (2) those whose main concern is to marvel at the remarkable record achieved by what they regard as America's model minority; and (3) those that seek to describe the Nisei world in social scientific terms.

Roger Daniels is the foremost practitioner of the first school. *The Politics of Prejudice* (1966) is a cleanly crafted study of the California anti-Japanese movement and its national implications. Like much of Daniels's work, and by his own admission, this is not so much a history of Japanese Americans as a history of White Americans acting badly toward their Japanese countrymen. *Politics of Prejudice* is less a social history—it provides only a sketchy portrait of the lives of Japanese Americans—than it is a political history; it is excellent. Daniels followed with *Concentration Camps U.S.A.* (1971; later *Concentration Camps: North America* [1981]), *The Decision to Relocate the Japanese Americans* (1975), *Prisoners without Trial* (1993), and a host of articles and editing projects. Nearly all seem designed to combat the political manifestations of White racism.[13]

The Denver newspaperman Bill Hosokawa is the most prominent proponent of the second point of view. His three major books, *Nisei: The Quiet Americans* (1969), *East to America: A History of the Japanese in the United States* (1980, with Robert Wilson), and *JACL in Quest of Justice* (1982), are paeans of praise to the Nisei generation and to the JACL. William Petersen chimed in with an influential *New York Times* article, "Success Story: Japanese-American Style" (1966), and a book, *Japanese Americans* (1971). The JACL leader Mike Masaoka highlighted his own role in *They Call Me Moses Masaoka* (1987). Recent historians have fought with Hosokawa and his colleagues about their sanguine view of the JACL and of Nisei struggles.[14]

Authors such as William Caudill, George DeVos, Leonard Broom, John Kitsuse, and Stanford Lyman wrote descriptive, social scientific studies of contemporary Japanese Americans during the 1950s and 1960s. These culminated in 1969 in Harry Kitano's *Japanese Americans* (rev. ed., 1976), a work that weds the historical base of the author's experience growing up in Japanese America to the theoretical base of Milton Gordon's ideas about ethnicity and assimilation. Some have argued that Kitano's assimilation-versus-pluralism model ought to be replaced by an internal colonialism model or the model proposed in this book, yet none can fail to see the authenticity of Kitano's rendering of Japanese American society.[15]

After about 1970, a new generation of scholars, many of them historians, began to address Japanese American history. Most of them, having come of age in the late 1960s and early 1970s in the context of the Asian American movement and leftist politics generally, carried activist visions of the purposes of scholarship. They had a hand in creating, and benefited from, unprecedented resources for scholarly work: Asian American studies programs around the country (in particular, the Asian American Studies Center at UCLA); archival sources such as the Japanese American Research Project at UCLA; bibliographical tools; the Asian American Studies Association; and publishing venues such as *Amerasia Journal,* the University of Hawai'i Press, and others.[16]

Like many of their generation, they made the gestalt shift from the consensus ideas of such scholars as Richard Hofstadter and Arthur Schlesinger Jr. to the power-conflict models of William Appleman Williams, Herbert Gutman, and others. They tended to address social rather than political history and wanted to create an understanding of social life from the bottom up. They treated Japanese Americans as actors rather than pawns. Their perspectives and concerns reflected not only their personal convictions about history but also trends in American historical studies in general.[17]

A few writers began to use the techniques of the new social history. There was a blossoming of oral history, after the fashion of Studs Terkel's celebrated histories of World War II and the Depression.[18] Some scholars showed themselves willing to pursue the panoply of quantitative techniques used by econometric historians.[19] More important, Japanese American historians tried, like historians in other fields, to give voice to the voiceless. One thinks particularly of Yuji Ichioka and Donald Hata's attempts to portray the lives of lumpen proletarians of the Issei generation.[20] Dennis Ogawa, Gary Okihiro, and Valerie Matsumoto have written community studies of Hawai'i, the Santa Clara Valley, and the San Joaquin Valley, respectively. There is need for a large number of such studies, to flesh out our knowledge of the variety among Japanese Americans and to test theoretical constructs.[21]

Most particularly, scholars have begun to study the immigrant generation. One is grateful for the groundwork laid by Masakazu Iwata and for more recent work by John Modell, Yasuo Wakatsuki, Akemi Kikumura, and Yoshiko Uchida.[22] But preeminently this territory belongs to Yuji Ichioka. After more than two decades of carefully building the foundations, brick by brick, for understanding the Issei, Ichioka in 1988 published *The Issei*, a first-rate institutional history that, together with more evocative accounts such as Uchida's, lays a base for future studies of Japanese immigrants. One aspect of Issei history that has been too little treated is the background to emigration, although Alan Moriyama and Yasuo Wakatsuki have made an effective start here.[23]

Labor history has been a particular preoccupation of the new group of scholars, and of some older writers as well. One reason is simply that most Japanese of the immigrant generation were laborers, at least in the beginning; to tell their story is to write labor history. Another reason is probably related to the leftward bent of much of the currently middle-aged generation of ethnic studies scholars. More than most historians of earlier generations, they tend to see the working class as critically important. Like E. P. Thompson and a host of historians in other fields, Japanese American historians have begun to look at the working class as a distinct entity. Some of the labor studies, such as those by Karl Yoneda, Yuji Ichioka, and John Modell, focus specifically on Japanese Americans. Others, such as Ronald Takaki's *Pau Hana* (1983) and Cletus Daniel's *Bitter Harvest* (1982), offer suggestive comparisons with other laboring groups.[24]

Even as some scholars have turned their attention to the working class, others have come to an understanding of the Japanese *middle* class as a class phenomenon. Edna Bonacich and John Modell have done the most work in this area, in *The Economic Basis of Ethnic Solidarity* (1980). Their concentration on middle-class formation is part of a larger trend in historical studies, of which the writings of such people as Mary Ryan and Paul Johnson are representative.[25]

Gender and family studies have been other areas of great growth in the historical profession in recent years. On feminist issues, Evelyn Nakano Glenn and Valerie Matsumoto have emerged as the major scholars for Japanese American studies. Glenn has written articles and a book on Japanese American women and domestic service over the course of the twentieth century; Matsumoto has produced a finely tuned study of a Japanese farming community over several decades that is especially sensitive to gender perspectives. The most exciting work on Japanese American family life comes from Sylvia Yanagisako: *Transforming the Past* (1985) is not only a stimulating social history of the Japanese American family but also a significant step forward in the study of American kinship. Joan Hori, Laurie Mengel, Yuji Ichioka, Akemi Kikumura, Yoshiko Uchida, Mei Nakano, and John Modell have all done significant work on women's and family studies.[26] Along with class, gender, and local histories have come a few studies of ethnic subgroups within the Japanese American group, specifically of Okinawans, both in Hawai'i and on the U.S. mainland.[27]

Theoretical work has been another encouraging area of growth in the past decade and a half. Historians have been involved here, but the lead has been taken by sociologists, in particular Edna Bonacich. One thinks especially of her theory of the split labor market and her 1984 book, with Lucie Cheng, on international labor migration, *Labor Immigration under Capitalism,* in which she and Cheng try to rearrange our view of immigration dynamics. They want us to eschew the functionalist equilibrium model of balanced but independent push and pull factors and to substitute a power-conflict model of a global market economy. Their argument—not a new one—contends that capitalist development in the United States caused a demand for cheap labor at the same time that its international manifestation—imperialism—displaced colonized peoples in the Third World, who then came to fill jobs in the United States. It is a suggestive theory, although the book's essays, by the authors' own admission, only begin to test the theory's accuracy. Regardless, it is refreshing to read the work of scholars who make their theoretical base explicit; most previous students of Japanese American history simply slid into an unacknowledged dependency on functionalist thinking. The book represents more systematic thinking about Japanese American workers than has been done before; it is therefore in many respects an important step forward over previous efforts, such as the antiracism school of the 1960s. Yet it runs the risk of minimizing the importance of racism—and of culture and ideology generally. Like any system, it highlights some important new understandings even as it tends to obscure others. This danger is equally present in Bonacich's idea of Japanese Americans as a "middleman minority." The middleman minority concept has engendered debate pitting Bonacich and her colleagues, John Modell and Harry Kitano, against other scholars such as Eugene Wong, David O'Brien, and Stephen Fugita.[28]

If these are the places we have been, where ought we to go next? For one thing, we could make fuller use of some of the resources at our disposal. Many scholars have used the marvelous files of the Japanese American Research Project at UCLA (though more often the English- than the Japanese-language documents) and the Japanese American Evacuation and Resettlement Study at Berkeley. Far fewer have availed themselves of the documents in the University of Washington archives, the Bishop Museum in Honolulu, or the dozens of oral histories at California State University, Fullerton. In time, the more than 200 oral histories of the Nisei Aging Project will make their way into the University of Washington's collection.[29] Only a few scholars have used the hundreds of 1920s-era life stories in the Survey of Race Relations Papers at Stanford. In addition, many of the Berkeley documents, including several large boxes of lengthy interviews that go far beyond the prison camp experience, have been declassified since 1975 but have not been much used.[30] There are also several published volumes of interviews that have yet to be mined.[31]

In addition to sources untapped, there are topics untouched by practitioners of Japanese American history. Recent emphases on theory and class analysis seem to have moved us beyond our formerly single-minded fixation on the World War II prison camp experience, although there will probably always be people working on that subject. One only hopes they will examine new data or treat new issues.[32]

Many other topics need treatment. The field needs more work on family and women's issues. The picture of Japanese American history will be much fuller as scholars write more community studies. Also needed are more evocations of the fabric of Issei life of the sort Akemi Kikumura has provided in her story of her mother's life. The Survey of Race Relations Papers might provide raw material for several studies of Issei culture and social structure.

Cultural history is a field almost wholly neglected to date. Even though a significant subgroup of the historical profession has been consumed with the ideas of the new cultural history, almost none of their preoccupations have made their way into work on Japanese Americans.[33] Richard Chalfen's study of family photographs and Eileen Tamura's of the Nisei generation in Hawai'i are the only books that operate comfortably in a postmodernist vein. It is striking that one of the few sharp-edged cultural reinterpretations of Japanese American history is not by a cultural historian but by two sociologists who are deeply wedded to social scientific methodology and show not the slightest postmodernist tendencies. Stephen Fugita and David O'Brien argue that the persistence of Japanese American ethnicity in the face of extraordinary assimilation is due to a particular Japanese cultural trait, and they trace the development of that trait through the course of Japanese American history. How interesting it would be for Japanese American culture to become the subject of scholars with a postmodernist paradigm.[34]

A serious study of Nisei teen subculture would be useful, and not hard to do. Bill Hosokawa has churned up some of the data for this subject, and there is a lot of material in the archives at Berkeley and UCLA, as well as in the stories of Toshio Mori, but no one has yet dealt with it in analytical fashion.[35] A cultural interpretation of the Issei generation would be within the grasp of a scholar whose Japanese is good enough to read the abundant community newspapers. There is no good study of Japanese Americans that focuses on the period after World War II. Several uneven sociological papers look at the immediate return to prewar homes, but no one takes the story much past 1950.[36] We need studies of Japanese Americans in places other than the West Coast and Hawai'i. Tooru Kanazawa, Sandra Taylor, and Thomas Walls have started on Alaska, Utah, and Texas, respectively, but this is only a beginning.[37] There are only two studies that touch on the important immigration of Japanese businesspeople and their families in the last two decades.[38] It is time for a historian to look at the Sansei generation. William Wei and Yen Le Espiritu have made a start, with political accounts of the 1960s Asian consciousness movement, but those have not done much to illumine the Sansei world specifically.[39]

Studies of Japanese American institutions are not plentiful. Yuji Ichioka has investigated the Japanese Association and labor unions. Jere Takahashi, Bill Hosokawa, and Paul Spickard have written about the JACL. John Hawkins and Mariko Takagi have started on the language schools, and Thomas James on education in the concentration camps. Brian Hayashi's excellent dissertation on Japanese American Protestants before World War II will soon be a book, but aside from that and Tetsuden Kashima's rudimentary description of Buddhism, there is very little on religion or churches, less that is up-to-date, and nothing that is historically analytical. And churches have been important to the Japanese American community. Can it have been accidental, for instance, that between 10 and 25 percent of Japanese emigrants were Christians, compared to less than 1 percent of the Japanese population at large? Similarly, agricultural associations, other civic organizations, community newspapers, and the like are nearly virgin territory in need of study.[40]

The dominant image of the Nisei generation in the 1930s and 1940s is in need of revision—not because it is wrong, but because it does not tell the whole story. The picture conveyed by the JACL-oriented studies of a group of "quiet Americans," well-behaved, hardworking, patriotic, and intent upon assimilation, is certainly more true than not. But there were other types of Nisei whose stories have not been fully told. There were liberal intellectuals who were not nearly so conservative as the JACL. The Kibei, born in America, raised in Japan, and often quite out of place on their return to America, have not yet found their chronicler. Then there was that tiny group of zoot-suiters, prostitutes, and others whose aggressive and outlandish behavior—whose very existence, in fact—so embarrassed other Nisei that they appear nowhere in published accounts. All these others at variance with the dominant image of the Nisei are also part of the larger picture.[41]

It is important to move in the direction of comparison with other ethnic groups, Asian as well as non-Asian, if we are to come to a better understanding of what is unique to Japanese American experience and what has been shared by other peoples in similar circumstances. The work being done on Japanese in South America and the few studies on Japanese Canadians constitute steps toward meaningful comparisons with Japanese experiences in other countries.[42] More thematic studies comparing the experiences of several American groups are needed. While it is important, for political and conceptual reasons, to continue to stress the commonalities among Asian Americans, it is also important, for conceptual if not political reasons, to note contrasts among Asian American groups, and between Japanese Americans and other peoples in the United States and abroad.[43] Finally, scholars should begin to work on projects that embody not just careful scholarship but genuine comparison, and ultimately synthesis and integration. It is hoped that this book is an example of that kind of writing.

Notes and References

one

1. Paul R. Spickard, "The Illogic of American Racial Categories," in *Racially Mixed People in America,* ed. Maria P. P. Root (Newbury Park, Calif.: Sage, 1992), 12–23.

2. The description of ethnic group formation, persistence, and change presented here is based on the work of Stephen Cornell, particularly on a soon-to-be-published paper titled "The Variable Ties That Bind: On Structure and Content in Ethnic Processes," *Ethnic and Racial Studies* (1996), and on several years of discussions with Professor Cornell.

3. For ethnicity as interests, see Joe Feagin, *Racial and Ethnic Relations,* 3rd ed. (Englewood Cliffs, N.J.: Prentice-Hall, 1988). For ethnicity as culture, see Robert E. Park, *Race and Culture* (Glencoe, Ill.: Free Press, 1949). For ethnicity as institutions, see Richard D. Alba, *Italian Americans* (Englewood Cliffs, N.J.: Prentice-Hall, 1985).

two

1. Note that this interpretation, while common among scholars of Japanese history, differs substantially from that of David O'Brien and Stephen Fugita in *The Japanese American Experience* (Bloomington: Indiana University Press, 1991).

2. "Kimigaiyo," in *Things Japanese,* trans. Basil H. Chamberlain, quoted in *Kodansha Encyclopedia of Japan,* vol. 5 (Tokyo: Kodansha, 1983), 336.

3. Quoted in Chizuko Lampman, *The East,* vol. 2, no. 4 (1966):71–75; cited in Harry H. L. Kitano, *Japanese Americans,* 2nd ed. (Englewood Cliffs, N.J.: Prentice-Hall, 1976), 13–14.

4. For people who lived and worked primarily in Japan, I present their family names first and personal names second, as is Japanese usage. For people who lived and worked primarily in the United States, I follow the American convention of citing the personal name and then the family name. Thus, Fukuzawa Yukichi was Yukichi of the Fukuzawa family.

5. Quoted in Irokawa Daikichi, *Kindai Kokka no Shuppatsu* (The Beginnings of the Modern Nation-State) (Tokyo, 1966), 378–79; quoted in Mikiso Hane, *Peasants, Rebels, and Outcastes: The Underside of Modern Japan* (New York: Pantheon, 1982), 23–24.

6. Yamamoto Shigemi, *Aa Nomugi-toge,* 90–91; quoted in Hane, *Peasants, Rebels, and Outcastes,* 182.

7. Yasuo Wakatsuki, "Japanese Emigration to the United States, 1866–1924," *Perspectives in American History* 12 (1979):407–11.

8. Alan Moriyama, *Imingaisha: Japanese Emigration Companies and Hawai'i* (Honolulu: University of Hawai'i Press, 1985), 160.

9. Occupation and class data are taken from Wakatsuki, "Japanese Emigration to the United States," 481–509.

10. *Teikoku Statistical Annual,* cited in ibid., 490.

11. *Historical Statistics of the United States, Colonial Times to 1970,* pt. 1 (Washington, D.C.: Government Printing Office, 1975), 379–80.

12. George DeVos and Hiroshi Wagatsuma, *Japan's Invisible Race,* rev. ed. (Berkeley: University of California Press, 1972), 200–221.

13. Yuji Ichioka, "Ameyuki-san: Japanese Prostitutes in Nineteenth-Century America," *Amerasia Journal* 4, no. 1 (1977):1–21; Laurie Mengel, "Not Just Picture Brides: Independent Japanese Women Immigrants" (paper presented to the Association for Asian American Studies, Honolulu, March 26, 1996).

14. Dorothy S. Thomas, Charles Kikuchi, and James Sakoda, *The Salvage* (Berkeley: University of California Press, 1952), 607–9.

15. Wakatsuki, "Japanese Emigration to the United States," 510.

16. Yamato Ichihashi, *Japanese Immigration: Its Status in California* (San Francisco: Marshall Press, 1915), 14.

17. "Honpo Imin Hawai'i Toko Ikken" (Concerning Travel of Japanese Emigrants to Hawai'i), Diplomatic Record Office, index 3.8.2.20 (5), quoted in Wakatsuki, "Japanese Emigration to the United States," 473–74.

18. "Kakuken Iminkaisha Yori Fukushima-Ken Shorui Shintatsunegai Tsuzuri" (File of Requests from Emigration Companies of All Prefectures for Fukushima Prefecture's Documents), Fukushima Prefectural Library, quoted in Wakatsuki, "Japanese Emigration to the United States," 476.

19. "Chikuzan in America," *Tokyo Keizai Zasshi,* no. 1606 (August 1911), quoted in Wakatsuki, "Japanese Emigration to the United States," 459–60.

three

1. Quoted in Kazuo Ito, *Issei: A History of Japanese Immigrants in North America,* trans. Shinichiro Nakamura and Jean S. Gerard (Seattle: Japanese Community Service, 1973), 21.

2. Leonard Dinnerstein and David M. Reimers, *Ethnic Americans,* 3rd ed. (New York: Harper & Row, 1988), 206–12.

3. Alan Moriyama, *Imingaisha: Japanese Emigration Companies and Hawai'i* (Honolulu: University of Hawai'i Press, 1985), 43, 70.

4. Ethnic Studies Oral History Project, *Stores and Storekeepers of Paia and Puunene, Maui* (Honolulu: University of Hawai'i Ethnic Studies Department, 1980), 399, quoted in Ronald Takaki, *Strangers from a Different Shore* (Boston: Little, Brown, 1989), 133.

5. Moriyama, *Imingaisha,* 97.

6. Derek Bickerton and William H. Wilson, "Pidgin Hawaiian," in *Pidgin and Creole Languages,* ed. Glenn G. Gilbert (Honolulu: University of Hawai'i Press, 1967), 61–76.

7. *Hawai'i Herald,* February 2, 1973, quoted in Takaki, *Strangers from a Different Shore,* 145.

8. Patsy Y. Nakayama, "A Walk through Honolulu's Little Tokyo," *Hokubei Mainichi,* February 2, 1990.

9. Yuji Ichioka, "Japanese Immigrant Labor Contractors and the Northern Pacific and the Great Northern Railroad Companies, 1898–1907," *Labor History* 21, no. 3 (1980):326–27.

10. Quoted in Ito, *Issei,* 32.

11. Quoted in ibid., 293–94.

12. Masakazu Iwata, "The Japanese Immigrants in California Agriculture," *Agricultural History* 36 (1962):25–37.

13. Quoted in Ito, *Issei,* 361.

14. Yuji Ichioka, *Issei* (New York: Free Press, 1988), 84–90; Ito, *Issei,* 743–805.

15. Yuji Ichioka, "Ameyuki-san: Japanese Prostitutes in Nineteenth-Century America," *Amerasia Journal* 4 (1977):1–21; Joan Hori, "Japanese Prostitution in Hawai'i during the Immigrant Period," *Hawai'i Journal of History* 15 (1981):113–24.

16. Tomoko Yamazaki, *The Story of Yamada Waka: From Prostitute to Feminist Pioneer,* trans. Wakako Hironaka and Ann Kostant (Tokyo: Kodansha, 1985).

17. Asiatic Exclusion League of North America, *Preamble and Constitution, 1905,* quoted in Eliot G. Mears, *Resident Orientals of the American Pacific Coast* (Chicago: University of Chicago Press, 1928), 435.

18. Chester H. Rowell, "Chinese and Japanese Immigrants—A Comparison," in *Annals of the American Academy of Political and Social Science,* vol. 34, *Chinese and Japanese in America* (September 1909):223–30.

19. *San Francisco Chronicle,* 13 February–13 March 1905, passim, quoted in Roger Daniels, *Asian America* (Seattle: University of Washington Press, 1988), 116.

20. Quoted in Roger Daniels, *The Politics of Prejudice* (Berkeley: University of California Press, 1962), 34.

21. Quoted in ibid., 47.

22. Commissioner General of Immigration, *Report* (Washington, D.C., 1908), 125, quoted in Mears, *Resident Orientals,* 443.

23. I am grateful for permission, in this section and others dealing with the ethnicity model presented earlier, to reproduce material that appeared in my article "Japanese Americans: The Formation and Transformation of an Ethnic Group," in *New Visions in Asian American Studies,* ed. Franklin Ng et al. (Pullman: Washington State University Press, 1994), 159–72.

24. Wakatsuki, "Japanese Emigration to the United States," 470.

four

1. The number went back up to 60 percent in 1919, after the Japanese government banned the picture bride practice.

2. Moriyama, *Imingaisha,* 138; Eileen Sunada Sarasohn, ed., *The Issei* (Palo Alto, Calif.: Pacific Books, 1983), 21–22; Kazuko Nakane, *Nothing Left in My Hands: An Early Japanese American Community in California's Pajaro Valley* (Seattle: Young Pine Press, 1985), 1–2.

3. Quoted in Ito, *Issei,* 189–90.

4. Murray Morgan, *Skid Road* (New York: Viking, 1951), 58–66.

5. Sarasohn, *The Issei,* 106–39; Ito, *Issei,* 188–201.

6. Edward K. Strong, *Japanese in California* (Stanford, Calif.: Stanford University Press, 1933), 72.

7. Akemi Kikumura, *Through Harsh Winters: The Life of a Japanese Immigrant Woman* (Novato, Calif.: Chandler and Sharp, 1981), 30.

8. Ibid., 18.

9. David Mas Masumoto, *Country Voices: The Oral History of a Japanese Family Farm Community* (Del Rey, Calif.: Inaka Countryside Publications, 1987), 129.

10. Ichihashi, *Japanese Immigration,* 21; Gretchen Tuthill, "A Study of the Japanese in the City of Los Angeles" (M.A. thesis, University of Southern California, 1924), 79; Strong, *Japanese in California,* 98.

11. Strong, *Japanese in California,* 133.

12. Ibid., 89, 133.

13. Mei T. Nakano, *Japanese American Women: Three Generations, 1890–1990* (Berkeley: Mina Press, 1990), 24.

14. Hyman Kublin, *Asian Revolutionary: The Life of Sen Katayama* (Princeton, N.J.: Princeton University Press, 1964), 47–87.

15. Ito, *Issei,* 631–42.

16. Strong, *Japanese in California,* 98.

17. John Modell, "Tradition and Opportunity: The Japanese Immigrant in America," *Pacific Historical Review* 40 (1971):177.

18. John Modell, *The Economics and Politics of Racial Accommodation: The Japanese of Los Angeles, 1900–1942* (Urbana: University of Illinois Press, 1977), 99.

19. Tetsuya Fujimoto, *Crime and Delinquency among the Japanese-Americans* (Tokyo: Chuo University Press, 1978), 72.

20. Quoted in Ito, *Issei,* 24, 27.

21. Quoted in ibid., 494–95.

22. Quoted in ibid., 471.

23. Ichioka, *Issei,* 151–52.

24. Ronald W. López, "The El Monte Berry Strike of 1933," *Aztlan* 1 (1970):101–14.

25. Quoted in Kitano, *Japanese Americans,* 17.

26. Edna Bonacich and John Modell, *The Economic Basis of Ethnic Solidarity: Small Business in the Japanese American Community* (Berkeley: University of California Press, 1980), 38–39. Bonacich and Modell's title is exactly backward. Their data demonstrate quite conclusively, not the "economic basis of ethnic solidarity" among Japanese Americans, but the ethnic basis of their economic solidarity.

27. Quoted in S. Frank Miyamoto, *Social Solidarity among the Japanese in Seattle,* rev. ed. (1939; Seattle: University of Washington Press, 1984), 20.

28. Quoted in ibid., 20–21.

29. Ibid., 21.

30. Quintard Taylor, "Blacks and Asians in a White City: Japanese Americans and African Americans in Seattle, 1890–1940," *Western Historical Quarterly* 22 (1991):401–29; Modell, *Racial Accommodation,* 113–19.

31. Quoted in Ito, *Issei,* 523.

32. Sarasohn, *The Issei,* 81.

33. Yamato Ichihashi, *The Japanese in the United States* (Stanford, Calif.: Stanford University Press, 1932), 106–15; Evelyn Nakano Glenn, "Occupational Ghettoization: Japanese American Women and Domestic Service, 1905–1970," *Ethnicity* 8 (1981):352–86; Tuthill, "The Japanese in Los Angeles," 79; Nobuya Tsuchida, "Japanese Gardeners in Southern California, 1900–1941," in *Labor*

Immigration under Capitalism: Asian Workers in the United States before World War II, ed. Lucie Cheng and Edna Bonacich (Berkeley: University of California Press, 1984), 435–69.

34. Eleanor Gluck, "An Ecological Study of the Japanese in New York City" (M.A. thesis, Columbia University, 1940), 28–29; Michiji Ishikawa, "A Study of Intermarried Japanese Families in U.S.A.," *Cultural Nippon* 3 (Tokyo, 1935), 457–87.

35. Miyamoto, *Social Solidarity,* 63, 64.

36. Strong, *Japanese in California,* 53.

37. Quoted in Miyamoto, *Social Solidarity,* 25.

38. Ivan H. Light, *Ethnic Enterprise in America: Business and Welfare among Chinese, Japanese, and Blacks* (Berkeley: University of California Press, 1972), 64.

39. Quoted in Fumiko Fukuoka, "Mutual Life and Aid among the Japanese in Southern California with Special Reference to Los Angeles" (M.A. thesis, University of Southern California, 1937), 19.

40. Masakazu Iwata, "The Japanese Immigrants in California Agriculture," *Agricultural History* 36 (1962):33.

41. Miyamoto, *Social Solidarity,* 22.

42. Karl Yoneda, *Ganbatte: Sixty-Year Struggle of a Kibei Worker* (Los Angeles: UCLA Asian American Studies Center, 1983).

43. Ito, *Issei,* 729.

44. Ichioka, *Issei,* 160–61.

45. Tetsuden Kashima, *Buddhism in America* (Westport, Conn.: Greenwood, 1977).

46. Quoted in Miyamoto, *Social Solidarity,* 56.

47. Quoted in Jitsuichi Masuoka, "Race Attitudes of the Japanese People in Hawai'i" (M.A. thesis, University of Hawai'i, 1931).

48. Strong, *Japanese in California,* 171.

49. Ibid., 168–75.

50. Tetsuya Fujimoto argues that the low Issei crime rate was due to class composition: as a group of mainly petty entrepreneurs, they were insulated from fluctuations in the economic cycle and therefore did not become unemployed laborers whose circumstances would encourage a resort to crime. *Crime and Delinquency.*

51. Robert Higgs, "Landless by Law: Japanese Immigrants in California Agriculture to 1941," *Journal of Economic History* 38 (1978):215.

52. Quoted in Daniels, *Politics of Prejudice,* 21.

53. Quoted in ibid., 99.

54. Quoted in Higgs, "Landless by Law," 224.

55. Quoted in Dennis M. Ogawa, *From Japs to Japanese: The Evolution of Japanese-American Stereotypes* (Berkeley: McCutchan, 1971), 13.

56. Quoted in ibid., 14.

57. *Los Angeles Times,* 1 November 1920, quoted in ibid., 15.

58. Quoted in Chotoku Toyama, "The Life History as a Social Document," 27 May 1924, Major Document No. 312, Survey of Race Relations Papers, Hoover Institution Archives, Stanford University.

59. *Los Angeles Examiner,* 23 July 1916, quoted in Ogawa, *Japs to Japanese,* 17.

60. Quoted in Higgs, "Landless by Law," 215.

61. "Issei's House Named National Historic Landmark," *Hokubei Mainichi*, 2 July 1991.

62. *Ozawa v. United States*, 13 November 1922, in Mears, *Resident Orientals*, 507–14.

63. Quoted in Yuji Ichioka, "The 1921 Turlock Incident," in *Counterpoint*, ed. Emma Gee (Los Angeles: UCLA Asian American Studies Center, 1976), 195–99.

64. Quoted in Ichioka, *Issei*, 249–50.

65. Quoted in Ito, *Issei*, 478.

66. Higgs, "Landless by Law," 222.

67. Quoted in Ichioka, *Issei*, 233.

68. These suggestions are admittedly speculative. A great deal of work needs to be done on Japanese American religion and language behavior.

five

1. The information for this walking tour is drawn from the *Seattle City Directory* for 1940, and from the author's recollections of growing up in this community in the 1960s.

2. Darrel Montero, *Japanese Americans: Changing Patterns of Ethnic Affiliation over Three Generations* (Boulder, Colo.: Westview, 1980), 39.

3. For a discussion of Japanese family structure in Meiji and Taisho Japan, see Chie Nakane, *Kinship and Economic Organization in Rural Japan*, Monographs on Social Anthropology No. 32 (London: London School of Economics, 1967). For an analysis of the ways the Japanese American family differed from its counterpart in Japan, and in particular for thoughtful observations on the roles of women in Japanese American families, see Evelyn Nakano Glenn, *Issei, Nisei, War Bride* (Philadelphia: Temple University Press, 1986), 201–18.

4. Kikumura, *Through Harsh Winters*, 8–9.

5. Quoted in Forrest E. LaViolette, *Americans of Japanese Ancestry* (Toronto: Canadian Institute of International Affairs, 1945), 21.

6. Kitano, *Japanese Americans*, 44.

7. Toshio Mori, *The Chauvinist and Other Stories* (Los Angeles: UCLA Asian American Studies Center, 1979), 73.

8. Quoted in LaViolette, *Americans of Japanese Ancestry*, 23.

9. Paul R. Spickard, *Mixed Blood: Intermarriage and Ethnic Identity in Twentieth-Century America* (Madison: University of Wisconsin Press, 1989), 91–92.

10. Quoted in LaViolette, *Americans of Japanese Ancestry*, 23.

11. Kitano, *Japanese Americans*, 122–36.

12. Noreen Sakai*, interview with the author, Honolulu, November 1994.

13. Kitano, *Japanese Americans*, 125–26.

14. All quoted in Ito, *Issei*, 589–90.

15. Quoted in Modell, *Racial Accommodation*, 160. Defenders of Japanese Americans against White criticism were often careful to point out—even to exaggerate—the Americanizing task of the language schools. See LaViolette, *Americans of Japanese Ancestry*, 52–56; and Bill Hosokawa, *Nisei: The Quiet Americans* (New York: Morrow, 1969), 160–61.

16. Quoted in Masumoto, *Country Voices*, 133.

17. Monica Sone, *Nisei Daughter* (Boston: Little, Brown, 1955), 22–23.

18. S. Frank Miyamoto, "Problems of Interpersonal Style among the Nisei," *Amerasia Journal* 13, no. 2 (1986–87):31–32. The other psychologists, anthropologists, and sociologists Miyamoto cites are William Caudill, "Japanese American Personality and Acculturation," *Genetic Psychology Monographs* 45 (1952):3–102; George A. DeVos, "A Quantitative Rorschach Assessment of Maladjustment and Rigidity in Acculturating Japanese Americans," *Genetic Psychology Monographs* 52 (1955):51–87; Abe Arkoff, "Need Patterns in Two Generations of Japanese Americans in Hawai'i," *Journal of Social Psychology* 50 (1959):75–79; Kitano, *Japanese Americans,* 103–5; Stanford Lyman, "Generation and Character: The Case of the Japanese Americans," in Lyman, *The Asian in the West* (Reno: University of Nevada Press, 1970), 81–97; LaViolette, *Americans of Japanese Ancestry,* 169–70; and E. K. Strong, *The Second-Generation Japanese Problem* (Stanford, Calif.: Stanford University Press, 1934), 175.

19. R. A. Sasaki, *The Loom and Other Stories* (Minneapolis: Graywolf Press, 1991), 17–18, 20–21.

20. Yoshiko Uchida, *The Invisible Thread* (New York: Julian Messner, 1991), 13.

21. Quoted in Sarasohn, *The Issei* 270.

22. Daisuke Kitaga, *Issei and Nisei: The Internment Years* (New York: Seabury, 1967), 27–29.

23. LaViolette, *Americans of Japanese Ancestry,* 141; Christie W. Kiefer, *Changing Cultures, Changing Lives: An Ethnographic Study of Three Generations of Japanese Americans* (San Francisco: Jossey-Bass, 1974), 95–129.

24. Quoted in LaViolette, *Americans of Japanese Ancestry,* 142.

25. See, for example, William C. Smith, *The Second Generation Oriental in America* (Honolulu: Institute of Pacific Relations, 1927).

26. Uchida, *Invisible Thread,* 14; Kitagawa, *Issei and Nisei,* 26; John Okada, *No-No Boy* (Rutland, Vt.: Tuttle, 1957), 34–35.

27. Reginald Bell, *Public School Education of Second-Generation Japanese in California* (Stanford, Calif.: Stanford University Press, 1935), 35–61.

28. Quoted in Smith, *Second-Generation Orientals,* 7–8.

29. Mei Nakano, *Japanese American Women* (Sebastopol, Calif.: Mina Press, 1990), 105; Sasaki, *The Loom,* 22–23.

30. Quoted in Ichihashi, *Japanese in the United States,* 345.

31. Quoted in Smith, *Second-Generation Oriental,* 22; Modell, *Racial Accommodation,* 165. Kawai was technically an Issei by birth but came to America as a young child and regarded himself a Nisei.

32. Nakano, *Japanese American Women,* 111.

33. Toshio Mori, *Yokohama, California* (Caldwell, Idaho: Caxton Printers, 1949; Seattle: University of Washington Press, 1985).

34. Quoted in Hosokawa, *Nisei,* 164–65.

35. Modell, *Racial Accommodation,* 166–67; Hosokawa, *Nisei,* 166.

36. Valerie Matsumoto, "Desperately Seeking 'Deirdre': Gender Roles, Multicultural Relations, and Nisei Women Writers of the 1930s," *Frontiers* 12 (1991): 19–32.

37. Hosokawa, *Nisei,* 164.

38. Quoted in Smith, *Second-Generation Oriental,* 17.

39. Quoted in Nakano, *Japanese American Women,* 117.

40. Taishi Matsumoto, "The Protest of a Professional Carrot Washer," *Kashu Mainichi*, 4 April 1937, quoted in John Modell, "Class or Ethnic Solidarity: The Japanese American Company Union," *Pacific Historical Review* 38 (1969):195.

41. Quoted in Strong, *Second-Generation Japanese Problem*, 237.

42. Modell, *Racial Accommodation*, 130–32.

43. Ibid., 131.

44. Quoted in Sone, *Nisei Daughter*, 120–21.

45. Quoted in Strong, *Second-Generation Japanese Problem*, 7, 230.

46. Sone, *Nisei Daughter*, 124.

47. Quoted in Ichihashi, *Japanese in the United States*, 360–61.

48. This section is based on Paul R. Spickard, "Twice Immigrants: Kibei in Prewar America and Japan" (unpublished manuscript).

49. John Stephan, *Hawai'i under the Rising Sun: Japan's Plans for Conquest after Pearl Harbor* (Honolulu: University of Hawai'i Press, 1984), 41.

50. Bradford Smith, *Americans from Japan* (Philadelphia: Lippincott, 1948), 253.

51. Quoted in "The Structure of Community Relationships," R20.42, Japanese American Evacuation and Resettlement Papers, Bancroft Library, University of California at Berkeley.

52. Paul R. Spickard, "Not Just the Quiet People: The Nisei Underclass" (unpublished manuscript).

53. Quoted in Bill Hosokawa, *JACL in Quest of Justice* (New York: Morrow, 1982), 279–80.

SIX

1. Allan Beekman, "Nikkei Killed by 'Friendly Fire' on Dec. 7, 1941," *Hokubei Mainichi*, 28 December 1991; James Koba's story was told to me in 1992 at Honolulu First Chinese Church of Christ, by a Chinese American ex-prizefighter who had lost to Koba the previous Tuesday.

2. Ken Moritomi,* personal communication with the author, Boston, 1974.

3. This section is adapted from Paul R. Spickard, "The Nisei Assume Power: The Japanese American Citizens League, 1941–1942," *Pacific Historical Review* 52 (1983):147–74.

4. Quoted in A. H. Leighton, *The Governing of Men* (1945; Princeton, N.J.: Princeton University Press, 1968), 19.

5. Jeanne Wakatsuki Houston and James D. Houston, *Farewell to Manzanar* (Boston: Houghton Mifflin, 1973), 6.

6. Spickard, "Nisei Assume Power," p. 157. This information is corroborated by a study of JACL files commissioned and then suppressed by the JACL in the 1990s; see Deborah Lim, "Draft Report to the Presidential Select Committee on Resolution No. 7 to the JACL National Convention" (San Francisco, 1990).

7. Quoted from Floyd K. Takeuchi, "Activist Wants AJA Group to Apologize," *Honolulu Star Bulletin*, 15 October 1991, A-6.

8. John A. Herzig, "Japanese Americans and MAGIC," *Amerasia Journal* 11, no. 2 (1984):47–55; Bob Kumamoto, "The Search for Spies: American Counterintelligence and the Japanese American Community, 1931–1942," *Amerasia Journal* 6, no. 2 (1979):45–75.

9. This argument is laid out with considerably more subtlety and detail in Spickard, "Nisei Assume Power."

10. Roger Daniels, *Prisoners without Trial: Japanese Americans in World War II* (New York: Hill and Wang, 1993), 28.

11. Cited in Roger Daniels, *Concentration Camps, USA: Japanese Americans and World War II* (New York: Holt, Rinehart and Winston, 1971), 33–34.

12. Quoted in Morton Grodzins, *Americans Betrayed: Politics and the Japanese Evacuation* (Chicago: University of Chicago Press, 1949), 27.

13. Grodzins, 27.

14. Quoted in Jacobus tenBroek, Edward N. Barnhart, and Floyd W. Matson, *Prejudice, War, and the Constitution* (Berkeley: University of California Press, 1954), 75.

15. Quoted by Togo Tanaka in Arthur A. Hansen and Betty E. Mitson, eds., *Voices Long Silent* (Fullerton, Calif.: California State University Oral History Project, 1974), 94–95.

16. Daniels, *Prisoners without Trial,* 30.

17. Quoted in Allan R. Bosworth, *America's Concentration Camps* (New York: Norton, 1967), 171.

18. Quoted in Audrie Girdner and Anne Loftis, *The Great Betrayal* (New York: Macmillan, 1969), 118–19.

19. Quoted in ibid., 115.

20. Except Mike Masaoka; he was allowed to remain free and to travel around the country. See Spickard, "Nisei Assume Power."

21. Quoted in Peter Irons, ed., *Justice Delayed: The Record of the Japanese American Internment Cases* (Middletown, Conn.: Wesleyan University Press, 1989), v.

22. Quoted in Peter Irons, *Justice at War* (New York: Oxford, 1983), 84.

23. Justice Frank Murphy reversed his earlier opinion in the Hirabayashi case, this time characterizing the evacuations as an abuse of constitutional power. He concluded: "All residents of this nation are kin in some way by blood and culture to a foreign land. Yet they are primarily and necessarily a part of this new civilization of the United States. They must accordingly be treated at all times as the heirs of the American experiment and as entitled to all of the rights and freedoms granted by the Constitution." Daniels, *Prisoners without Trial,* 61–62.

24. Lim, "Draft Report," sect. IIA.

25. Altogether, the War Relocation Authority handled 120,313 people, including those taken by the FBI to Immigration and Naturalization Service camps and then transferred to the WRA; those born in camps; and others not part of the spring 1942 imprisonment. See appendix, table 18.

26. Houston and Houston, *Farewell to Manzanar,* 10–11.

27. Quoted in Girdner and Loftis, *Betrayal,* 524–25.

28. Miné Okubo, *Citizen 13660* (New York: Columbia University Press, 1946; Seattle: University of Washington Press, 1983), 33–36.

29. Sandra C. Taylor, *Jewel of the Desert: Japanese American Internment at Topaz* (Berkeley: University of California Press, 1993), 80.

30. Okubo, *Citizen 13660,* 117–18.

31. Ibid., 122.

32. Quoted in Irons, *Justice at War,* 101–2.

33. Houston and Houston, *Farewell to Manzanar,* 78–79.

34. Charles Kikuchi, *The Kikuchi Diary,* ed. John Modell (Urbana: University of Illinois Press, 1973), 62.

35. Ibid., 82, 119, 122.

36. Quoted in Edward H. Spicer et al., *Impounded People: Japanese Americans in the Relocation Centers* (Tucson: University of Arizona Press, 1969), 105.

37. Houston and Houston, *Farewell to Manzanar,* 47–51.

38. Paul R. Spickard, "Injustice Compounded: Amerasians and Non-Japanese Americans in World War II Concentration Camps," *Journal of American Ethnic History* 5, no. 2 (1986):5–22; "Voluntary Internee Dies at 67," *Hokubei Mainichi,* 11 January 1992.

39. Yoshiko Uchida, *Desert Exile* (Seattle: University of Washington Press, 1984), 97.

40. Orin Starn, "Engineering Internment: Anthropologists and the War Relocation Authority," *American Ethnologist* 13 (1986):700–720; Spicer et al., *Impounded People.*

41. D. S. Thomas, Richard Nishimoto et al., *The Spoilage* (Berkeley: University of California Press, 1946). Cf. Uji Ichioka, ed., *Views from Within: The Japanese American Evacuation and Resettlement Study* (Los Angeles: UCLA Asian American Studies Center, 1989).

42. John J. McCloy, letter to Alexander Micklejohn, 30 September 1942, quoted in Richard Drinnon, *Keeper of Concentration Camps* (Berkeley: University of California Press, 1987), 36.

43. Kitano, *Japanese Americans,* 73.

44. Michi Weglyn, *Years of Infamy: The Untold Story of America's Concentration Camps* (New York: Morrow, 1976), 123.

45. Quoted in Lim, "Draft Report," n.p.

46. Quoted in Thomas, Nishimoto et al., *Spoilage,* 57–58.

47. War Relocation Authority, Community Analysis Section, Community Analysis Notes No. 1, "From a Nisei Who Said 'No,'" 15 January 1944.

48. Thomas, Kikuchi, and Sakoda, *Salvage,* 616–25.

49. Girdner and Loftis, *Betrayal,* 342.

50. Daniels, *Prisoners without Trial,* 73.

51. Dorothy Kuniko Takechi, "The Nisei in Denver, Colorado: A Study in Personality Adjustment and Disorganization" (M.A. thesis, Fisk University, 1945); Michael Daniel Albert, "Japanese American Communities in Chicago and the Twin Cities" (Ph.D. dissertation, University of Minnesota, 1980), 147; Mitziko Sawada, "After the Camps: Seabrook Farms, New Jersey, and the Resettlement of Japanese Americans, 1944–47," *Amerasia Journal* 13, no. 2 (1986–87), 117–36.

52. Thomas, Kikuchi, and Sakoda, *Salvage,* 616; Leonard Broom and Ruth Riemer, *Removal and Return* (Berkeley: University of California Press, 1949), 36.

53. Quoted in Valerie Matsumoto, "Japanese American Women during World War II," *Frontiers* 8, no. 1 (1984):6–14.

54. Sone, *Nisei Daughter,* 219.

55. Uchida, *Desert Exile,* 149.

56. Okubo, *Citizen 13660,* 208–9.

57. Roger Daniels, "Forced Migrations of West Coast Japanese Americans, 1942–1946: A Quantitative Note," in *Japanese Americans from Relocation to Redress,* ed. Roger Daniels, et al. (Salt Lake City: University of Utah Press, 1986), 72–74.

58. Yoneda, *Ganbatte,* 145.

59. Thelma Chang, "A Legacy of Bravery: The 442nd Comes Home," *Honolulu Advertiser,* 21 March 1993.

60. Not all the Nisei soldiers were heroes. Some of the others are described in Tamotsu Shibutani, *The Derelicts of Company K* (Berkeley: University of California Press, 1978).

61. J. K. Yamamoto, "Belated Recognition Given to Heart Mountain Draft Resisters," *Hokubei Mainichi,* 18 July 1992.

62. This story is told ably and in great detail in Thomas and Nishimoto et al., *Spoilage.*

63. Gary Okihiro makes this argument, with some important qualifications, in "Religion and Resistance in America's Concentration Camps," *Phylon* 45 (1984):220–33.

64. Quoted in U.S. Commission on Wartime Relocation and Internment of Civilians, *Personal Justice Denied* (Washington, D.C.: Government Printing Office, 1982), 248–49.

65. Daniels, *Prisoners without Trial,* 85.

66. Quoted in Thomas and Nishimoto et al., *Spoilage,* 363–70.

67. "The Japanese Americans," *Race Relations* 2, no. 6 (January 1945):162–63.

68. Daniel K. Inouye, *Journey to Washington* (Englewood Cliffs, N.J.: Prentice-Hall, 1967), 207–8.

69. Quoted in Sarasohn, *The Issei,* 239.

70. Houston and Houston, *Farewell to Manzanar,* 97–98, 102.

71. Sandra C. Taylor, "Evacuation and Economic Loss," in *Japanese Americans: From Relocation to Redress,* ed. Roger Daniels, Sandra C. Taylor, and Harry H. L. Kitano (Salt Lake City: University of Utah Press, 1986), 163–67.

72. Houston and Houston, *Farewell to Manzanar,* 133–34.

73. Daniel I. Okimoto, *American in Disguise* (New York: Walker/Weatherhill, 1971).

74. Amy Iwasaki Mass, "Socio-Psychological Effects of the Concentration Camp Experience on Japanese Americans," *Bridge* (Winter 1978):61–63.

75. Donna K. Nagata, *Legacy of Injustice* (New York: Plenum, 1993).

76. Kitagawa, *Issei and Nisei;* Spickard, "Nisei Assume Power."

77. Spickard, "Nisei Assume Power"; Thomas, Kikuchi, and Sakoda, *The Salvage,* 607–9; Kiefer, *Changing Cultures, Changing Lives.*

seven

1. David Mura, "In Search of the Real Nisei," *Hokubei Mainichi,* 22 December 1989.

2. Quoted in Sarasohn, *The Issei,* 237, 249–50.

3. Hosokawa, *JACL in Quest of Justice,* 283.

4. Masumoto, *Country Voices,* 62–75.

5. Mura, "Real Nisei"; Weglyn, *Years of Infamy,* 273; "Documentary on Fred Korematsu in the Works," *Hokubei Mainichi,* 2 April 1991.

6. "Japanese American Success Story: Out-Whiting the Whites," *Newsweek,* 21 June 1971, cited in Tetsuden Kashima, "Japanese American Internees Return, 1945 to 1955: Readjustment and Social Amnesia," *Phylon* 41 (1980):114.

7. Virginia B. Hertzler, "A Sociometric Study of Japanese Students in a Polyethnic High School" (M.A. thesis, University of Washington, 1949).

8. Houston and Houston, *Farewell to Manzanar,* 121–23, 133.

9. Floyd K. Takeuchi, "Hilo High Graduate Earns Respect of His Profession," *Honolulu Star Bulletin,* 23 September 1991; Barbara Hiura, "Reflections of a Yomiuri Giant and S. F. 49er," *Hokubei Mainichi,* 7 January 1993.

10. Willam H. Warren, "Maps: A Spatial Approach to Japanese American Communities in Los Angeles," *Amerasia Journal* 13, no. 2 (1986–87):137–51.

11. Valerie J. Matsumoto, *Farming the Homeplace: A Japanese American Community in California, 1919–1982* (Ithaca, N.Y.: Cornell University Press, 1993), 156–58.

12. Kitano, *Japanese Americans,* 89–90.

13. "Nisei Parade for Wallace at Gilmore," *California Eagle,* 7 October 1948.

14. Spickard, *Mixed Blood,* 121–58.

15. Stephen S. Fugita and David J. O'Brien, *Japanese American Ethnicity* (Seattle: University of Washington Press, 1991), 125.

16. Darrel Montero and Gene N. Levine, "Third Generation Japanese Americans: Prospects and Portents" (paper presented to the Pacific Sociological Association, San Jose, Calif., 1974).

17. "Report: Asians More Educated but Earn Less," *Hokubei Mainichi,* 19 September 1992.

18. William Petersen, "Success Story, Japanese-American Style," *New York Times Magazine* (9 January 1966):21.

19. Jeff Hudson, "JA Author Currently Working on First Novel," *Hokubei Mainichi,* 24 September 1991.

20. "Thomas's Statements about Asians Criticized," *Hokubei Mainichi,* 17 September 1991; "Report: AAs Face Glass Ceiling in Silicon Valley," *Hokubei Mainichi,* 23 September 1993.

21. "Success Story of One Minority Group in U.S." *U.S. News and World Report,* 26 December 1966.

22. Montero and Levine, "Third Generation Japanese Americans," 5.

23. Quoted in "Fresno Forum Examines Nisei-Sansei Transition," *Hokubei Mainichi,* 30 August 1994.

24. Both quoted in Fumiko Hosokawa, *The Sansei* (San Francisco: R&E Research Associates, 1978), 103.

25. Jan Masaoka, "I Forgot My Eyes Were Black," in *Asian Women* (Berkeley: University of California Asian American Studies, 1971), 57–59.

26. Cynthia L. Nakashima, "An Invisible Monster: The Creation and Denial of Mixed-Race People in America," in *Racially Mixed People in America,* ed. Maria P. Root (Newbury Park, Calif.: Sage, 1992), 162–78.

27. For intermarriage and people of mixed ancestry, see Spickard, *Mixed Blood.*

28. Ron Chew, "After 41 Years, a Wealth of Memories," *International Examiner,* 2 May 1990. For Issei and Nisei aging, see also Donna L. Leonetti, *Nisei Aging Project Report* (Seattle: University of Washington, 1983); Randall Jay Kendis, *An Attitude of Gratitude: The Adaptation to Aging of the Elderly Japanese in America* (New York: AMS Press, 1989); Darrel Montero, "The Elderly Japanese American: Aging among the First Generation Immigrants," *Genetic Psychology Monographs* 101 (1980):99–118.

29. Quoted in Nakano, *Japanese American Women,* 221.

30. George Johnston, "UCLA Grants Don Nakanishi Tenure," *Pacific Citizen,* 2 June 1989.

31. Amy Uyemura, "The Emergence of Yellow Power in America," *Gidra* (October 1969), excerpted in *Roots: An Asian American Reader,* ed. Amy Tachiki et al. (Los Angeles: UCLA Asian American Studies Center, 1971), 9–13.

32. William Wei, *The Asian American Movement* (Philadelphia: Temple University Press, 1993), 15.

33. "JACL Says Bill Would Hurt Legal Immigrants," *Hokubei Mainichi,* 24 March 1994.

34. Holly Uyemoto, *Rebel without a Clue* (New York: Crown, 1989).

35. Dean Takehara, "1991 Was a Deadly Year for Southern California Nikkei," *Hokubei Mainichi,* 14 January 1992.

36. Arthur Zich, "Japanese Americans: Home at Last," *National Geographic* (April 1986):518; "Study Reveals New Details about Japanese Immigrants," *Hokubei Mainichi,* 7 October 1993; Todd Barrett, "Mastering Being in America: Japanese Are Flocking to U.S. Business Schools," *Newsweek* (5 February 1990); "Report: 40,700 Japanese College Students in U.S." *Hokubei Mainichi,* 27 November 1992.

37. John Schwartz, "The 'Salarymen' Blues," *Newsweek* (9 May 1988); Merry White, *The Japanese Overseas: Can They Go Home Again?* (New York: Free Press, 1988); Richard W. Anderson, "Sam Kusumoto: This Mind of Minolta Has an American Heart," *Pinnacle* (May-June 1991):8–15.

38. Fugita and O'Brien, *Japanese American Ethnicity,* 141–64.

39. Francis Fukuyama, *The End of History and the Last Man* (New York: Free Press, 1992).

40. Quoted in Daniels, *Prisoners without Trial,* 132.

41. James K. Okutsu, [review of *In Search of Hiroshi* by Gene Oishi], *Amerasia Journal* 15, no. 2 (1989):214.

42. Donna K. Nagata, "The Japanese American Internment: Exploring the Transgenerational Consequences of Traumatic Stress," *Journal of Traumatic Stress* 3, no. 1 (1990):47–69; see also Nagata, *Legacy of Injustice.*

43. There was also some talk of calling for reparation payments to descendants of African American slaves, although little came of that; see David Ellen, "Payback Time: Reparations for Slavery?" *New Republic* 201 (31 July 1989):10–11.

44. Quoted in Irons, *Justice Delayed,* 25–26, 41, 46.

45. The full report is Deborah Lim, "Draft Report to the Presidential Select Committee on Resolution No. 7 to the JACL National Convention" (San Francisco, 1990). As late as 1994, former JACL President Cressey Nakagawa was justifying the whitewash; see J. K. Yamamoto, "Ex-JACL President's Remarks on 'Lim Report,'" *Hokubei Mainichi,* 5 August 1994.

46. U.S. Commission on Civil Rights, *Civil Rights Issues Facing Asian Americans in the 1990s* (Washington, D.C.: Government Printing Office, 1992), 25–28.

47. "Different Version of Shooting Given by Witness," *Hokubei Mainichi,* 3 November 1992.

48. *Morning Edition,* National Public Radio, 27 February 1992.

Bibliographic Essay

1. I should make clear from the outset that I am speaking here only of the work on Japanese American history that has been done in English. For the work being done in Japanese, see Yuji Ichioka, "Recent Japanese Scholarship on the

Origins and Causes of Japanese Immigration," *Immigration History Newsletter* 15, no. 2 (November 1983):2–5.

2. Yamato Ichihashi, *Japanese Immigration: Its Status in California* (San Francisco: Marshall Press, 1915); Ichihashi, *The Japanese in the United States* (Stanford, Calif.: Stanford University Press, 1932; New York: Arno, 1969); Shotaro Frank Miyamoto, *Social Solidarity among the Japanese in Seattle* (1939; Seattle: University of Washington Press, 1984); Emil T. H. Bunjie, *The Story of Japanese Farming in California* (Berkeley, 1937); Sakichi Chijiwa, "A Social Survey of the Japanese Population in Palo Alto and Menlo Park" (M.A. thesis, Stanford University, 1933); Michinari Fujita, "The Japanese Association in America," *Sociology and Social Research* 13 (1929):211–28; Ganki Kai, "Economic Status of the Japanese in California" (M.A. thesis, Stanford University, 1922); Kanichi Kawasaki, "The Japanese Community of East San Pedro Terminal Island" (M.A. thesis, University of Southern California, 1931); Kiichi Kanzaki, *California and the Japanese* (San Francisco: Japanese Association of America, 1921); H. A. Millis, "Some Economic Aspects of Japanese Immigration," *American Economic Review* 5 (1915):787–804; Kaizo Naka, "Social and Economic Conditions among Japanese Farmers in California" (M.S. thesis, University of California, Berkeley, 1913); Shichiro Matsui, "Economic Aspects of the Japanese Situation in California" (M.A. thesis, University of California, Berkeley, 1922); Jean Pajus, *The Real Japanese in California* (Berkeley, Calif.: Gillick, 1937); Edward K. Strong, "Japanese in California: Based on a Ten Percent Survey of Japanese in California and Documentary Evidence from Many Sources," *Stanford University Publications* [University Series, Education-Psychology] 1, no. 2 (1933):185–372; Chotoku Toyama, "The Japanese Community in Los Angeles" (M.A. thesis, Columbia University, 1926). The only bona fide historical study was Ernest K. Wakukawa, *A History of the Japanese People of Hawai'i* (Honolulu: Toyoshoin, 1938).

3. Kiyoshi K. Kawakami, *The Real Japanese Question* (New York: Macmillan, 1921); Kawakami, "The Naturalization of Japanese: What It Would Mean to the United States," *North American Review* 185, no. 617 (June 1907):394–402; Kawakami, "How California Treats the Japanese," *Independent* 74 (1913):1019–22; Kawakami, "Japan and the United States," *Atlantic Monthly* 119, no. 5 (May 1917):671–81; Kawakami, *Japan in World Politics* (New York: Macmillan, 1917); Kawakami, "Japan in a Quandary," *North American Review* 219, no. 821 (April 1924):474–85; Kawakami, *Asia at the Door* (New York: Fleming H. Revell, 1941); American Association of Political and Social Science, *Annals* 34, no. 2 (September 1909), and 93, no. 1 (January 1921); Manchester E. Boddy, *Japanese in America* (Los Angeles: 1921); Sidney L. Gulick, *The American Japanese Problem* (New York: Scribner's, 1914); Toyokichi Iyenaga and Kennosuke Sato, *Japan and the California Problem* (New York: Putnam's, 1921); Japanese Association of the Pacific Northwest, *Japanese Immigration: An Exposition of Its Real Status* (Seattle: 1907); H. A. Millis, *The Japanese Problem in the United States* (New York: Macmillan, 1915); Ichiro Tokutomi, *Japanese-American Relations* (New York: Macmillan, 1922).

4. Edward K. Strong, *The Second-Generation Japanese Problem* (Stanford, Calif.: Stanford University Press, 1934); Emory S. Bogardus and Robert H. Ross, "The Second-Generation Race Relations Cycle," *Sociology and Social Research* 24 (1940):357–63; Jitsuichi Masuoka, "Race Relations and Nisei Problems," *Sociology and Social Research* 30 (1946):452–59; John Okada, *No-No Boy* (Rutland, Vt.: Tuttle, 1957; Seattle: University of Washington Press, 1980); Daisuke Kitagawa, *Issei and Nisei: The Internment Years* (New York: Seabury, 1967); Monica Sone, *Nisei Daughter* (Boston, Little, Brown, 1953; Seattle: University of Washington Press, 1979); John Modell, ed., *The Kikuchi Diary: Chronicle from an American Concentration Camp* (Urbana: University of Illinois Press, 1973); George DeVos, "A Comparison of the

Personality Differences in Two Generations of Japanese Americans by Means of the Rorschach Test," *Nagoya Journal of Medical Science* 17 (1954):153–265; Forrest E. LaViolette, *Americans of Japanese Ancestry: A Study of Assimilation in the American Community* (Toronto: Canadian Institute of International Affairs, 1945); Tsutomu Obana, "Problems of American-Born Japanese," *Sociology and Social Research* 19 (November-December 1934):161–65.

5. Dorothy S. Thomas and Richard Nishimoto et al., *The Spoilage: Japanese-American Evacuation and Resettlement during World War II* (1946; Berkeley: University of California Press, 1969); Dorothy S. Thomas, Charles Kikuchi, and James Sakoda, *The Salvage* (Berkeley: University of California Press, 1952); Jacobus tenBroek, Edward N. Barnhart, and Floyd Matson, *Prejudice, War, and the Constitution* (Berkeley: University of California Press, 1954); Eugene V. Rostow, "The Japanese American Cases—A Disaster," *Yale Law Journal* 54 (1945):489–533; Leonard Bloom and Ruth Riemer, *Removal and Return: The Socio-Economic Effects of the War on Japanese Americans* (1949; Berkeley: University of California Press, 1973); Morton Grodzins, *Americans Betrayed: Politics and the Japanese Evacuation* (Chicago: University of Chicago Press, 1949); Leonard Broom and John I. Kitsuse, *The Managed Casualty: The Japanese-American Family in World War II* (1956; Berkeley: University of California Press, 1973).

6. U.S. Army, Western Defense Command and Fourth Army, *Final Report: Japanese Evacuation from the West Coast, 1942* (Washington, D.C.: Government Printing Office, 1943; Salem, N.H.: Ayer, 1979); U.S. Congress, House Select Committee Investigating National Defense Migration, *Hearings* (Washington, D.C.: Government Printing Office, 1942); U.S. Department of the Interior, War Relocation Authority, *The Evacuated People: A Quantitative Description* (Washington, D.C.: Government Printing Office, 1946); U.S. Congress, House Select Committee Investigating National Defense Migration, *National Defense Migration, Fourth Interim Report* (Washington, D.C.: Government Printing Office, 1942); U.S. Congress, House Select Committee Investigating National Defense Migration, *National Defense Migration* (Washington, D.C.: Government Printing Office, 1942); U.S. Department of the Interior, War Relocation Authority, *Community Analysis Reports*, nos. 1–19 (October 1942–June 1946); U.S. Department of the Interior, War Relocation Authority, *Administrative Highlights of the WRA Program* (Washington, D.C.: Government Printing Office, 1946); U.S. Department of the Interior, War Relocation Authority, *Wartime Exile: The Exclusion of the Japanese Americans from the West Coast* by Ruth McKee (Washington, D.C.: Government Printing Office, 1946); U.S. Department of the Interior, War Relocation Authority, *Community Government in War Relocation Centers* (Washington, D.C.: Government Printing Office, 1946); U.S. Department of the Interior, War Relocation Authority, *Impounded People: Japanese Americans in the Relocation Centers* (Washington, D.C.: Government Printing Office, 1946); U.S. Department of the Interior, War Relocation Authority, *Legal and Constitutional Phases of the WRA Program* (Washington, D.C.: Government Printing Office, 1946); U.S. Department of the Interior, War Relocation Authority, *The Relocation Program* (Washington, D.C.: Government Printing Office, 1946); U.S. Department of the Interior, War Relocation Authority, *WRA: A Story of Human Conservation* (Washington, D.C.: Government Printing Office, 1946); U.S. Department of the Interior, War Relocation Authority, *The Wartime Handling of Evacuee Property* (Washington, D.C.: Government Printing Office, 1946); U.S. Department of the Interior, War Relocation Authority, *People in Motion: The Postwar Adjustment of the Evacuated Japanese-Americans* (Washington, D.C.: Government Printing Office, 1947).

7. Miné Okubo, *Citizen 13660* (Seattle: University of Washington Press, 1983; Columbia University Press, 1946), autobiographical words and drawings; Allan R.

Bosworth, *America's Concentration Camps* (New York: Norton, 1967); Spicer et al., *Impounded People;* Audrie Girdner and Anne Loftis, *The Great Betrayal* (London: Macmillan, 1969); Maisie and Richard Conrat, *Executive Order 9066: The Internment of 110,000 Japanese Americans* (Cambridge, Mass.: MIT Press, 1972), photo essay; Jeanne Wakatsuki Houston and James D. Houston, *Farewell to Manzanar* (New York: Houghton Mifflin, 1973), popular autobiography; Michi Weglyn, *Years of Infamy: The Untold Story of America's Concentration Camps* (New York: Morrow, 1976); Sandra C. Taylor, *Jewel of the Desert: Japanese American Internment at Topaz* (Berkeley: University of California Press, 1993). Others in the mainstream include Robert M. O'Brien, *The College Nisei* (Palo Alto, Calif.: Pacific Books, 1949); Toshio Yatsushiro, *Politics and Cultural Values: The World War II Japanese Relocation Centers and the United States Government* (New York: Arno, 1968), reprint of a 1953 dissertation; Norman R. Jackman, "Collective Protest in Relocation Centers," *American Journal of Sociology* 63 (1957):264–72; Takeo Kaneshiro, comp., *Internees: War Relocation Center Memoirs and Diaries* (New York: Vantage, 1976); Douglas W. Nelson, *Heart Mountain* (Madison: State Historical Society of Wisconsin and University of Wisconsin, Department of History, 1976); Bob Kumamoto, "The Search for Spies: American Counterintelligence and the Japanese American Community, 1931–1942," *Amerasia Journal* 6, no. 2 (1979):45–76; Edward Miyakawa, *Tule Lake* (Waldport, Oreg.: House by the Sea Publishing, 1979); Chester Tanaka, *Go for Broke: A Pictorial History of the Japanese American 100th Infantry Battalion and the 442nd Regimental Combat Team* (Richmond, Calif.: JACP, 1981); Yoshiko Uchida, *Desert Exile: The Uprooting of a Japanese-American Family* (Seattle: University of Washington Press, 1982); Donald Edward Collins, *Native American Aliens: Disloyalty and Renunciation of Citizenship by Japanese Americans during World War II* (Westport, Conn.: Greenwood, 1985); John Christgau, *"Enemies": World War II Alien Internment* (Ames: Iowa State University Press, 1985); John Christgau, "Collins versus the World: The Fight to Restore Citizenship to Japanese American Renunciants of World War II," *Pacific Historical Review* 54 (1985):1–31; Georgia Day Robertson, *The Harvest of Hate* (New York: Lynx Books, 1986); Deborah Gesensway and Mindy Roseman, *Beyond Words: Images from America's Concentration Camps* (Ithaca, N.Y.: Cornell University Press, 1987); Masayo Umezawa Duus, *Unlikely Liberators: The Men of the 100th and 442nd* (Honolulu: University of Hawai'i Press, 1987); Thomas James, *Exile Within: The Schooling of Japanese Americans, 1942–1945* (Cambridge, Mass.: Harvard University Press, 1987).

8. Roger Daniels, *Concentration Camps USA: Japanese Americans and World War II* (New York: Holt, Rinehart and Winston, 1971); Daniels, *Prisoners without Trial: Japanese Americans in World War II* (New York: Hill and Wang, 1993). At several key points, Daniels follows the lead of Stetson Conn, "Japanese Evacuation from the West Coast," in *The United States Army in World War II: The Western Hemisphere: Guarding the United States and Its Outposts,* ed. Stetson Conn, Rose C. Engleman, and Byron Fairchild (Washington, D.C.: Government Printing Office, 1964).

9. Raymond Okamura, "Revisions in Japanese American History: Review of Books Published in 1976," *Journal of Ethnic Studies* 5 (1977):112–15; Gary Okihiro, [review of *Years of Infamy* by Michi Weglyn], *Amerasia Journal* 4 (1977):167–71.

10. Gary Okihiro, "Japanese Resistance in America's Concentration Camps: A Reevaluation," *Amerasia Journal* 2 (1973):20–34; Okihiro, [review of *Years of Infamy* by Weglyn]; Okihiro, "Tule Lake under Martial Law: A Study of Japanese Resistance," *Journal of Ethnic Studies* 5 (1977):71–85; Okihiro and Julia Sly, "The Press, Japanese Americans, and the Concentration Camps," *Phylon* 44 (1983):66–83; Okihiro, "Religion and Resistance in America's Concentration Camps," *Phylon* 45 (1984):220–33; Paul R. Spickard, "The Nisei Assume Power: The Japanese American Citizens League, 1941–1942," *Pacific Historical Review* 52 (1983):147–74; Yuji Ichioka, ed., *Views from Within: The Japanese American Evacuation*

and Resettlement Study (Los Angeles: UCLA Asian American Studies Center, 1989); Richard Nishimoto, *Inside an American Concentration Camp: Japanese American Resistance at Paton, Arizona*, ed. Lane Ryo Hirabayashi (Tucson: University of Arizona Press, 1995). Okihiro has recently brought his formidable analytical powers to bear on the Hawaiian scene in *Cane Fires: The Anti-Japanese Movement in Hawai'i, 1865–1945* (Philadelphia: Temple University Press, 1991).

11. JACL National Committee for Redress, *The Japanese American Incarceration: A Case for Redress* (San Francisco: Japanese American Citizens League, 1978); "Rites of Passage: The Commission Hearings, 1981," *Amerasia Journal* 8, no. 2 (1981):53–106; Commission on Wartime Relocation and Internment of Civilians, *Personal Justice Denied* (Washington, D.C.: Government Printing Office, 1982); Peter Irons, *Justice at War: The Story of the Japanese American Internment Cases* (New York: Oxford, 1983); John Tateishi, *And Justice for All: An Oral History of the Japanese American Detention Camps* (New York: Random House, 1984); Roger Daniels, Sandra Taylor, Harry Kitano, eds., *Japanese Americans: From Relocation to Redress* (Salt Lake City: University of Utah Press, 1986; Seattle: University of Washington Press, 1991); William Minoru Hohri, *Repairing America: An Account of the Movement for Japanese-American Redress* (Pullman: Washington State University Press, 1988); Leslie T. Hatamiya, *Righting a Wrong: Japanese Americans and the Passage of the Civil Liberties Act of 1988* (Stanford, Calif.: Stanford University Press, 1993). Cf. *Papers of the United States Commission on Wartime Relocation and Internment of Civilians* (Frederick, Md.: University Publications of America); Peter Irons, ed., *Justice Delayed: The Record of the Japanese American Internment Cases* (Middletown, Conn.: Wesleyan University Press, 1989); Nobuya Tsuchida, *American Justice: Japanese American Evacuation and Redress Cases* (Minneapolis: University of Minnesota Asian/Pacific American Learning Resource Center, 1988); and Yasuko I. Takezawa, *Breaking the Silence: Redress and Japanese American Ethnicity* (Ithaca: Cornell University Press, 1995).

12. Ken Adachi, *The Enemy That Never Was: A History of the Japanese Canadians* (Toronto: McClelland and Stewart, 1976); Joy Kogawa, *Obasan* (Boston: Godine, 1981). See also David B. Iwaasa, "The Japanese in Southern Alberta, 1941–1945," *Alberta History* 24, no. 3 (1976):5–19; W. Peter Ward, "British Columbia and the Japanese Evacuation," *Canadian Historical Review* 57 (1976):289–308; Barry Broadfoot, *Years of Sorrow, Years of Shame: The Story of the Japanese Canadians in World War II* (Toronto: Doubleday, 1977); Roger Daniels, "The Japanese Experience in North America: An Essay in Comparative Racism," *Canadian Ethnic Studies* 9 (1977):91–100; M. Ann Sunahara and Glenn T. Wright, "The Japanese Canadian Experience in World War II: An Essay on Archival Sources," *Canadian Ethnic Studies* 11 (1979):78–87; Tomoko Makabe, "Canadian Evacuation and Nisei Identity," *Phylon* 41 (1980):116–25; Roger Daniels, *Concentration Camps: North America* (Malabar, Fla.: Krieger, 1981), a reissue of his 1971 book, with an additional section on the Canadian camps; Ann Gomer Sunahara, *The Politics of Racism: The Uprooting of Japanese Canadians during the Second World War* (Toronto: Lorimer, 1981); Daniel J. O'Neil, "American versus Canadian Policies toward Their Japanese Minorities during the Second World War," *Comparative Social Research* 4 (1981):111–34. For a related story in another country, see C. Harvey Gardiner, *Pawns in a Triangle of Hate: The Peruvian Japanese and the United States* (Seattle: University of Washington Press, 1981).

13. Roger Daniels, *The Politics of Prejudice: The Anti-Japanese Movement in California and the Struggle for Japanese Exclusion* (Gloucester, Mass.: Peter Smith, 1966; New York: Atheneum, 1968); Daniels, *Concentration Camps U.S.A.* (New York: Holt, Rinehart and Winston, 1971); Daniels, *Concentration Camps: North America* (Malabar, Fla.: Krieger, 1981); Daniels, *The Decision to Relocate the Japanese Americans*

(Philadelphia: Lippincott, 1975); Daniels, "The Decision to Relocate the North American Japanese: Another Look," *Pacific Historical Review* 51 (1982):71–77; Daniels, ed., *American Concentration Camps: A Documentary History of the Relocation and Incarceration of Japanese Americans, 1941–1945*, 9 vols. (New York: Garland, 1989). In *The Politics of Prejudice*, Daniels stood on the shoulders of a number of students of the anti-Japanese movement: Larry Nepomuceno, "Japanese Restriction in California, 1900–1913" (M.A. thesis, University of California, Berkeley, 1939); Carey McWilliams, *Prejudice: Japanese-Americans: Symbol of Racial Intolerance* (Boston: Little, Brown, 1944); Rebecca B. Gruver, "Japanese-American Relations and the Japanese Exclusion Movement, 1900–1934" (M.A. thesis, University of California, Berkeley, 1956); James B. Kessler, "The Political Factors in California's Anti-Alien Land Legislation, 1912–1913" (Ph.D. dissertation, Stanford University, 1958). Another recent Daniels work is *Asian America: Chinese and Japanese in the United States since 1850* (Seattle: University of Washington Press, 1988). A much less measured writer on the racism theme is Richard Drinnon, *Keeper of Concentration Camps: Dillon S. Myer and American Racism* (Berkeley: University of California Press, 1987).

14. Bill Hosokawa, *Nisei: The Quiet Americans* (New York: Morrow, 1969); Robert A. Wilson and Bill Hosokawa, *East to America: A History of the Japanese in the United States* (New York: Morrow, 1980); Hosokawa, *JACL in Quest of Justice: The History of the Japanese American Citizens League* (New York: Morrow, 1982); William Petersen, "Success Story: Japanese-American Style," *New York Times Magazine* (9 January 1966):20–21ff.; Petersen, *Japanese Americans* (New York: Random House, 1971); Mike Masaoka, with Bill Hosokawa, *They Call Me Moses Masaoka* (New York: Morrow, 1987). My dissent from Hosokawa's view is in "The Nisei Assume Power." See also William Caudill and George DeVos, "Achievement, Culture, and Personality: The Case of the Japanese-Americans," *American Anthropologist* 58 (1956):1102–26; Kazuo Miyamoto, *Hawai'i: End of the Rainbow* (Rutland, Vt.: Tuttle, 1964); Jim Yoshida, with Bill Hosokawa, *The Two Worlds of Jim Yoshida* (New York: Morrow, 1972); Frank F. Chuman, *The Bamboo People: The Law and Japanese-Americans* (Chicago: Japanese American Citizens League, 1976).

15. William A. Caudill, "Japanese American Personality and Acculturation," *Genetic Psychology Monographs* 45 (1952):3–102; George DeVos, "A Quantitative Rorschach Assessment of Maladjustment and Rigidity in Acculturating Japanese-Americans," *Genetic Psychology Monographs* 51–52 (1955):1–87; Leonard Broom and John I. Kitsuse, "The Validation of Acculturation: A Condition to Ethnic Assimilation," *American Anthropologist* 57 (1955):44–48; Stanford M. Lyman, "Generation and Character: The Case of the Japanese-Americans," in Lyman, *The Asian in the West* (Reno, Nev.: Western Studies Center, 1970); Harry H. L. Kitano, *Japanese Americans: The Evolution of a Subculture* (Englewood Cliffs, N.J.: Prentice-Hall, 1969; 2nd ed., 1976). A further step in this line is Darrel Montero, *Japanese Americans: Changing Patterns of Ethnic Affiliation over Three Generations* (Boulder, Colo.: Westview Press, 1980).

16. Bibliographical tools include Isao Fujimoto et al., *Asians in America: A Selected Annotated Bibliography* (Davis, Calif.: University of California, Department of Applied Behavioral Sciences, 1971; rev. ed.); Yuji Ichioka et al., *A Buried Past: An Annotated Bibliography of the Japanese American Research Project Collection* (Berkeley: University of California Press, 1974); Mitsugu Matsuda, *The Japanese in Hawai'i, 1868–1967: A Bibliography of the First Hundred Years* (Honolulu: University of Hawai'i Social Science Research Institute, 1968); Yasuo Sakata, *Footsteps of the Issei: An Annotated Checklist of the Manuscript Holdings of the Japanese American Research Project Collection* (Los Angeles: UCLA Asian American Studies Center, 1992); and John Liu and Glenn Omatsu's annual (since 1978) "Selected Bibliography" in *Amerasia Journal*. (Gary Okihiro started the series in 1977.) On the publishing front, the

University of Hawai'i Press has been extremely active. Other presses to contribute significantly have included the University of Washington Press, Temple University Press, the University of California Press, R&E Research Associates, the California State University-Fullerton Oral History Program, and UCLA's Asian American Studies Center. The University of Illinois Press and Stanford University Press have promising new series as well. The *Pacific Historical Review* has also published a number of important articles on Japanese American history.

17. See Richard Hofstadter, *The American Political Tradition* (New York: Knopf, 1948); Hofstadter, *The Age of Reform* (New York: Knopf, 1955); Arthur M. Schlesinger Jr., *The Age of Jackson* (Boston: Little, Brown, 1945); Schlesinger, *The Cycles of American History* (Boston: Houghton Mifflin, 1986); William Appleman Williams, *The Tragedy of American Diplomacy* (New York: World, 1959); Herbert Gutman, *Power and Culture: Essays on the American Working Class* (New York: Pantheon, 1987).

18. Valerie J. Matsumoto, *Farming the Home Place: A Japanese American Community in California, 1919–1982* (Ithaca, N.Y.: Cornell University Press, 1993); Linda Tamura, *The Hood River Issei* (Urbana: University of Illinois Press, 1994); Tateishi, *And Justice for All*; Arthur A. Hansen and Betty E. Mitson, eds., *Voices Long Silent: An Oral Inquiry into the Japanese American Evacuation* (Fullerton, Calif.: California State University, Fullerton, Oral History Project, 1974); Arthur A. Hansen, Sue Kunitomi Embrey, and Betty Kulberg Mitson, *Manzanar Martyr: An Interview with Harry Y. Ueno* (Fullerton, Calif.: California State University, Fullerton, Oral History Project, 1986); David Mas Masumoto, *Country Voices: The Oral History of a Japanese American Family Farm Community* (Del Rey, Calif.: Inaka Countryside Publications, 1987); Eileen Sunada Sarasohn, ed., *The Issei: Portrait of a Pioneer* (Palo Alto, Calif.: Pacific Books, 1983); United Okinawan Association of Hawai'i, *Uchinanchu: A History of Okinawans in Hawai'i* (Honolulu: Ethnic Studies Program, University of Hawai'i, 1981); Michiyo Lang et al., *Issei Christians* (Sacramento: Issei Oral History Project, 1977); Jessie A. Garrett and Ronald C. Larson, eds., *Camp and Community: Manzanar and the Owens Valley* (Fullerton, Calif.: California State University, Fullerton, Oral History Project, 1977). Garrett's work demonstrates the danger of ethnic history done by people outside of, and out of touch with, ethnic communities. The editors record uncritically many comments of White Owens Valley residents that are clearly racist, and they show little recognition of how racist their material is (indeed, their original title for the book was "Jap Camp").

19. For example, John Modell, *The Economics and Politics of Racial Accommodation: The Japanese of Los Angeles, 1900–1942* (Urbana: University of Illinois Press, 1977); Edna Bonacich and John Modell, *The Economic Basis of Ethnic Solidarity: Small Business in the Japanese American Community* (Berkeley: University of California Press, 1980); Evelyn Nakano Glenn, "The Dialectics of Wage Work: Japanese-American Women and Domestic Service, 1905–1940," *Feminist Studies* 6 (1980):432–71; Glenn, "Occupational Ghettoization: Japanese American Women and Domestic Service, 1905–1970," *Ethnicity* 8 (1981):352–86; Glenn, *Issei, Nisei, War Bride: Three Generations of Japanese American Women in Domestic Service* (Philadelphia: Temple University Press, 1986); Alan Moriyama, "The Causes of Emigration: The Background of Japanese Emigration to Hawai'i, 1885–1894," in *Labor Immigration under Capitalism: Asian Workers in the United States before World War II*, ed. Lucie Cheng and Edna Bonacich (Berkeley: University of California Press, 1984), 248–76; Nobuya Tsuchida, "Japanese Gardeners in Southern California, 1900–1941," in Cheng and Bonacich, *Labor Immigration under Capitalism*, 435–69.

20. Donald T. Hata Jr., *Undesirables, Early Immigrants, and the Anti-Japanese Movement in San Francisco, 1892–1893* (New York: Arno, 1979); Yuji Ichioka, "Ameyuki-san: Japanese Prostitutes in Nineteenth-Century America," *Amerasia*

Journal 4, no. 1 (1977):1–21; Ford H. Kuramoto, *A History of the Shonien, 1914–1972: An Account of a Program of Institutional Care of Japanese Children in Los Angeles* (San Francisco: R&E Research Associates, 1976).

21. Dennis Ogawa, ed., *Kodomo No Tame Ni* (Honolulu: University of Hawai'i Press, 1978); Timothy J. Lukes and Gary Y. Okihiro, *Japanese Legacy: Farming and Community Life in California's Santa Clara Valley* (Cupertino, Calif.: California History Center, 1985); Matsumoto, *Farming the Homeplace.* See also Barbara Yasui, "The Nikkei in Oregon, 1834–1940," *Oregon Historical Quarterly* 76 (1975):225–57; Masumoto, *Country Voices;* Kazuko Nakane, *Nothing Left in My Hands: An Early Japanese American Community in California's Pajaro Valley* (Seattle: Young Pine Press, 1986).

22. Masakazu Iwata, "The Japanese Immigrants in California Agriculture," *Agricultural History* 36 (1967):25–37; Iwata, *Planted in Good Soil: A History of the Issei in United States Agriculture,* 2 vols. (New York: Peter Lang, 1991); John Modell, *Economics and Politics of Racial Accommodation;* John Modell, "Japanese-Americans: Some Costs of Group Achievement," in *Ethnic Conflict in California History,* ed. Charles Wollenberg (Los Angeles: Tinnon-Brown, 1970), 101–19; Yasuo Wakatsuki, "The Japanese Emigration to the United States, 1866–1924," *Perspectives in American History* 12 (1979):389–516; Akemi Kikumura, *Through Harsh Winters: The Life of a Japanese Immigrant Woman* (Novato, Calif: Chandler and Sharp, 1981); Kikumura, *Promises Kept: The Life of an Issei Man* (Novato, Calif.: Chandler and Sharp, 1991); Yoshiko Uchida, *Picture Bride* (New York: Simon and Schuster, 1987). See also Tooru Kanazawa, *Sushi and Sourdough* (Seattle: University of Washington Press, 1989); Yuzo Murayama, "The Economic History of Japanese Immigration to the Pacific Northwest, 1890–1920" (Ph.D. dissertation, University of Washington, 1982); Yukiko Kimura, *Issei: Japanese Immigrants in Hawai'i* (Honolulu: University of Hawai'i Press, 1988); Mitziko Sawada, "Culprits and Gentlemen: Meiji Japan's Restrictions of Emigrants to the United States, 1891–1909," *Pacific Historical Review* 60 (1991):339–59. Two books on Japanese foreign adventurism also tell of the Issei generation in Hawai'i: Hilary Conroy, *The Japanese Frontier in Hawai'i, 1868–1898* (Berkeley: University of California Press, 1953); and John J. Stephan, *Hawai'i under the Rising Sun: Japan's Plans for Conquest after Pearl Harbor* (Honolulu: University of Hawai'i Press, 1984). One book, not on the Issei, but important to understanding the 1910s and 1920s, is Sandra C. Taylor, *Advocate of Understanding: Sidney Gulick and the Search for Peace with Japan* (Kent, Ohio: Kent State University Press, 1984).

23. Yuji Ichioka, "A Buried Past: Early Issei Socialists and the Japanese Community," *Amerasia Journal* 1, no. 2 (1971):1–25; Ichioka, "Ameyuki-san;" Ichioka, "The Early Japanese Immigrant Quest for Citizenship: The Background of the 1922 Ozawa Case," *Amerasia Journal* 4, no. 2 (1977):1–22; Ichioka, "Japanese Associations and the Japanese Government: A Special Relationship, 1909–1926," *Pacific Historical Review* 49 (1977):409–38; Ichioka, "Amerika Nadeshiko: Japanese Immigrant Women in the United States, 1900–1924," *Pacific Historical Review* 49 (1980):339–57; Ichioka, "Japanese Immigrant Labor Contractors and the Northern Pacific and the Great Northern Railroad Companies, 1898–1907," *Labor History* 21 (1980):325–50; Ichioka, "An Instance of Private Japanese Diplomacy: Suzuki Bunji, Organized American Labor, and Japanese Immigrant Workers, 1915–1916," *Amerasia Journal* 10, no. 1 (1983):1–22; Ichioka, "Japanese Immigrant Response to the 1920 California Alien Land Law," *Agricultural History* 58 (1984):157–78; Ichioka, "Attorney for the Defense: Yamato Ichihashi and Japanese Immigration," *Pacific Historical Review* 55 (1986):192–225; Ichioka, *The Issei: The World of the First Generation Japanese Immigrants, 1885–1924* (New York: Free Press, 1988); Alan Takeo Moriyama, *Imingaisha: Japanese Emigration Companies and Hawai'i* (Honolulu: University of Hawai'i Press, 1985); Moriyama, "The Causes of Emigration," in

Cheng and Bonacich, *Labor Immigration under Capitalism;* Don and Nadine Hata, "George Shima: 'The Potato King of California,'" *Journal of the West* 25 (January 1986):55–63.

24. Karl Yoneda, "100 Years of Japanese Labor History in the U.S.A.," in *Roots: An Asian American Reader,* ed. Amy Tachiki et al. (Los Angeles: UCLA Asian American Studies Center, 1971), 150–58; Karl Yoneda, *Ganbatte: Sixty-Year Struggle of a Kibei Worker* (Los Angeles: UCLA Asian American Studies Center, 1983); Ichioka, "Japanese Immigrant Labor Contractors"; Ichioka, "An Instance of Private Japanese Diplomacy"; John Modell, "Class or Ethnic Solidarity: The Japanese American Company Union," *Pacific Historical Review* 38 (1969):193–206; Ronald Takaki, *Pau Hana: Plantation Life and Labor in Hawai'i* (Honolulu: University of Hawai'i Press, 1983); Cletus E. Daniel, *Bitter Harvest: A History of California Farmworkers, 1870–1944* (Ithaca, N.Y.: Cornell University Press, 1981; Berkeley: University of California Press, 1982); Stephen S. Fugita and Daniel J. O'Brien, "Economics, Ideology, and Ethnicity: The Struggle between the United Farm Workers Union and the Nisei Farmers League," *Social Problems* 25 (1977):146–56; Robert Higgs, "Landless by Law—Japanese Immigrants in California Agriculture to 1941," *Journal of Economic History* 38 (1978):205–26; Linda C. Majka and Theo J. Majka, *Farm Workers, Agribusiness, and the State* (Philadelphia: Temple University Press, 1982); Y. Murayama, "Contractors, Collusion, and Competition: Japanese Immigrant Railroad Laborers in the Pacific Northwest, 1898–1911," *Explorations in Economic History* 21 (1984):290–305.

25. Bonacich and Modell, *Economic Basis of Ethnic Solidarity;* Burton Bledstein, *The Culture of Professionalism: The Middle Class and the Development of Higher Education in America* (New York: Norton, 1976); Stuart M. Blumin, "The Hypothesis of Middle-Class Formation in Nineteenth-Century America," *American Historical Review* 90 (1985):399–438; Paul Boyer, *Urban Masses and Moral Order in America, 1820–1920* (Cambridge, Mass.: Harvard University Press, 1978); Paul Johnson, *A Shopkeeper's Millenium: Society and Revivals in Rochester, New York, 1815–1837* (New York: Hill and Wang, 1978); Mary P. Ryan, *Cradle of the Middle Class: The Family in Oneida County, New York, 1790–1865* (New York: Cambridge, 1981).

26. Glenn, *Issei, Nisei, War Bride;* Glenn, "Dialectics of Wage Work"; Glenn, "Occupational Ghettoization"; Matsumoto, *Farming the Homeplace;* Sylvia Junko Yanagisako, *Transforming the Past: Tradition and Kinship among Japanese Americans* (Stanford, Calif.: Stanford University Press, 1985); Yanagisako, "Two Processes of Change in Japanese American Kinship," *Journal of Anthropological Research* 31 (1975):196–224; Joan Hori, "Japanese Prostitution in Hawai'i during the Immigration Period," *Hawaiian Journal of History* 15 (1981):113–24; Laurie Mengel, "Not Just Picture Brides: Independent Japanese Women Migrants" (paper presented to the Association for Asian American Studies, Honolulu, 26 March 1996); Ichioka, "Amerika Nadeshiko"; Ichioka, "Ameyuki-san"; Kikumura, *Through Harsh Winters;* Uchida, *Picture Bride;* Mei Nakano, *Japanese American Women: Three Generations, 1890–1990* (Sebastopol, Calif.: Mina Press, 1990); Valerie Matsumoto, "Japanese American Women during World War II," *Frontiers* 8 (1984):6–14; John Modell, "The Japanese-American Family: A Perspective for Future Generations," *Pacific Historical Review* 37 (1968):67–82; Tomoko Yamazaki, *The Story of Yamada Waka: From Prostitute to Feminist Pioneer* (Tokyo: Kodansha International, 1985).

27. Ben Kobashigawa, trans., *History of the Okinawans in North America* (Los Angeles: Okinawan Club of North America and UCLA Asian American Studies Center, 1988); United Okinawan Association, *Uchinanchu.*

28. Edna Bonacich, "A Theory of Ethnic Antagonism: The Split Labor Market," *American Sociological Review* 37 (1972):547–59; Tomoko Makabe, "The

Theory of the Split Labor Market: A Comparison of the Japanese Experience in Brazil and Canada," *Social Forces* 59 (1981):786–809; Cheng and Bonacich, *Labor Immigration under Capitalism;* Bonacich, "A Theory of Middleman Minorities," *American Sociological Review* 38 (1973):583–94; Harry H. L. Kitano, "Japanese Americans: The Development of a Middleman Minority," *Pacific Historical Review* 43 (1974):500–519; Bonacich, "Small Business and Japanese American Ethnic Solidarity," *Amerasia Journal* 2 (1975):96–113; Bonacich and Modell, *Economic Basis of Ethnic Solidarity;* David J. O'Brien and Stephen S. Fugita, "Middleman Minority Concept: Its Explanatory Value in the Case of the Japanese in California Agriculture," *Pacific Sociological Review* 25 (1982):185–204; Eugene F. Wong, "Asian American Middleman Minority Theory: The Framework of an American Myth," *Journal of Ethnic Studies* 13 (1985):51–88. Bonacich and Kitano take their inspiration regarding the middleman minority theory from Hubert Blalock Jr., *Toward a Theory of Minority Group Relations* (New York: Wiley, 1967), 79–84.

29. For a description of that project, see Donna L. Leonetti, *Nisei Aging Project Report* (Seattle: Nisei Aging Project, 1983), which is on the shelf in the UCLA University Research Library.

30. Japanese American Research Project (JARP), Department of Special Collections, University Research Library, UCLA; Japanese Evacuation and Resettlement Study, Bancroft Library, University of California, Berkeley; Japanese American Collection, Archives, University of Washington Library; Oral History Collection, California State University, Fullerton; Survey of Race Relations Papers (SRR), Hoover Institution Archives, Stanford University (the Survey of Race Relations also includes material on Filipino and Chinese Americans). These papers formed the basis of Eliot Grinnell Mears, *Resident Orientals on the American Pacific Coast* (Chicago: University of Chicago Press, 1928), but have since been used only tangentially by such scholars as John Modell, *Economics and Politics of Racial Accommodation;* Ronald Takaki, *Strangers from a Different Shore* (Boston: Little, Brown, 1989); and Paul Spickard, *Mixed Blood: Intermarriage and Ethnic Identity in Twentieth-Century America* (Madison: University of Wisconsin Press, 1989). See also Robert Ezra Park, "A Race Relations Survey," in Park, *Race and Culture* (Glencoe, Ill.: Free Press, 1950), 158–65.

31. Jitsuichi Masuoka, *Orientals and Their Cultural Adjustment* (Nashville: Fisk University, 1946); Kazuo Ito, *Issei: A History of Japanese Immigrants in North America,* trans. Shinichiro Nakamura and Jean S. Gerard (Seattle: Japanese Community Service, 1973); Daphne Marlatt, ed., *Steveston Recollected* (Victoria: Provincial Archives of British Columbia, 1975); United Okinawan Association, *Uchinanchu;* Dorothy Kuniko Takchi, "The Nisei in Denver, Colorado: A Study in Personality Adjustment and Disorganization" (M.A. thesis, Fisk University, 1945). See also the oral histories listed above at n. 18.

32. One recent study with a promising new focus is psychologically rather than historically constructed: Donna K. Nagata, *Legacy of Injustice: Exploring the Cross-Generational Impact of the Japanese American Internment* (New York: Plenum, 1993).

33. See Lynn Hunt, ed., *The New Cultural History* (Berkeley: University of California Press, 1989); Natalie Zemon Davis, *The Return of Martin Guerre* (Cambridge, Mass.: Harvard University Press, 1984); Robert Darnton, *The Great Cat Massacre and Other Episodes in French Cultural History* (New York: Random House, 1984).

34. Richard Chalfen, *Turning Leaves: The Photograph Collections of Two Japanese American Families* (Albuquerque: University of New Mexico Press, 1991); Eileen H. Tamura, *Americanization, Acculturation, and Ethnic Identity: The Nisei Generation in*

Hawai'i (Urbana: University of Illinois Press, 1994); Stephen S. Fugita and Daniel J. O'Brien, *Japanese American Ethnicity: The Persistence of Community* (Seattle: University of Washington Press, 1991); O'Brien and Fugita, *The Japanese American Experience* (Bloomington: Indiana University Press, 1991).

35. Hosokawa, *Nisei;* Toshio Mori, *Yokohama, California* (Caldwell, Idaho: Caxton.Printers, 1949; Seattle: University of Washington Press, 1985); Mori, *The Chauvinist and Other Stories* (Los Angeles: UCLA Asian American Studies Center, 1979).

36. Emory S. Bogardus, "Resettlement Problems of Japanese-Americans," *Sociology and Social Research* 29 (1945):218–66; Toru Matsumoto, *Beyond Prejudice: A Story of the Church and Japanese-Americans* (New York: Friendship Press, 1946); Emory S. Bogardus, "The Japanese Return to the West Coast," *Sociology and Social Research* 31 (1947):226–33; U.S. War Relocation Authority, *People in Motion;* Thomas et al., *The Salvage;* Sone, *Nisei Daughter;* Midori Nishi, "Changing Occupance of the Japanese in Los Angeles County, 1940–1950" (Ph.D. dissertation, University of Washington, 1955); Yoshiko Uchida, *Journey Home* (New York: Atheneum, 1978); Tetsuden Kashima, "Japanese American Internees Return, 1945–1955: Readjustment and Social Amnesia," *Phylon* 41 (1980):107–15; Kevin Allen Leonard, "'Is This What We Fought For?': Japanese Americans and Racism in California, The Impact of World War II," *Western Historical Quarterly* 21 (1990):463–82.

37. Kanazawa, *Sushi and Sourdough;* Sandra C. Taylor, "Leaving the Concentration Camps: Japanese American Resettlement in Utah and the Intermountain West," *Pacific Historical Review* 60 (1991):169–94; Thomas K. Walls, *The Japanese Texans* (San Antonio: University of Texas, Institute of Texan Cultures, 1987). See also Stephen S. Fugita and Henry T. Tanaka, "The Japanese American Community in Cleveland," in *Encyclopedia of Cleveland,* ed. D. D. Van Tassel (Bloomington: Indiana University Press, 1987); Michael D. Albert, "Japanese American Communities in Chicago and the Twin Cities" (Ph.D. dissertation, University of Minnesota, 1980); George E. Pozzeta and Harry A. Kersey Jr., "Yamato Colony: A Japanese Presence in South Florida," *Tequesta* 36 (1976):66–77; Mark J. Gehrie, "Childhood and Community: On the Experience of Young Japanese Americans in Chicago," *Ethos* 4 (1976), 353–83.

38. Merry White, *The Japanese Overseas: Can They Go Home Again?* (New York: Free Press, 1988); Evelyn Iritani, *An Ocean Between Us* (New York: Morrow, 1994).

39. Yen Le Espiritu, *Asian American Panethnicity* (Philadelphia: Temple University Press, 1992); William Wei, *The Asian American Movement* (Philadelphia: Temple University Press, 1993). Some sociologists and anthropologists have been at work on the Sansei: Minako K. Maykovich, *Japanese American Identity Dilemma* (Tokyo: Waseda University Press, 1972); Hilla K. Israeli, "An Exploration into Ethnic Identity: The Case of Third-Generation Japanese Americans" (Ph.D. dissertation, UCLA, 1976); Fumiko Hosokawa, *The Sansei* (Palo Alto, Calif.: R&E Research Associates, 1978); Hisako Matsuo, "Identificational Assimilation of Japanese Americans," *Sociological Perspectives* 35 (1992):505–23; Mark Gehrie, "Sansei: An Ethnography of Experience" (Ph.D. dissertation, Northwestern University, 1973). Other forays into the Sansei world include Cynthia Kadohata, *The Floating World* (New York: Viking, 1989); David Mura, *Turning Japanese: Memoirs of a Sansei* (New York: Atlantic Monthly Press, 1991); Lydia Minatoya, *Talking to High Monks in the Snow* (New York: HarperCollins, 1992); Janie Hitomi Takaki, "The Later Generations: How Has the Internment of Japanese in America Impacted Them?" (M.S.W. thesis, California State University, Long Beach, 1988); and Kaoru Oguri

Kendis, *A Matter of Comfort: Ethnic Maintenance and Ethnic Style among Third-Generation Japanese Americans* (New York: AMS Press, 1989).

40. Ichioka, *The Issei;* Jere Takahashi, "Japanese American Responses to Race Relations: The Formation of Nisei Perspectives," *Amerasia Journal* 9, no. 1 (1982):29–57; Hosokawa, *JACL in Quest of Justice;* Spickard, "Nisei Assume Power"; John N. Hawkins, "Politics, Education, and Language Policy: The Case of Japanese Language Schools in Hawai'i," *Amerasia Journal* 5, no. 1 (1978):39–56; Mariko Takagi, "Moral Education in Prewar Japanese Language Schools in Hawai'i" (M.A. thesis, University of Hawai'i, 1987); James, *Exile Within;* Brian Masaru Hayashi, "'For the Sake of Our Japanese Brethren': Assimilation, Nationalism, and Protestantism among the Japanese of Los Angeles, 1895–1942" (Ph.D. dissertation, UCLA, 1990); Hayashi, *For the Sake of the Japanese Brethren* (Stanford, Calif.: Stanford University Press, 1995); Tetsuden Kashima, *Buddhism in America: The Social Organization of an Ethnic Religious Institution* (Westport, Conn.: Greenwood, 1977); Kosei Ogura, "A Sociological Study of the Buddhist Churches in North America, with a Case Study of a Gardena, California, Congregation" (M.A. thesis, University of Southern California, 1932); Robert F. Spencer, "Japanese Buddhism in the United States, 1940–1946: A Study in Acculturation" (Ph.D. dissertation, University of California, Berkeley, 1946); Toru Matsumoto and Marion O. Lerrigo, *A Brother Is a Stranger* (New York: John Day, 1946); Matsumoto, *Beyond Prejudice;* Leonard D. Cain, "Japanese-American Protestants: Acculturation and Assimilation," *Review of Religious Research* 3 (1962):113–21; Lester E. Suzuki, *Ministry in the Assembly and Relocation Centers of World War II* (Berkeley: Yardbird, 1979); Thomas, *The Salvage,* 607–9; Stephen S. Fugita and David J. O'Brien, "Economics, Ideology, and Ethnicity: The Struggle between the United Farm Workers and the Nisei Farmers League," *Social Problems* 25 (1977):146–56; Dorothy A. Stroup, "The Role of the Japanese-American Press in Its Community" (M.A. thesis, University of California, Berkeley, 1960). Yuji Ichioka and others organized a conference on Nisei in the Japanese American press during the 1930s, held in Los Angeles in 1985 (*Hokubei Mainichi,* 1 January 1986).

41. Tamotsu Shibutani gives some sense of Nisei who failed to live up to the ideal in *The Derelicts of Company K: A Sociological Study of Demoralization* (Berkeley: University of California Press, 1978). Considerable data on the zoot-suiters and their playmates can be found in Charles Kikuchi's resettler interviews in the Japanese American Evacuation and Resettlement Study papers at the Bancroft library in Berkeley. One Kibei's letters have been published in Mary Kimoto Tomita, *Dear Miye: Letters Home from Japan* (Stanford, Calif.: Stanford University Press, 1995).

42. On South America: James L. Tigner, "Japanese Immigration into Latin America: A Survey," *Journal of Interamerican Studies and World Affairs* 23 (1981):457–82; Tigner, "Japanese Settlement in Eastern Bolivia and Brazil," *Journal of Interamerican Studies and World Affairs* 24 (1982):496–517; Tigner, "The Ryukyuans in Argentina," *Hispanic American Historical Review* 47 (1967):203–24; Tigner, "The Ryukyuans in Bolivia, *Hispanic American Historical Review* 43 (1963):206–9; Tigner, "Sindo Remmei: Japanese Nationalism in Brazil," *Hispanic American Historical Review* 41 (1961):515–32; Tigner, "The Ryukyuans in Peru, 1906–1952," *The Americas* 25 (July 1978):20–44; Yukio Fujii and T. Lynn Smith, *The Acculturation of Japanese Immigrants in Brazil* (Gainesville: University of Florida Press, 1959); Philip Staniford, *Pioneers in the Tropics: The Political Organization of Japanese in an Immigrant Community in Brazil* (New York: Humanities Press, 1973); D. Hastings, "Japanese Emigration and Assimilation in Brazil," *International Migration Review* 3 (1969):32–52; H. Saito, "The Integration and Participation of the Japanese and Their Descendants in Brazilian Society," *International Migration* 14 (1976):183–97;

H. D. Sims, "Japanese Postwar Migration to Brazil," *International Migration Review* 6 (1972):246–65; R. J. Smith et al., eds., *The Japanese and Their Descendants in Brazil: An Annotated Bibliography* (Sao Paulo: Centro de Estudos Nipo-Brasileiros, 1967); N. R. Stewart, *Japanese Colonization in Eastern Paraguay* (Washington, D.C.: National Academy of Sciences, 1967); S. I. Thompson, "Religious Conversions and Religious Zeal in an Overseas Enclave: The Case of the Japanese in Bolivia," *Anthropological Quarterly* 41 (1968):201–8; Thompson, "Separate but Superior: Japanese in Bolivia," in *Ethnic Encounters: Identities and Contexts,* ed. G. L. Hicks and P. E. Leis (North Scituate, Mass.: Duxbury Press, 1977); Nobuya Tsuchida, "The Japanese in Brazil, 1908–1941" (Ph.D. dissertation, UCLA, 1978); Karen Tei Yamashita, *Brazil Maru* (Minneapolis: Coffee House Press, 1992).

On Canada: Adachi, *Enemy That Never Was;* Joy Kogawa, *Itsuka* (New York: Doubleday, 1992); Kogawa, *Obasan;* Iwaasa, "Japanese in Southern Alberta"; Ward, "British Columbia and the Japanese Evacuation"; Broadfoot, *Years of Sorrow, Years of Shame;* Sunahara and Wright, "Japanese Canadian Experience"; Makabe, "Canadian Evacuation and Nisei Identity"; Daniels, *Concentration Camps: North America;* Sunahara, *Politics of Racism;* Roger Daniels, "Chinese and Japanese in North America: The Canadian and American Experiences Compared," *Canadian Review of American Studies* 17 (1986):173–86; O'Neil, "American versus Canadian Policies."

43. Examples of comparative studies of American ethnic groups are Takaki, *Pau Hana;* Daniel, *Bitter Harvest;* Spickard, *Mixed Blood;* Drinnon, *Keeper of Concentration Camps;* Charles M. Wollenberg, *All Deliberate Speed: Segregation and Exclusion in California Schools, 1855–1975* (Berkeley: University of California Press, 1976); Ivan H. Light, *Ethnic Enterprise in America* (Berkeley: University of California Press, 1972); Quintard Taylor, "Blacks and Asians in a White City: Japanese Americans and African Americans in Seattle, 1890–1940," *Western Historical Quarterly* 22 (1991):401–29.

Index

The Author

Paul R. Spickard is professor of history, associate dean of the College of Arts and Sciences for the social sciences, and director of the Pacific Islander Americans Research Project at Brigham Young University-Hawai'i. He is also director of research for the Institute for Polynesian Studies.

Professor Spickard received an A.B. degree from Harvard and his M.A. and Ph.D. degrees from the University of California, Berkeley. The author of two dozen articles and scores of papers on topics in American ethnic history, particularly Asian American history, he is also the author or editor of five books on American ethnic history and related topics, including *Mixed Blood: Intermarriage and Ethnic Identity in Twentieth-Century America* (1989). He has won four teaching awards, as well as an Outstanding Book Award from the Gustavus Myers Center for the Study of Human Rights in the United States (1990).

A native of Seattle, he now resides in Kaneohe, Hawai'i, with his two children, Naomi Siu-Mei Spickard and Daniel Mun-Wah Spickard.